ORTHO'S GUIDE TO DECKS & PATIOS

Created and Designed by
the Editorial Staff of Ortho Books

Author
Eric Clough

Editor
David Toht

Illustrator
Tony Davis

ORTHO BOOKS

Publisher
Robert B. Loperena

Editorial Director
Christine Jordan

Manufacturing Manager
Ernie S. Tasaki

Editors
Robert J. Beckstrom
Michael D. Smith

Managing Editor
Sally W. Smith

Prepress Supervisor
Linda M. Bouchard

**Sales & Marketing
Manager**
David C. José

Graphics Coordinator
Sally J. French

Publisher's Assistant
Joni Christiansen

Address all inquiries to:
Ortho Books
Box 5006
San Ramon, CA 94583-0906

° 1996 Monsanto Company
All rights reserved

1	2	3	4	5	6	Softcover
96	97	98	99	2000	01	

1	2	3	4	5	6	Hardcover
96	97	98	99	2000	01	

ISBN 0-89721-312-2 Softcover
ISBN 0-89721-315-7 Hardcover
Library of Congress Catalog Card
Number 96-67630

THE SOLARIS GROUP
2527 Camino Ramon
San Ramon, CA 94583

Contributing Authors
T. Jeff Williams
Sharon Ross
Robert J. Beckstrom
Mark and Beverly Bremer

Editorial Coordinator
Cass Dempsey

Copyeditor
Elizabeth von Radics

Proofreader
David Sweet

Indexer
Trisha Lamb Feuerstein

Contributing Illustrators
Rik Olson
Dany Galgani
Ron Hildebrand
Pamela Drury-Wattenmaker
Angela Hildebrand

Separations by
Color Tech Corp.

**Lithographed in
the USA by**
Banta Book Group

Thanks to:
California Redwood Association, for photographs on pages 6, 30, 50, 60–61, and 284
City College of San Francisco
Deborah Cowder
Designer Showcase of the Benefit Guild of the East Bay
The San Francisco Decorator Showcase
Alisa D. Gean, M.D.
Jana Olsen
Randy and Carolyn Shane
David Van Ness
Katharine and Dan Whalen

Photo Stylists
Names of stylists are followed by the page numbers on which their work appears.
L=Left; T=Top
Sara Slavin: 4–5
JoAnn Masaoka Van Atta: 111

Photographers
Names of photographers are followed by the page numbers on which their work appears.
William Aplin: 55, 227TL, 227BL
Archadeck: 64
Scott Atkinson: 266, 268
Carol Bernson: 260
Dennis Bettencourt: 227BR
Laurie Black: 281, 289, 292
John Blaustein: 104
Ernest Braun: 6, 50, 60–61, 284
Richard Christman: 25, 75, 76, 83
Josephine Coatsworth: 8, 17, 119, 211, 286
Alan Copeland: 59, 117, 118, 129, 153, back cover center
Crandall & Crandall: Front cover, 7, 38, 80, 91, 92, 107T, 107B, 170, 227TR, 243, 295
Stephen Cridland: 109
John Edwards Photography: 16, 84
Julius Fava: 242
Derek Fell: 3CT, 9, 10, 47, 194–195, 202, 209, 294
David Goldberg: 13, 62, 77, 256, 291
Saxon Holt: 1, 18–19, 20, 28, 33, 74, 86, 213, back cover right
Jerry Howard/Positive Images: 52, 253
Balthazar Korab: 30
Michael Landis: 3T, 48, 93, 94–95, 97, 169, 206, 234
Fred Lyon: 4–5, back cover left
Michael McKinley: 106, 233, 276, 278, 280, 282, 283, 293
James McNair: 238
Douglas Muir: 53
John Neubauer: 288
Geoffrey Nilsen: 70, 102, 111, 114, 137, 166, 172, 285
Ortho Photo Library: 46, 49, 78, 265
Robert Perron: 273
Kenneth Rice: 3B, 14, 15, 90, 236, 274–275
Carol Simowitz: 254
David Stone, Photo/Nats: 245
Jeff Stone: 88, 89
Tom Tracy: 87
Jessie Walker: 3CB, 262–263
Jeff Williams: 12
Doreen L. Wynja: 85

**Architects, Builders,
and Designers**
Archadeck: 64
Artistic Lighting of San Rafael: 276, 282
Timothy R. Bitts & Assoc.: 284
Blue Sky Design: 107T
Jack Chandler: 15
Gary Cushenberry: 60–61
Decks by Kiefer: 50
Environmental Creations, Inc.: 107B
Dan Fix Landscape Construction: 236
Carolyn A. Guy, Barbara Argabright, and Peter Tourtelotte: 90
Eric Haesloop, William Turnbull Associates: 266
Dan Hasselgrave, Structura: 273
Chris Hecht: 25
John Herbst, Jr., and Associates: 38, 170
Bill Hollborn: 256
Richard Julin & Associates: 285
Rick Kiefel: 109
Christopher Westbrook Klos: 6
McKinney's Custom Deck and Patio: 3CB, 262–263
Rudyard Morley, Distinctive Lighting: 281
Jan Moyer Lighting Design: 3B, 274–275
Roger Peters: 30
Jeff Stone, Landscape Architect: 88, 89
Harry A. White Lighting Design: 280

Front Cover
This well-landscaped site is enhanced by a two-level redwood deck and a brick patio.

Title Page
A simple deck, designed with taste and imagination, can be very charming.

Back Cover
Left: This hillside deck makes use of space that is otherwise too steep to use.
Center: Accurate measurement is vital to successful construction of either a patio or a deck.
Right: This pool patio looks like stone, but it's really concrete.

CONTENTS

THE JOYS OF OUTDOOR LIVING

This deck extends the outdoor living area of the house into a space that was otherwise unavailable. The deck can be used for sitting, dining, or visiting, and greatly increases the number of people that can be accommodated at a summer party.

Through the ages, people have created many forms of shelter, inspired by both necessity and pleasure. Where mild weather prevails, many of these living areas have been outdoors. Although decks and patios may seem relatively innovative, they are part of a rich design tradition that has its roots in ancient Egypt, Greece, and China. Today's explosion of designs for outdoor living has turned houses inside out. People are exuberantly extending their lifestyles to include outdoor cooking, eating, sleeping, bathing, playing, partying, and working. They've discovered that decks or patios can serve the myriad purposes that indoor rooms do. And they've found that these outdoor additions are by far the least expensive way to expand the living space of their home.

Simply put, decks and patios are outdoor floors—platforms with an almost endless variety of uses. A deck is an aboveground wood structure whereas a patio rests on the ground and may be surfaced with a variety of materials.

This book itself rests on solid ground—the firm idea that you can design your own deck or patio and build it yourself. You may never have gone through the design process of the professional landscape architect, and you may rarely have dealt with lumber and concrete in the raw. But with this book in hand, you'll learn the procedures and practical information—and gain the confidence—to conceive, plan, and construct outdoor living spaces that are perfectly suited for you and your home.

TAKING INDOOR FUNCTIONS OUTDOORS

Decks and patios are most commonly used as extensions of interior spaces for living, working, and eating. The outdoor cooking area, which usually centers around a grill and may include built-in storage cabinets and even sinks, is an extension of the kitchen. Other deck and patio areas take on the intimate character of a family room, with comfortable furniture arranged in a manner conducive to conversation and entertainment. Much like a living room, a deck can be a quiet adult haven, complete with a fire pit, comfortable seating, and subtle lighting. On the other hand, a sunny patio with an adjacent climbing structure and sandbox can be a delightful play area for children.

The combination of a spa or hot tub with a swimming pool is common in outdoor living spaces.

Specific areas of a deck or patio can have more than one use. A sunny breakfast nook can double as an entry court. A boardwalk that connects the house to the deck and garden can also serve as a play ramp for kids or a display area for perennial flowers. Some patios and decks have several levels, serving to separate functions, age groups, and activities. Stairways can be sculptural links among them.

Often decks and patios can go beyond the function of interior rooms. Where else but on a deck or patio could you have a hot soak under the stars? Hot tubs and spas are a popular feature on many decks, an outgrowth of the Japanese *furó*, or honorable bath. Though there are many sizes and shapes on the market, most tubs are at least 3 feet deep and 4 feet in diameter. Filled with water heated to about 110° F, they relax muscles and soothe arthritic pain. A spa can be located off the master bedroom for private

adult use, or situated outside the family room and accessible to children and friends. Some designers have enclosed saunas, or Finnish steam baths, in the underpinnings of decks. Others design outdoor rooms with entertainment in mind: soirees, music, children's puppet shows, readings—even outdoor movies.

Outdoor rooms can be furnished seasonally for sleeping under the stars, with hammocks, waterbeds, or gym mats. Where interior space is at a premium, decks and patios can house laundry facilities, storage sheds, pet shelters, and even garbage cans. The ways that decks and patios extend interior rooms are limited only by space, access, and weather.

In addition to extending the interior living environment, decks and patios serve many normal outdoor functions. Herb and vegetable gardens can be planted in containers or as focal points in patio gardens. Decks can include a potting shed or

Outdoor cooking and dining adds special pleasure to meals in fine weather.

This small patio area, designed for privacy and serenity, is equally suitable for quiet conversation or solitary contemplation.

greenhouse. A rear deck may be the ideal place to keep the dog—outdoors but close to the house. Decks and patios can be lawn substitutes, reducing the amount of regular maintenance. Adjacent to swimming pools, decks and patios offer an area for lounging and sunbathing.

Best of all, there is a certain magic about the way decks and patios provide shelter while remaining very much part of the outdoors. A sense of roomlike enclosure is created with the imaginative use of existing elements—a fence or the boughs of a nearby tree, a screen or lattice,

or a wall of the house. Walls of outdoor rooms can be suggested by trees, potted plants, railings, elevation changes, and other interruptions to one's field of vision. The ceiling of an outdoor room may be the canopy of a large spreading tree, strings of lights, vines on lattice, a canvas-covered trellis, or simply the open sky. The plane of the floor—wood decking or the patio surface—can be visually extended by non–walking surfaces such as water or plantings. The moods of outdoor rooms are influenced by light, temperature, plants, and views. Make the best of those influences and you have magic indeed.

A BRIEF HISTORY OF OUTDOOR LIVING

History offers countless precedents for delight in outdoor living spaces. They demonstrate the strong attraction people have long felt for enjoying everyday living out of doors. These precedents offer many cues for designing your deck or patio.

Earthly Paradise

Religious writings abound with descriptions of gardenlike rooms. The most celebrated, of course, is the Garden of Eden, in which there was "every tree that is pleasant to the sight and good for food"—a sanctuary from the wilds beyond. The imagery of Eden has been an inspiration for outdoor rooms through the ages. In designing modern garden spaces, Eden is still a cultural inspiration for balance and goodness.

Mohammed perpetuated the notion of paradise gardens and filled his with fountains and groves of trees. Glades of flowers and the splashing of water, rare in Islamic countries, came to symbolize the essence of heaven.

The paradise garden reached its height of development in the Persian formal designs called *glorietas.* These rectangular enclosures featured elaborate and intricate patterns of flower plantings, gravel paths, and water courses. Many of the designs have been preserved in the patterns of Persian rugs. As time passed, the glorieta as a design genre appeared in India and Spain, and later in Mexico and California, where it evolved into the patio and the patio court.

In your deck or patio paradise, you may want to incorporate elements unique to your environment. Perhaps the shaded and cascading character of a brook can be imitated in a deck with several levels

stepping down to a canvas-canopied enclosure. Or if your site is on a craggy hillside, a protected patio simulating a flat rock outcropping might be in keeping with the natural surroundings.

Oases and Hanging Gardens

Among the oldest recorded gardens in the world are the oases of Egypt. They comprised rare shade, water, plants, beauty, and food. These gardens were simple rectangles with rows of plants and paths, but they were the beginnings of great outdoor rooms. In Mesopotamia, the celebrated Hanging Gardens of Babylon were actually oases constructed as

The steep stairs of this patio wall create an opportunity for a "hanging" garden.

roof terraces. The gardens rose to a height of 300 feet and covered 4 acres. They provided great views and cooling breezes that washed over the plants and people.

Can Babylon be an inspiration as you design your deck or patio? Think of how you can change the space with structures that alter the direction of views or the character of the topography. Is the site flat and seemingly uninteresting? You might be inspired to make raised planter boxes, pump some water to create a small waterfall, or build a multilevel deck stepping down to a patio, simulating the effect of the Hanging Gardens.

Roman Courtyards

Because of the pleasant Mediterranean climate throughout the Roman Empire, outdoor living continued unabated in marketplaces, public baths, stadiums, and residences. The dominant residential architectural style featured an atrium—a patio or central courtyard—containing fountains, sculpture, and plantings. Often the atrium walls were painted with murals of landscapes or heroic scenes. At Pompeii on the Bay of Naples, lava from Mount Vesuvius covered residential atriums in A.D. 79, preserving their beauty for centuries until recent excavations revealed it. With the rise and fall of empires in Asia Minor and the Mediterranean, the Persian garden as a design form—the glorieta—migrated to North Africa and then to Spain with the Moors. There the Roman atrium was combined with the paradise garden in the thirteenth century. An early example is the Court of the Lions at Granada's Alhambra palace, where channels of water not only run through courtyards but also into and through some rooms, functioning as an effective albeit primitive form of air conditioning. Romans solved the age-old problem of how to tie indoor space to outdoor atriums by using paving or pools as links.

Chinese Gardens

In China, gardens evolved as miniature representations of awesome nature. Scaled-down mountain ranges, lakes, and trees could be enjoyed from benches and open pavilions. Such gardens became beloved places of contemplation—right in the center of the home. Developing from this tradition, the Japanese refined the contemplation garden with sand and rock painstakingly positioned to represent natural balance and form. The great Zen gardens were intended to be viewed from prearranged vantage points, where decks and pavilions were sited. Domestic gardens became very refined as well. They were the most private area of the home, where guests were seldom invited and where meditation would be uninterrupted.

Contemplation areas on decks or pavilions were carefully sited to take advantage of views that could be framed and screened with trees or shrubs. If a site overlooking a great valley and distant mountain range was marred by neighboring houses, designers situated the deck so that it directed views between the rooftops. By screening the roofs with shrubs and fences, the viewer's eye was diverted.

European Gardens

In Europe during the Middle Ages, walled towns and castles afforded little space for outdoor living. The tiny, crooked streetscapes of medieval enclosures teemed with activity, and the small outdoor rooms in these enclosed settlements had to be used intensively. Herbs were grown in beds, fish were raised in ponds, and trees were carefully

Opposite: The formal pattern, central fountain, and use of tile in this patio are typical of the gardens of the eastern Mediterranean. This style migrated to North Africa and then entered Western culture when the Moors invaded Spain.

In this courtyard garden, the Moorish roots of Mexican style are evident in the fountain, the privacy walls, and the paving. Southwest Pueblo influence, however, has modified the design to create a comfortable and informal outdoor sitting area.

placed to give shade from the summer heat. The planner of a roof deck or a small urban patio can learn a lot from the tiny outdoor spaces of Europe's medieval towns.

New World Patios

Evolved from Persian traditions of outdoor living, patios came into the United States from Mexico with the Spanish. Courtyards were closely linked to the living space of the house and provided overflow space—just as the modern deck or patio does today. Some of these Spanish designs were cloisters, with deep eaves overhanging broad walks. In the courts themselves, there were wells, flowers, herbs, and trees as well as pleasant, shady places to sit. Because interior rooms often opened directly onto the courtyard, access was easy and it was the hub of the household.

OUTDOOR IMPROVEMENTS BEGIN WITH DREAMING

Consider creative landscape design to be an opportunity to make the best of the physical constraints of your site, providing you with more enjoyable living space. Golden Gate Park in San Francisco was once a series of sand dunes. Both Central Park in New York City and Disney World in Orlando were at one time swampy bogs. Most pieces of property can be improved upon in some way. You can often turn a limitation into an exciting opportunity. Enclose a noisy front entryway and it becomes a Moorish courtyard. Redirect the drainage in a swampy area and you have a beautiful meandering brook. Anchor a deck on a steep slope and you've added living

space where none existed before. You will find that there are creative landscape design solutions to most site problems.

Enjoy a Return on Financial Investment

Landscape installations are well worth the financial investment they require. A new landscape will likely increase the property value of your home when you decide to sell it. In addition, a well-planned landscape gives a positive first impression that may result in a faster sale. According to a recent study by the American Association of Nurserymen, an attractive yard can increase the value of a property by as much as 30 percent, with 12 percent being about average. Landscape conveniences, including automatic irrigation, lighting, and gates, can add immensely to the resale value. In addition, your new deck or patio may inspire your neighbors and hence raise the property values and overall image of the neighborhood.

Make a Personal Statement

Landscape design is an art and, like any art form, is a largely subjective endeavor. It reflects the artist's personality. Your landscape is a personal, creative statement. The form you give to your home's exterior reflects who you are. It speaks of your thoughts and wishes and provides insight into your personality. Like people, no two landscapes are exactly alike. Consider designing your landscape to be an opportunity to add living beauty to the world.

So, although there is a technical side to landscape design, the final product is meant for pleasure. Landscape design plays more than a merely functional role in society and our lives. It serves emotional needs as well. Your home landscape should refresh, relax, comfort, and uplift. And the knowledge that you have designed and installed the landscape yourself will make it all the more enjoyable.

Defining Your Needs Allow your imagination a wide latitude and make notes of what you want from an outdoor living space. Defining your needs can be an interesting and enjoyable process. If you share space with other people, the needs

Garden whimsy has long and venerable roots. This path of manhole covers (obtained from a junkyard) reflects its owners' personal style and sense of humor.

of the group and those of individuals must be carefully balanced. Perhaps your teenagers want a basketball court and you need a quiet place to write poetry. Can both needs be served?

Start with a checklist of group and individual needs. It might include some of the following:

Fireplace niche
Family room
Basketball hoop and court
Library (contemplation space)
Poolside
Dressing rooms
Storage
Herb garden
Vegetable garden
Bird feeder
Dog run
Hammock
Children's play equipment
Connecting spaces or stairs
Greenhouse

As you develop your design checklist, investigate all the possible use requirements for the outdoor space you are planning. One patio or deck cannot be all things to all people. The conflict between a basketball court and a poetry nook may be unresolvable, but this is what the creative design process is all about.

Be aware of the changing needs of a person or family over time. Grandma may be sprightly now, but will she be able to negotiate a steep staircase to the deck in a few more years? Dad's present hobby of raising orchids in the kitchen window would be enhanced and expanded if he had a small greenhouse. The preschoolers probably won't need the sandbox after next summer. Could it become a barbecue area?

Discuss these questions in detail. Try to develop solutions that meet not only obvious needs but unspoken desires as well. A wish to sleep outdoors on a summer night might never get articulated because it may seem silly, but some free discussion and gentle probing may make that fantasy a reality.

Would your family entertain more if your house did not feel so crowded when friends dropped in? Paving stones and a lawn tough enough to take some traffic can create a low-cost outdoor room that can accommodate half the neighborhood on a balmy night. Simple lighting can extend the hours of effective use—and add drama to the space. Used artfully, lighting can transform surrounding elements such as trees and fences into magical entities that enhance and enchant an outdoor space.

Opposite: Children can play in the sandbox or ride tricycles on the lower patio level while parents keep an eye on them from the adjacent seating area.

A patio can provide one of the most sought-after outdoor living areas: a sunny spot for conversation or reading.

The plentiful greenery that screens this brick patio buffers sound and endows it with a feeling of secluded privacy.

Consider wind patterns. Will a deck or patio need to be shielded? Wind screens can be both functional and decorative. Where practical, hedging and trees are often more efficient—as well as more attractive—than solid walls.

Privacy and sound buffering should also be included in your design checklist. Plants absorb sound well and can provide almost total privacy. Solid materials such as stone can deflect sound, but a sheet of plywood might act like a drumhead and amplify certain frequencies. Study the conditions and seek professional advice in this area if it is warranted. Most sounds can be controlled, but others, such as from jet airplanes, present serious challenges.

Besides functional needs, do some preliminary thinking about the site. Consider what aspects of the landscape you *don't* want to change. Explore the question of what affect the proposed addition will have on the existing house and garden. Will drainage patterns be changed dramatically? A concrete slab is a solid surface that might accumulate and divert a large volume of water—water that your present lawn simply absorbs. Will a new roof structure cast shade on your vegetable garden or block natural light to the family room? Will an exposed-aggregate patio hurt trees that are well worth preserving? As paving diverts needed moisture from tree roots and destroys their ability to breath, decks are better than patios if a floor surface will abut a tree.

BALLPARK BUDGETING

At the low end of your potential costs, gravel or a seeded lawn area costs relatively little. Recycled materials such as slabs of concrete from an old driveway or bricks salvaged from a demolished building cost little except some intensive labor. Poured concrete is next in terms of construction material cost. Masonry products and clear redwood decking are among the more costlier materials. Expensive pavings such as marble or polished granite top the list.

Once you have a preliminary idea of what you want, you can estimate expenses by determining the likely cost of the materials involved. Double that amount if you plan to contract out the work. Budget should not excessively inhibit your design, however. The beauty of outdoor structures is that they can be added a little at a time, very much at your own speed and without disrupting indoor life. An overall plan can be implemented over many years. (For a detailed overview of the steps of planning and budgeting a project, see page 267.)

So set some goals, put them in the back of your mind, and then let your creative self work toward the ideal design solution.

This large patio was given enough slope, or pitch, to drain rain runoff into the lawn, thereby preventing water from collecting on the surface.

DESIGNING DECKS & PATIOS

The first step in planning is to measure and evaluate the existing situation. After mapping the site, make notes of potential deck or patio sites and the factors that affect them, such as sun or shade, access to the house, and good or bad views.

The planning process, which results in a final site plan, consists of three major creative activities: survey, evaluation, and design. In the survey, you make a base plan of the existing site, analyze the site conditions, assess your needs and objectives, and identify the resources available to carry out the design. Evaluation is the examination of accumulated information in search of design ideas. Design is the result of all this work—the creation of actual designed form. The main objective of all these activities is to free you from preconceptions about design forms—to observe, criticize, and make design decisions that will customize your future outdoor rooms. You will be engaged in all three of these activities throughout the process and go back and forth among them. If you've been dreaming at all about your new deck or patio, you have already begun the design process (see page 12). In this chapter you will learn how to move your design forward in a systematic way. It's an exciting process that can result in an outdoor environment custom-made for your needs and the built-in resources of your site.

SURVEYING YOUR SITE

Successful designs often result from dropping all preconceptions and approaching a problem with an open mind. To do this on your own site requires taking a fresh and objective look. Take some time to observe the potential locations for your deck or patio. You may want to build a combined deck and patio, or just one or the other. It might be close to the house or freestanding out in "the back forty." In any case, search out all potential sites.

One way to choose possible locations is to stroll through the areas you might use and pick several places just for sitting and relaxing. Walk a looping trail if you have a very large property, identifying sites and evaluating them from different angles. If your lot is small,

Use a tape measure to determine distances between significant points, such as from the corner of the house to where the fence meets the house.

you'll likely be limited to only two or three possible locations. Sit for a while in each. Move from one position to another. You may be surprised how much you will see that you hadn't noticed before. Look for problems and possibilities. Think of this observation process as a circling trail where you will find new and exciting details each time you walk it and pause to look anew.

As you study the potential sites, imagine what the views to and from them would be with a patio or deck at various elevations. Can you connect the garden to the house with a deck and thus make better access between them? How will it look from inside the house? From the street? Climb a stepladder to check out views, and lay out hoses or string lines to mark possible sites.

Is the street side the sunniest or most spacious part of the lot? Maybe you can make it private with fencing and plantings and create in the newly reclaimed space an image-enhancing deck or patio. The space might serve as a link between the public sidewalk and the private patio directly adjacent to the house. It may be that you have only enough room to make a private entryway or court. But at certain times of the day, that little space may be ideal for an outdoor room. Consider how you can design the space to serve your needs and convey the image you want for the home.

PREPARING A BASE PLAN

Now that you have studied the existing conditions of your lot, translate your observations into plan drawings. Architectural plans are drawings that show an area from a bird's-eye view—that is, looking directly down on the site. Such a plan will help you see planting areas, lawns, paths, and the house and how they relate to one another. Even if you are building only a small deck or patio, the municipality where you live will probably want drawn plans before issuing a building permit. The more complete the plans, and the more accurate the information, the happier the building officials will be.

The first thing you will need to begin your drawings is an accurate base plan. A complete base plan will show the correct property line, any easements or underground utilities on the lot, contours (lines that connect points of similar elevation, indicating the formation and slope of the land), existing trees and shrubs that you plan to save, the outline of the house, and any paths or structures on the property.

Finding Existing Records

The local building department or assessor's office may have a copy of your plat plan on file. This plan normally would not show your house or any improvements made to the lot, but would indicate a property line and any underground utilities or easements. If your house was designed by an architect or builder, that office may have a plan of your property that you can copy. Old plans should be verified to ensure that whatever is indicated is still part of the landscape and that any new structures or plantings are included.

If a copy of your plat plan is not available, you may need to have your property professionally surveyed. A topographic survey will show the property boundaries and contour lines of the site. This is particularly important if the lot is on a steep slope. A relatively flat site will not need a plan that shows contours, although accurate grade elevations will be necessary. The location and depth of existing underground storm drains on or off the property may be needed as well.

Drawing the Base Plan

Many aspects of drawing a base plan can easily be done freehand, but drafting tools will enable you to draw straight lines, precise angles, and circles. Even a freehand plan must be drawn to scale. Scaling aids accuracy when you are locating areas on a plan, helps you visualize the relative size of landscape elements, and is necessary for determining the amount of materials needed for construction. It's a good idea to get the correct tools for producing accurate plans right from the beginning—you will need them for the working drawings as well.

For the purposes of accuracy, your final working drawings should be measured with a ruler or, better, an architect's scale. This handy tool calibrates dimensions directly to the scale you are using. For example, if you are using a scale in which ¼ inch equals 1 foot, the architect's scale would represent a 4-foot length as 1 inch, an 8-foot length as 2 inches, and so on. You can draw most of your plan freehand, then use the architect's scale, triangle, and T square to establish angles and dimensions.

With masking tape, attach two pieces (one for padding) of graph tracing paper to a flat table or drawing board. Use rolled tracing paper for quick sketch studies as you work through the process. For full overlays, use additional pieces of graph tracing paper. The circle template and compass allow you to measure and draw any circular forms you choose to use in your designs. A soft-lead pencil is ideal for making the early freehand sketches. The harder pencils give a finer line and thus are more suitable for the later, precise drawings. Keep these sharp.

The first priority is to get your ideas down on paper. For this reason, the concept design should be done freehand. The mechanical aids are best kept for the final site plan of known facts and the working drawings that show exact dimensions and conditions.

DRAFTING TOOLS

Start with these basic tools: one 8-inch by 24-inch pad of 1,000h tracing paper with ¼-inch graph lines; one roll of tracing paper 14 inches wide; one transparent adjustable triangle, 8 inches or larger; a ruler; a T square; some masking tape; 6B drawing pencil for rough sketching; grade F drafting pencils for finished drawings; a compass; and an art-gum eraser. An architect's scale is recommended. You may also want a circle template and another with various sizes of squares and rectangles.

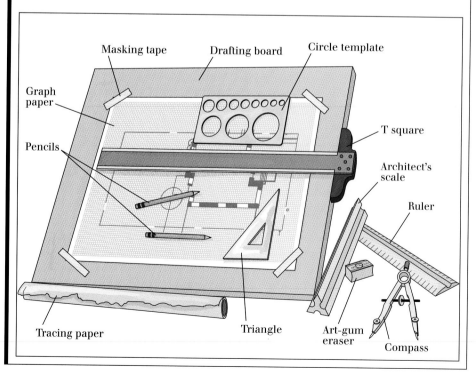

Masking tape · Drafting board · Circle template

Graph paper

Pencils

T square

Architect's scale

Ruler

Tracing paper

Triangle

Art-gum eraser

Compass

Choosing a Scale

To draw plans to scale, you will need graph paper, with each square representing a set measurement. A scale of 1 square equaling 6 feet is an especially easy scale to work with when roughly measuring activity areas in your yard, as 6 feet is approximately two adult strides. For more-detailed drawings, you can use an architect's scale for converting real dimensions into a relative scale.

When choosing a scale, consider the size of your property and the amount of detail you need to show. A large lot will require the use of a smaller scale, such as 1 inch to 20 feet, in order for the entire site to fit on a single piece of paper. A smaller lot or detailed areas would be better depicted at a larger scale, such as $\frac{1}{8}$ or $\frac{1}{4}$ inch to 1 foot. Construction details should be drawn at a 1-inch-to-1-foot scale—or even larger for intricate details such as Victorian ornaments.

Measuring the Site

To begin measuring your site, you will need a baseline, or datum line, on which to base the measurements. A wall of the house or an adjacent building will make an adequate baseline. Draw this line to scale on a sheet of graph paper, being sure to leave enough room around it to include the rest of the lot. Always draw a north arrow on

TOOLS FOR MEASURING YOUR SITE

There are a few simple tools you will need to measure your site. The two most important are tape measures. At least one should be 100 feet. In addition, have a sturdy, 20-foot carpenter's tape.

■ You'll need a hammer or a small sledgehammer and an armload of pointed stakes (large nails or spikes can be used instead). You'll also need a willing assistant and a small bag of white flour or agricultural lime. Mark measured locations with a dab of flour or draw a line with it for easy visibility.

■ A roll of string is a necessity. Mason's twine can be pulled tight and will not stretch or sag when you are trying to establish critical vertical distances. Don't attempt to use rough binder twine. Some nylon and polypropylene string stretches and then stretches again.

■ A carpenter's level and a line (or string) level are necessary for establishing the contours of the site. Better yet, use a builder's transit even if you have to rent one. (If you have not used one before, be sure to have the equipment-rental person show you exactly how to set it up and then check it to be sure it is properly aligned.)

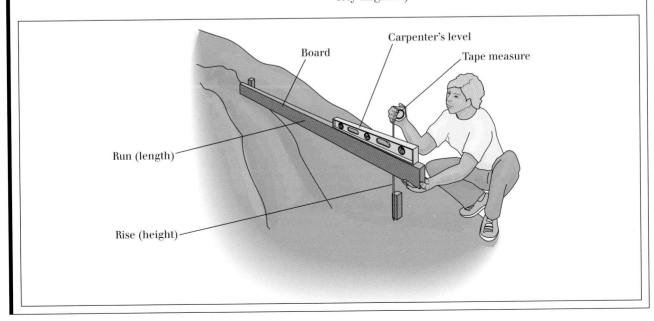

Carpenter's level

Board

Tape measure

Run (length)

Rise (height)

TRIANGULATION

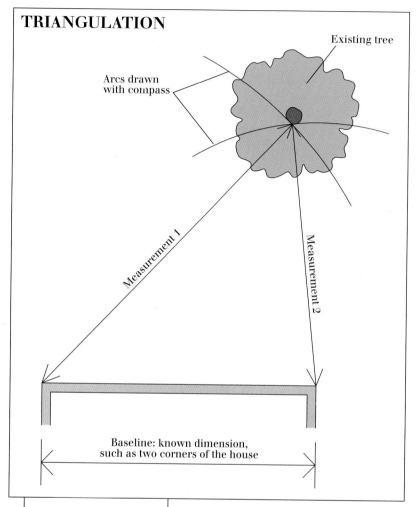

Existing tree

Arcs drawn
with compass

Measurement 1

Measurement 2

Baseline: known dimension,
such as two corners of the house

location and diameter of tree trunks and the spread of overhanging branches; shrubs; fences; overhead and underground utility lines; easements and setbacks; existing irrigation setups and hose bibbs; and any other structures on the lot. Mark down all of these locations as you measure them. To draw curved walks and driveways, locate a series of points along the curve and then draw a line connecting them. The more points you locate, the more accurate the curve will be.

In addition to horizontal dimensions, you may wish to include some vertical measurements on the base plan. The best way to do this is to set an elevation for the floor of the house and take the measurements from there. For example, assume that the finished floor of the house is at an elevation of 100 feet. If the deck is 6 inches below that, its elevation would be listed as 99 feet 6 inches. If the lawn is 1 foot below the deck, the elevation of the lawn would be 98 feet 6 inches. If the site has many elevation changes, you will need an accurate topographic survey produced to convey this information.

After you have taken all the measurements, trace this information onto a clean piece of paper as neatly as possible.

Measuring the house is fairly simple. Start by measuring the length of every section of the perimeter and then draw a corresponding outline. Locate all the windows and doors, and measure the height from the floor to thresholds, windowsills, and door tops. Measure the distance to the ground in all significant locations and indicate these dimensions on the plan. If ground level is 18 inches below the benchmark floor level of 100 feet, the notation for the grade at this point would be 98'6". By the same

all your plans and indicate the scale you are using. This is a standard practice that will make it easier for builders or city officials to read and understand your plans. It is also a standard convention to use the top of the drawing as the north direction; sun and shade patterns can then be determined at a glance.

With a photocopy of your rough plan, a pencil, and a tape measure in hand, head outside for some field work. Beginning from the baseline, use a 50- to 100-foot tape measure to locate everything on the lot that seems relevant. This includes the property line; all walls of the house, including the locations of doors and windows; the driveway and road; existing patio and paths; pool; the

notation system, the windowsill would be 102'6" if it is 30 inches from the floor.

Using the baseline as a starting point, stake out a grid of 10-foot squares, then locate other elements such as trees, outbuildings, pool, and paths in relation to this grid.

Another method of locating points on a plan is called triangulation. One 50-foot tape measure will do, but it is best to use two tape measures to save time. Attach the tapes to the fixed end points of the baseline, then walk each tape to the point you want to locate. Record each dimension and transfer it to the base plan, making an arc with a compass set for the correct scale distances. The intersection of the arcs is the exact placement of the measured point.

Use mason's twine and a line level to establish the relative height of each measured point and record this information on the plan. (Be sure to check the accuracy of the line level by checking it against a carpenter's level.) Holding one end of the line at the floor height of the house (represented as 100 feet on the plan), pull the line taut and raise and lower it until the bubble in the line level is centered. Then measure the distance from the string to the ground.

Climate Check

Climate and microclimate conditions will affect the design, location, and ultimate use of your patio or deck. Seasonal weather changes and the effects of varying temperature need to be considered. If time permits, keep a journal to establish the sun/shade patterns, rain and wind direction, and areas of standing water. Choose a location that avoids (or makes allowances for) damaging elements, such as swampy ground or strong wind,

and takes advantage of pleasant conditions, such as cool breezes, shade, and the warming sun.

If you don't have time for lengthy observation, it is possible to calculate solar angles for all seasons of the year. You can determine the amount of shade a structure or tree will cast for any day of the year. Check the local library for reference books on architectural standards or solar building techniques. These books often have charts on solar angles as well as clear descriptive examples of how to plot shade patterns. Before using the charts, consult a map or atlas to find out the approximate latitude of your community (the number of degrees your site is from the equator).

Plastic wind screens shelter this deck from the wind without blocking the view.

WORKING WITH MICROCLIMATES

PLOTTING THE SUN'S PATH

Summer shadow

Winter shadow

On June 21, the sun's angle from the horizon at noon is about 65° at the U.S. northern border and 85° at the southern border

E

N

S

W

On December 21, the sun's angle from the horizon at noon is about 20° at the U.S. northern border and 40° at the southern border

PLANNING FOR SHADE

North

BLOCKING BREEZES WHILE ADMITTING SUNLIGHT

Plastic panel or safety glass

DIFFUSING BREEZES WITH PARTIAL SCREENING

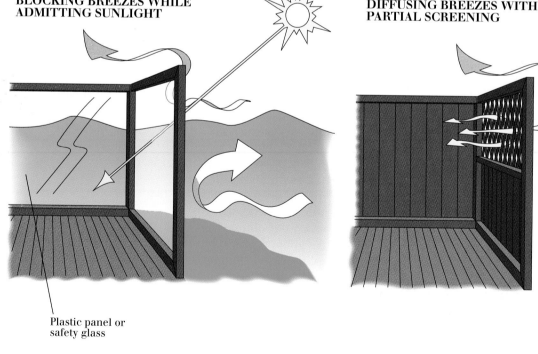

SEASONAL CHANGES IN THE PATH OF THE SUN

Angle of sun at
summer solstice

Angle of sun at
vernal and autumnal
equinoxes

Canada

United States

Angle of sun at
winter solstice

Although the angle of the sun
changes with the seasons, because of the curved surface of
the earth the angle is always
more acute the farther you live
from the equator

Summer sun

Summer sun

Equinox sun

The angle of the
sun in Washing-
ton, Michigan,
Maine, and other
northern-tier
states

Equinox sun

Winter sun

Winter sun

The angle of the sun
in Arizona, Texas,
Florida, and other
southern-tier states

For a very general idea of sun patterns using your drawing scale, draw a vertical line representing the height of the house, a tree, or any tall shade-producing object. At the base of this line, draw a horizontal line representing the floor of the outdoor living space. Then use an adjustable triangle to set an angle of 75 degrees from the horizontal and draw a line from the top of the one representing the house height to the one representing the deck or patio floor. Where these lines intersect is the outer extent of the house shadow cast in a northerly direction at noon, June 21—the summer solstice and the longest day of the year.

Note that 75 degrees is the angle of the noon sun about halfway between the southern and northern borders of the United States; it is approximately 65 degrees above the horizon at the northern border and 85 degrees at the southern border. At the winter solstice (the shortest day of the year) the solar noon angles are 20 degrees at the northern border and 40 degrees at the southern border.

Plot simple sun paths on the base plan so that as you work with preliminary designs, you will be conscious of basic sun/shade patterns at various times of the year.

In cold climates, find out the depth of the frost line for your area;

The time you spend carefully measuring and assessing the site will pay off in satisfaction when you are using the patio or deck.

building codes in some North American climate zones require that footings be 4 feet or more into the earth. Frost will heave paved surfaces, as will expanding clay. These conditions, which vary within regions, may affect underground drainage, the placement of footings and posts, and the construction of retaining walls. Building officials are usually very helpful if you discuss your plans with them before you complete your final drawings. Their advice is based on knowledge of local conditions and code requirements and should be listened

to carefully. Also consider unusual local hazards that may affect the deck design. In areas where heavy snows, earthquakes, hurricanes, or tornadoes occur, appropriate building codes and construction techniques must be followed carefully.

Drainage patterns should also be noted and marked on the base plan. As a general rule, water generated on one property should never drain onto adjoining properties. Most patio surfaces are nonabsorbent and simultaneously shed water and prevent the soil below them from absorbing and dissipating it. Some jurisdictions insist that surface run-off be diverted into storm sewers, dry wells, or retention ponds. Storm sewers are frequently inadequate to receive all the water from a drainage area at one time.

Note any specific soil conditions, such as perpetual dampness or the presence of clay, rocks, and sand. It is a good idea to remove the topsoil from the proposed patio site; topsoil is a poor bearing surface and is too precious to be covered with paving (it takes a forest about 100 years to create 1 inch of topsoil). Other underground conditions need to be noted as well. If low areas of the lot have been filled, note the depthand the type of material. Also note the location of septic tanks and fields. If the site is steep or soil conditions are unstable (as with new fill), you may want to ask a landscape architect to advise you on workable solutions for difficult problems.

SUPPLEMENTING THE BASE PLAN

Your nearly completed base plan is an important topographical record, but it tells only part of the story. Next you need to search out and record the less tangible—but still important—features by making a site analysis. Even if you are very familiar with your property, it's to your advantage to record all your observations. You may discover aspects of the lot that you had never thought about before. The better you understand what you have, the easier it will be to develop a sensitive and appropriate design solution.

To conduct a site analysis, overlay your base plan with a piece of tracing paper and use this to write down your observations. Note the following information: the location of sunny and shady spots; any areas with poor drainage; the direction of

SAMPLE BASE PLAN

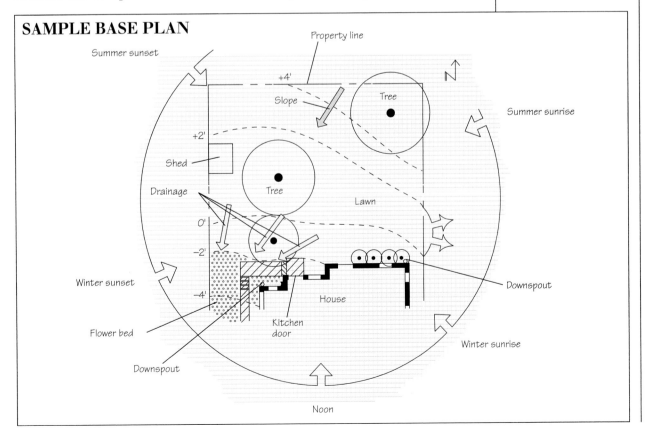

prevailing winds and wind-free areas; steep slopes and level areas; access points and circulation routes; and any features you might wish to accent, such as a rock outcropping or a pond. Include views too, noting the attractive ones and the ones you would like to block out. Also record any improvements you find desirable, such as getting more sun to a particular area or screening the patio from a neighbor's view. Note any trees or shrubs you'd like to remove, as well as those you want to retain. List any other structures or planting areas that you want to eliminate as well as things you may want to add, such as a pool or badminton court.

In addition, write on the drawing any feelings you have about particular areas of the yard. If there is one spot you especially like, circle it on the drawing. Likewise, if there is an area that is unattractive and needs improvement, indicate its location and describe it on the plan. Finally, show possible new access points, potential deck or patio locations, and desired paths.

Your Immediate Neighbors

The homes adjacent to yours will have an impact on your landscape design and installation. They will affect where you place plants as well as social, storage, and recreation areas.

Your next-door neighbors' landscapes may be attractive and appealing enough to act as a catalyst for your design. You may want to select similar plants and construction materials. This will add to the overall impact your landscape has on your home and neighborhood. If the disparity between styles is too great, the only answer may be to screen out your neighbors' landscapes.

You will want to take note of features in your neighbors' landscapes that will affect your design. Notice

the shade cast by neighboring buildings. In hot regions you can use the shade cast by the buildings next door to great advantage in your patio layout. Notice the location of areas in your neighbors' yards that are designated for socializing, recreation, quiet, storage, and children's play. You will want to consider these functional areas when designing your own. The success of an outdoor dining area planned for elegant entertaining could be destroyed, for example, if it is located just across the fence from a neighbor's garbage cans or dog run.

Your House

The outside of your house presents a particular identity, and the landscape structures should work to reflect that character. A truly successful landscape design melds architecture and environment. Determine whether the layout, materials used, or architectural details give your home a distinct style. Books from the local library may help you to correctly identify styles and details.

The relative size of your home is also important to bear in mind as you begin to create your design. A large house usually benefits from some vertical elements to provide balance and make it more aesthetically pleasing on a human scale. Conversely, if the house is small, very tall elements should be avoided, unless your intent is to lose the house within the landscape. Be careful not to build landscape structures that dwarf the house.

Spend some time simply looking out the windows of your home. Imagine what you would like to see in the new patio and its adjacent landscape. Also take note of the design of your home's interior. The coordination of interior design and exterior construction in the use of

Opposite: This redwood deck fits with the rest of the neighborhood, both in function and in the style and materials used.

color, texture, and plants can have a stunning effect.

Preserving the Best Features of Your Landscape

If your project involves remodeling or renovating an existing landscape, you'll have some preexisting elements that you want to integrate into the new design. Trees, paving, or structures may provide a starting point from which to work. Even if you think that nothing in the yard is salvageable, take the time to look at every feature before you begin demolition. Consider remodeling the house at the same time so indoor and outdoor spaces can interact with each other in a harmonious way. Perhaps you need a sliding glass door to access your new patio.

If your landscape has a personal or public history, you may decide to accentuate or preserve this identity. Whether it is the overall design that has historical value or just a single tree, let these earlier features inspire your creativity. Relocating a historical structure or plant is well worth the effort. A landscape with a history is a valuable personal and public treasure.

Preserving mature trees and shrubs can save you a great deal of money. See whether pruning isn't a better idea for an overgrown shrub; or if a small tree is in the center of the new deck site, consider transplanting—or even building the deck around it—as opposed to cutting it down. Make an extra effort to preserve the plants and structures you want to keep; these valuable assets are easily destroyed or damaged in the process of construction. Be sure to barricade existing trees near the new patio or deck to protect them; heavy equipment and careless workers can inflict serious accidental damage.

Designing Outdoor Structures on a New Lot

If you are at the blueprint stage or have just started to build your house, you have the freedom to alter or modify the plan to suit your wishes and needs. You can, for example, adjust entries, exits, walks, and driveways to better integrate them with your landscape choices. Look around your lot for existing features, such as large trees, rocks, and streams, that you can incorporate into your design. Make sure that the house construction accommodates these elements so you do not risk destroying them. Although you may feel that the design and construction of the house is taking up all of your creativity, try to decide on at least the major features of the landscape design, particularly deck and patio sites, while the house is being planned.

You can have some of the landscape construction done in conjunction with the building of the home while the equipment is on-site. For example, grading and other earth moving are considerably easier for a professional to do with a backhoe brought in for foundation work than for you to do later using a shovel and wheelbarrow.

After you've finished recording your observations, the base-plan overlay may be a confusing muddle of notes, arrows, and circles. If you wish, you can redraw your site analysis onto a clean sheet of tracing paper, including the rough outline of the lot, house, and other fixed points. Don't throw away your original, however; it will be helpful as you develop your ideas into a final site plan.

The natural sitting area of this yard would make a good spot for a deck. With careful planning, the deck could take advantage of the existing tree for shade.

BRAINSTORMING WITH BUBBLE DIAGRAMS

Now is the time to begin designing. Lay tracing paper over the base plan. Start with bubble diagrams (these can be circles, rectangles, and irregular forms) to sketch out where major elements in the design should be located and how they relate to each other. In doodling with the bubble shapes, feel free to brainstorm; these sketches are preliminary and most will be discarded. Don't be concerned with your drawing skills at this point. In fact, too much detail in the beginning can actually inhibit the design process, which involves getting spontaneous ideas on paper while they are fresh. Plan on drawing several different bubble diagrams. As you do so, look to the following case study for inspiration.

A Landscape Design Case Study

Keep in mind that with bubble diagrams, many sketches are prepared and discarded. Ideas should be allowed to flow freely from all who will use the area. Budget should be considered but not in any real detail. The two or three approaches you like best can be saved for further consideration. Here is an example of how the process works, and what kind of creative solutions should be explored before settling on a design.

Notice that this site slopes rather sharply to the rear and is presently not landscaped. There are three pines in the northwest corner, where the prevailing wind comes from. A small flowering crabapple tree thrives near the corner of the dining room. The best view is in

BUBBLE DIAGRAM

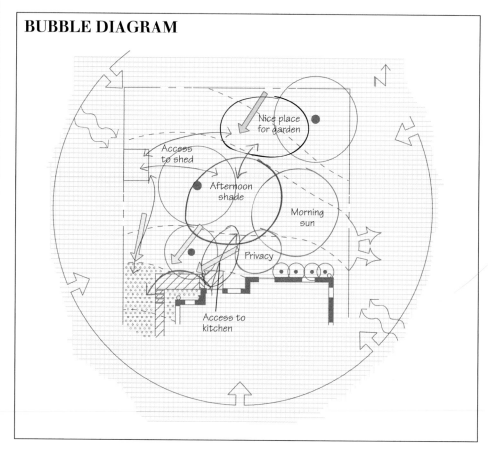

BASE PLAN OF CASE STUDY

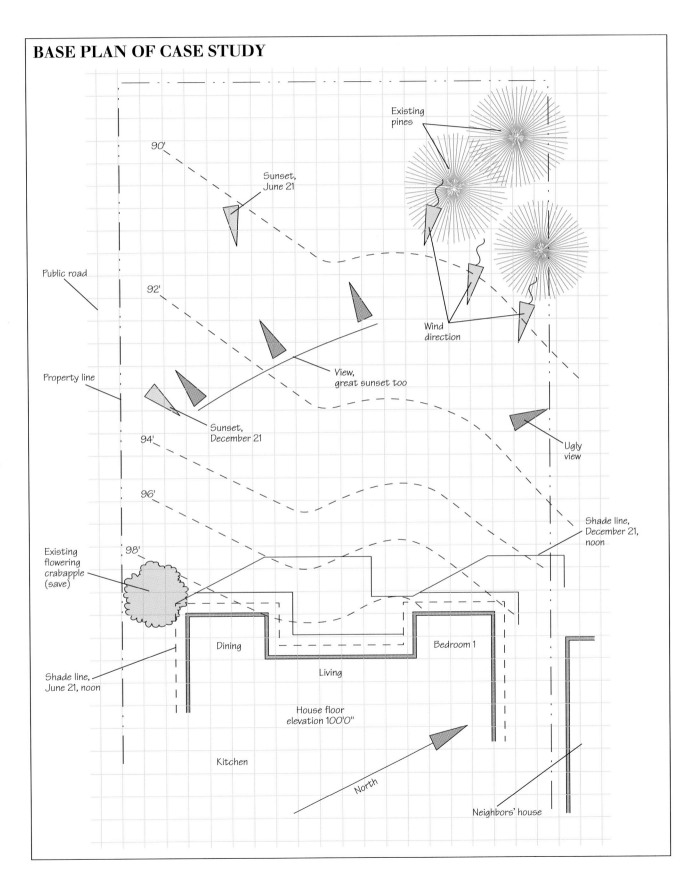

90'

Existing
pines

Sunset,
June 21

Public road

92'

Wind
direction

Property line

View,
great sunset too

Sunset,
December 21

Ugly
view

94'

96'

Shade line,
December 21,
noon

98'

Existing
flowering
crabapple
(save)

Dining

Bedroom 1

Shade line,
June 21, noon

Living

House floor
elevation 100'0"

Kitchen

North

Neighbors' house

BASIC PRINCIPLES FOR DESIGNING DECKS AND PATIOS

Keep it simple. Simple forms are easiest for people to relate to. For decks and patios, plain geometric shapes are the safest; rectangles or circular forms, or a combination of these simple shapes, will probably be most pleasing to the eye. Arcs can be effective when they are tangential to straight lines or to each other, making a smooth transition from one element to another. Curved forms are best when they can be related to a radius point. A free arc or curve with no clear center tends to look weak or confusing.

■ Repeat forms and materials. Designs tend to work best when a few materials are repeated in an interesting manner. For example, if every brick of a brick patio were a different color or shape, it would look confusing. But if the brick were common red with some charcoal-colored feature strips embedded, the design would be interesting and comfortably familiar. A repeating brick feature strip in a concrete patio is more effective than combining feature strips of stone, brick, marble, tile, or wood.

■ Create harmony. Suppose that one of the plant materials used in the yard is sprawling juniper, a common plant. If there was one at the front gate, a cluster of three near the front door, five near the steps to the deck, another individual plant near the patio, and a cluster of five at the rear of the garden, a person might not specifically remember the subtle repetition but would sense a harmony and wholeness in the overall design. A visual melody of form and texture would linger in the mind. Changes in varieties could enrich the pattern.

Contrast, when used well, can compliment the overall feeling of repetition and harmony. A bold form, a piece of sculpture, or a fountain can capture the eye and please the senses. Confusion results if these are overdone, however.

■ Scale. Architecture—the constructed environment—includes garden structures, decks, and patios as well as houses and larger buildings. Scale is one of the most important elements in architectural design, and the human form is one of the primary factors when considering architectural scale. The sense of scale can be quite different, depending on the intended use and the feeling one is expressing in the design. For example, a cathedral may be designed to create a sense of awe, a diminishment of the individual, but the pews must fit the human form.

If your house is large, the site broad and sweeping, a 10-by-10 deck might be dwarfed by its surroundings, so a larger size would be more appropriate. But in either case, the rise and run of the steps leading to it must be in scale with the walking patterns of human beings. It is necessary to size the design elements in relationship to each other and to the human scale.

■ Texture. As a deliberate design element, texture offers great opportunity for variations in the finished environment.

Light is the companion of texture—it is difficult to see the pattern and texture of a stone wall in the middle of the night (without an introduced light source), but the same stone wall will display impressive character if the sun rays slant across its face.

Even a lightly broomed patio floor will develop textural form when the broomed lines are at right angles to the setting sun and cast small shadow patterns on the surface.

■ Color. All materials used in construction and landscaping have a color that is uniquely their own. How you blend them on your palette is a matter of personal choice. The safe way is to blend colors, attempting to harmonize the elements in the design. Contrast can be exciting. A magenta bougainvillea against a stark white wall, or a piece of scarlet furniture on a bleached gray deck, lends stylish drama to a setting.

STANDARD DIMENSIONS

WALKWAYS AND STEPS

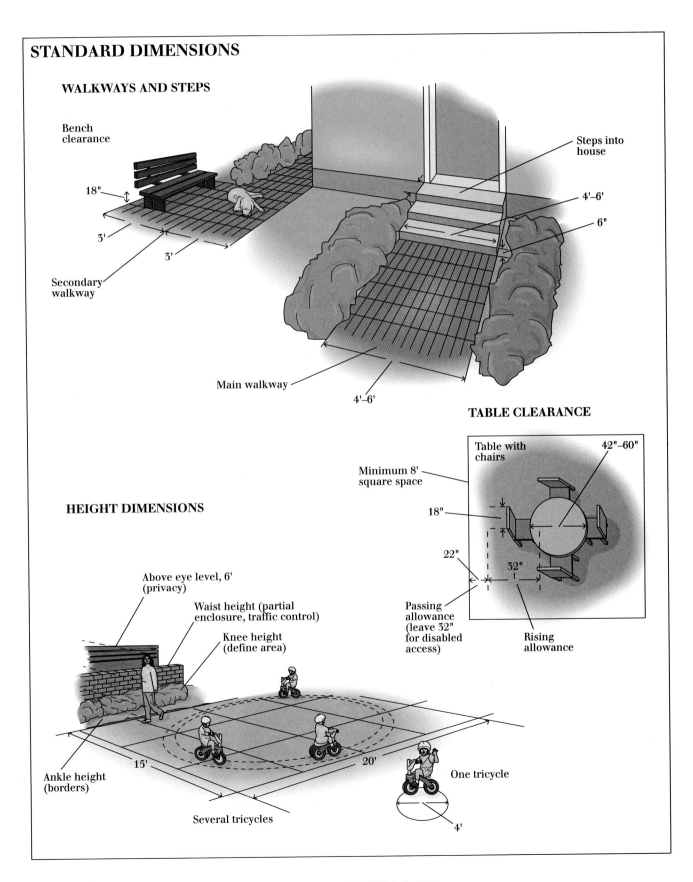

Bench clearance

18"

3'

3'

Secondary walkway

Steps into house

4'–6'

6"

Main walkway

4'–6'

TABLE CLEARANCE

Table with chairs

Minimum 8' square space

42"–60"

18"

22"

32"

Passing allowance (leave 32" for disabled access)

Rising allowance

HEIGHT DIMENSIONS

Above eye level, 6' (privacy)

Waist height (partial enclosure, traffic control)

Knee height (define area)

Ankle height (borders)

15'

20'

Several tricycles

One tricycle

4'

the west, where the sunsets are spectacular. The house will cast some winter shade on the central part of a patio or deck area, particularly in the winter months when the sun is low.

The contours show there is an 8-foot downward grade from the house floor (indicated as 100 feet) to the rear of the lot. This is substantial enough to require a retaining wall or two if there is to be any major flat area in the yard. The wish list for the homeowner of this property includes a lawn area with no more than a gentle slope from one side to the other. It also includes outdoor living areas in the form of decks or patios and an outdoor eating area accessible from the indoor dining room. At least a portion of the deck or patio areas should provide for year-round sunning, bordered by some shady retreats.

Bubble Diagram 1 The first bubble diagram proposes two potential deck areas attached to the house at the dining and living rooms at or near floor level. (In snow country or where winds are high, it would be good practice to build the deck 6 inches below the floor.)

An additional patio or terrace area is sketched into the diagram at a level 5 feet below the decks and far enough from the house to be in full sun throughout the year.

A retaining wall extends a relatively flat lawn area at a level of 91 feet. This would require a 3-foot cut at the wall and a 3-foot fill behind it. Another wall could be constructed near the 90-foot contour at the lower lawn or a 3-foot bank could be formed and planted with erosion-resistant ground cover.

This large lawn area, which is fairly level, would be suitable for badminton, volleyball, or croquet.

Two small decks can create lots of outdoor living area without overwhelming a small site or destroying too many trees.

BUBBLE DIAGRAM 1

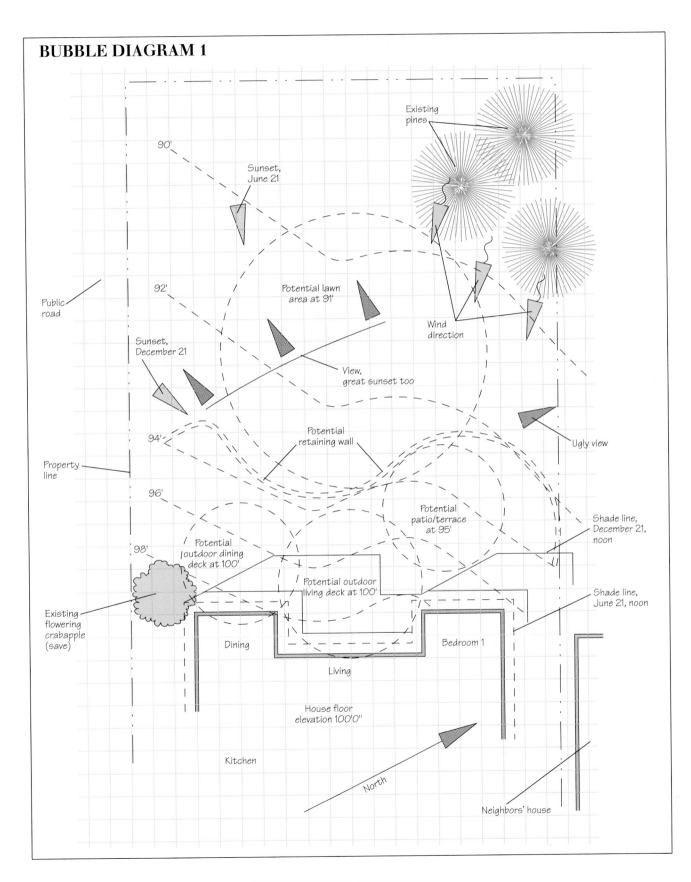

BUBBLE DIAGRAM 2

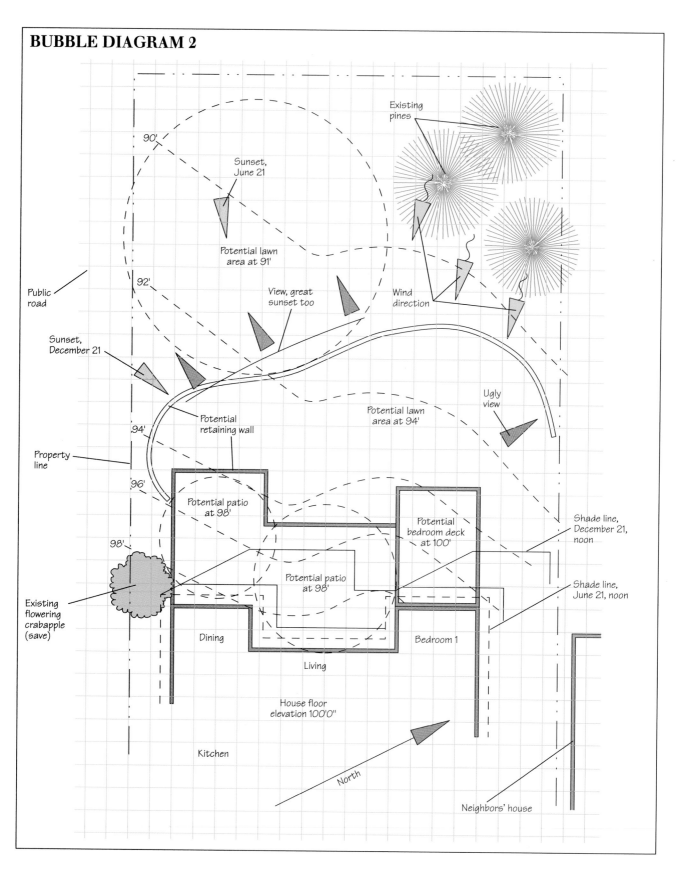

Bubble Diagram 2 This plan proposes that a patio make up most of the outdoor living area—actually a terrace with a retaining wall along the edge farthest from the house. A railing would be added to the top of the wall for safety. Another retaining wall separates the yard into two separate lawn areas, one 3 feet higher than the other. The plan includes a sundeck at the level of the bedroom, intended as a relatively private and separate space. The main terraces are 2 feet lower than the floor level to minimize the amount of fill needed.

Evaluating the Bubble Diagrams

The next important step is to consider the pros and cons of each approach and compare them for cost and practicability. The goal is to focus on one potential design and develop it into a full preliminary drawing. Then a rough cost estimate can be calculated.

The layout of bubble diagram 2 works well. The relationship of the patio and deck areas are in keeping with the wish list and the floor plan of the house. The railing needed for the patio area can be designed as a partial windbreak and if built with transparent materials will not block the view. The house will provide some shade for the patios, and an overhead shade structure would not be difficult to add later. The lawn areas are reasonably spacious even though they are bisected by a retaining wall.

The major argument against this design is the cost. Two retaining walls will be expensive to construct no matter what material is used. The walls indicated are each about 80 feet long and 4 feet high and will require footings. Quick calculations include a 5-foot wall (part of the wall should be below grade) and

a 3-foot-wide footing. In addition, at least 1 foot of earth fill will be required over the entire area—totaling about 6,000 square feet. That's nearly 225 cubic yards of earth. The cost of these alterations would be very high.

One budget-sparing alternative is to lower the grades by 1 foot. This would mean a 5-foot difference between the patio and the lawn area below. Because the patio is already 2 feet below the house floor, this is excessive. The plan is handsome and workable, but the cost is too high, especially in light of the fact that we have not yet considered the costs of constructing the patios and deck, the original purpose of the design exercise. Bubble diagram 1 seems to be the plan to pursue.

Two additional drawings are needed at this stage. These should be fairly detailed even though they are still in the preliminary design phase. Simply overlay the base plan with the selected bubble diagram and a new piece of tracing paper and continue with the design, using the base-plan grid to keep the drawing in scale. Check the measurements from time to time with an architect's scale.

The first drawing (see page 42) is a preliminary site plan, indicating all the major elements of the project. It doesn't depict framing specifics or exact details for retaining walls, though it does include landscape symbols for plants and trees, and double lines for fences, railings, and curbs. The more information included now, the more accurate the preliminary estimate will be.

The second drawing (see page 44) is a section of the site—a perspective representing a cross section of the base plan at the section line (marked *A* on the drawing). Draw this as if you are directly in

CASE STUDY PRELIMINARY SITE PLAN

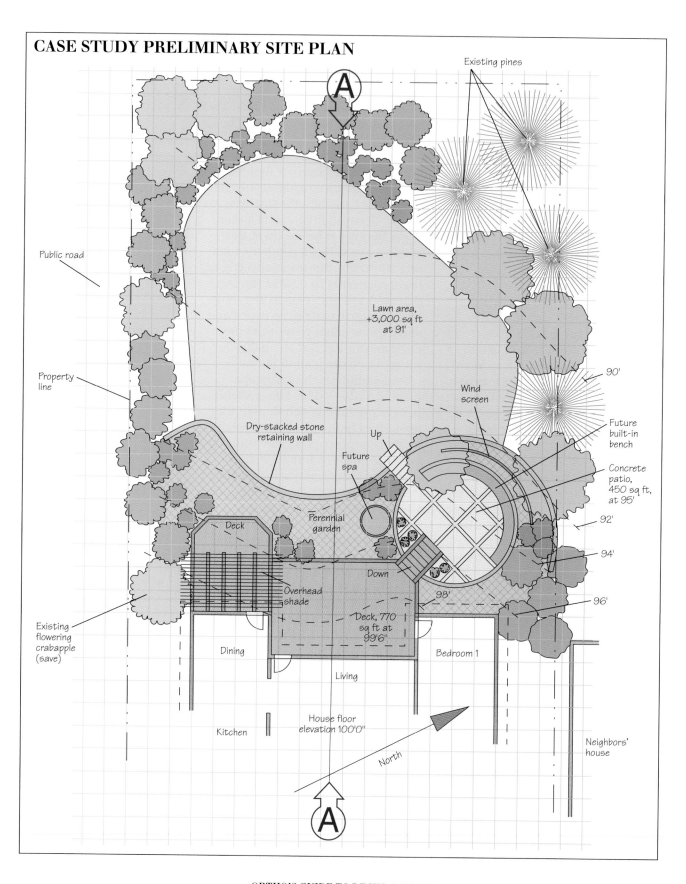

Existing pines

Public road

Lawn area,
+3,000 sq ft
at 91'

Property
line

90'

Wind
screen

Dry-stacked stone
retaining wall

Up

Future
spa

Future
built-in
bench

Concrete
patio,
450 sq ft,
at 95'

92'

Deck

Perennial
garden

94'

Down

96'

Overhead
shade

98'

Existing
flowering
crabapple
(save)

Deck, 770
sq ft at
99'6"

Dining

Bedroom 1

Living

Neighbors'
house

Kitchen

House floor
elevation 100'0"

North

A

front of, and level with, the area being viewed. This shows the existing grades, the relative height of the house floor, and the size of existing trees. It also shows the proposed construction elements.

This section drawing offers another way of viewing the site and the planned construction. It also helps establish actual finished grades. Section drawings are an excellent way to indicate how the various elements of the construction are supposed to go together. Later, a full set of working drawings will include numerous larger-scale sections for various details of the project.

For a preliminary plan, a deck is designed next to the house with direct access to the dining room, living room, and bedroom 1. This is a fairly large deck, providing ample room for entertaining and outdoor dining. A barbecue grill can easily be incorporated near the dining room, either worked into the final design or added later.

The trellised roof provides shade during the hot summer months, but for sun lovers part of the dining deck will get full summer sun from noon until sunset. The shady area could easily be extended over more of the deck, if desired.

The preliminary plan shows that the floor of the deck is 6 inches below the house floor. This prevents rain from driving under the doors and allows for snow buildup in colder climates. Where severe weather is not a major concern, however, a deck level with the house floor would allow easier accessibility.

Where the deck leads to the patio, the deck is about 4½ feet above the existing grade, so a short flight of stairs is needed. The patio is to be a transitional level between the deck and the lawn. This patio will be concrete with brick feature strips

and brick edging—an attractive design and considerably less expensive than an all-brick patio.

The wind screen along the patio is both practical and decorative. The screen itself could be designed in many ways and could support a mural, sculpture, or other type of outdoor art. In order to further protect the patio from the prevailing wind, some leafy trees are included to supplement the windbreak effect of the existing pines. A small tree added near the new patio will offer a bit of shade on a hot afternoon. As the design is refined and completed, a bench or other built-in furnishing could be added. The patio area would also be great for a children's play area, an adjacent small swimming pool, or a spa. Steps or a ramp connect the patio to the lawn area.

The serpentine retaining wall could be built of brick to match the feature strips in the patio, or of stone (especially if the site abounds in usable rocks), wood, concrete, or concrete blocks. The retaining effect could also be achieved with a shaped bank planted in ground cover for erosion control. However, for a 4-foot grade change, a shaped bank would need to be at least 6 feet wide. A bank steeper than that would be hard to stabilize with simple planting.

Cost Estimate At this point only a rough estimate of costs can be made. Additional features might be added: a barbecue grill, a bench, lighting, and irrigation. There might be a small pool or a spa. Some of these extras could involve substantial costs.

In order to prepare an accurate estimate, it is necessary to have a set of working drawings from which material lists can be prepared. At this stage the pertinent question is whether the proposed

CASE STUDY PRELIMINARY SECTION

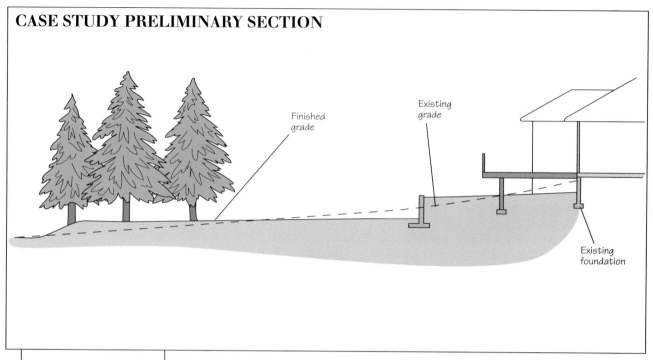

Finished grade

Existing grade

Existing foundation

design is affordable. Remember that between 50 and 60 percent of the contract estimate is labor. It should be reasonable to reduce the total price (calculated below) by 50 percent if you are going to do all the work yourself, and by 40 percent if you will have a contractor do just the grading.

If you are building a deck or patio yourself, you can take advantage of interesting design options that will not affect the budget. For example, the do-it-yourselfer can choose any pattern for a brick patio without affecting the cost. It takes about five bricks per square foot of patio floor (including an allowance for breakage and other waste), whether you choose a basket weave, herringbone, running bond, pinwheel, or double-helix pattern. If you were paying a bricklayer, however, the cost for the labor would vary according to the design you chose. A complicated or unusual pattern could double the cost of the work, as it simply takes more time to install.

DESIGNING ON A HUMAN SCALE

Human scale is the test that determines adequate space. For example, a deck off the master bedroom will be used by only two people. A reclining or semireclining person needs a space at least 7 feet long; 2 or 3 feet more are needed for another person to walk past. Thus, 9 or 10 feet is a comfortable distance for one dimension of this deck. Allowing about 3 feet for the width of a person, the chair they sit on, and a small table, as well as a 3-foot allowance for a door opening onto the deck, 9 or 10 feet are required for the other dimension. Therefore, a 10-by-10 deck or patio would be a reasonable minimum size for a two-person sunning area. This same 100 square feet can be moderately stretched in either direction—an 8-by-12 space might work just as well if the furnishings are set on a diagonal.

Another situation might call for a small outdoor eating area off the kitchen. Assume that four people will sit at a round table 42 inches in diameter. Between 2 and 2½ feet of depth (24 to 30 inches) is required for a seated person in a comfortable chair. Another 18 inches are required for traffic behind this person. So, assuming a person on either side of the table, the minimum distance across this eating area is a little less than 12 feet, so 12 by 12 would be a comfortable preliminary design size for this intimate outdoor eating area.

People at a party, most of whom are standing up and clustering in groups for conversation, need about 18 square feet each—a circle of about 4½ to 5 feet in diameter. So if your outdoor space is primarily a party area, allow about 900 square feet for every 50 guests. Use the same calculation for decks or paving around swimming pools.

If the patio or deck will be used primarily as an outdoor dining area for a family of four and their friends, you might plan on a 12-by-16-foot space for 8 to 10 people. In addition, for general use you'd want to allow 20 square feet for each of the 10 people. The total square feet needed for the dining area (*12 × 16 = 192*) plus that needed for general use (*20 × 10 = 200*) totals about 400 square feet. The same space could also accommodate a 25-person party quite comfortably.

Areas for sports and games can be creatively integrated into constructed outdoor rooms. Allow a 10-by-10-foot space and a wall for darts. An area for active table-tennis players needs to be 20 feet square.

CHALLENGING LANDSCAPES

Almost every landscape situation has some constraint or problem. You can turn some of these draw-

This deck, although tiny, still affords a comfortable outdoor sitting area amid the blooms of container-held plants.

backs into assets by choosing an appropriate design. You may have functional difficulties, such as noise or poor drainage, or aesthetic concerns, such as dilapidated plants or a bad view. Your landscape problem may be a small plot or even a complete lack of land.

Small Spaces

Although urban sites most frequently present a small-space challenge, in some cases a portion of a larger landscape, such as a side yard or enclosed patio, needs to be designed separately as a small space. If you choose to combine a separate small-space design within a larger context, the transition from one space to the other must be smooth and natural. Provide a sense of continuity among the various parts by using similar materials or plantings.

The greatest challenge in small-space design is scale. If possible, don't have walls or screens that overpower the space. Use several small planting pots instead of one oversized container. Use small-unit paving materials such as bricks instead of large pavers, and 2×4s for decking rather than 2×6s. Install lightweight, white metal furniture rather than bulky redwood or teak. Small, fine-textured plants, rather than broadleaf ones, are better for a small area. If your goal is to give the illusion of more space, try affixing mirrors to screens, fences, or house walls. Be careful that a mir-

ror does not face the sun and that the deception is not too obvious.

Most patios or decks include some horticultural elements. Plantings should tolerate the cramped conditions. If the landscape is in an urban area, you have the added constraints of smog, harsh winds, and limited sunlight. Consult the local garden center for plants that can thrive in these circumstances. In general, it is better for the unity of the landscape to keep plantings to the same species.

By the very nature of its size, the installation of a small-space landscape usually goes very quickly and, depending on the materials and objects you choose, requires little investment. The amount of maintenance will depend on the deck or patio materials you choose and the plants you install. Watering may be your most time-consuming

Masses of potted flowers take up limited space but create an illusion of size on this small deck by blurring its edges.

task, and even that can be minimized dramatically by choosing plants native to your region and microclimate.

Although many people think of small-space landscapes as a limitation, you should be aware of their advantages. Condensed space means that less of every material is needed, which is nice on the budget. In addition, the time needed for chores is lessened, meaning that you can have an attractive yard with plenty of time left over to enjoy it.

Balconies and Rooftops
Don't let a complete lack of land prevent you from creating an outdoor living space. Balconies and roofs present especially difficult situations, but they also offer great opportunities for specialty plants and added color while providing a place to get away from it all in the midst of the city. Along with the problems usually associated with small-space landscapes, balconies and rooftops have the added challenges of water, drainage, lighting, weight loads, and access. For instance, planters, large pots, and similar heavy objects must be kept over load-bearing walls or near the building edges.

When you add plants to your roof deck or balcony, choose ones that can tolerate crowded root conditions as well as wind, partial shade, and little water. Some plants are more tolerant of these conditions than others. Soil for pots and planters should be lightweight and continually supplied with fertilizer. Vines and ivies are good choices because they are tough, tolerant plants that can climb, screen, and provide blossoms or fragrant blooms without taking up a great deal of space.

Property Edges and Zero Lot Lines
Every piece of property has an edge, as do the various use areas within a landscape. Some boundaries present more difficulty than others—homes too close to the house next door, adjacent to a commercial or retail establishment, or next to a busy street. Zero-property-line problems occur when a building is constructed exactly on the lot line, presenting the homeowner next door with a tall, blank wall.

Making the best of a structure located close to a property line may

The space between a privacy wall and the wall of the house can be made more appealing with a few plants.

A lath fence creates quick and inexpensive privacy without the constricting feeling of a solid wall.

require cooperation among neighbors. If possible, grow a vine on the offending wall to soften the view. Trees or tall shrubs, if there is enough ground space, will also lessen the impact of a building.

The edge of your property may be wide enough to be a side yard, providing a small area for socializing. Narrow side yards are excellent for storage or as a pet area. If the sun exposure is good, you may opt to locate a vegetable garden here, out of sight from the rest of the landscape. A side yard just off a bedroom may make a secluded patio.

Designing for Privacy

This is as simple as laying out the areas you wish to cordon off. The position of landscape plantings,

fences, walls, and garden structures will divide private and public spaces. Constructed elements will yield instant privacy, whereas hedges and other planted screens will take months or possibly years to grow to the point where they provide adequate screening.

Plant screens can be the least expensive to install if you can afford to wait until they reach maturity. Do not use deciduous plant materials as visual buffers. Consider the overhead and eye-level views when you choose plantings. Coniferous trees normally grow slowly, but they screen from the ground level to several stories up. In time, however, many conifers lose their lower branches, making some form of additional understory planting

necessary. Views from above can be blocked with an arbor or grove of canopy trees, which offer the advantage of screening overhead but leave an open view at ground level.

Wood can also be an inexpensive way to create a privacy screen or baffle. With the wide range of design possibilities and colors of paint and stain, wood fences and screens will fit into almost any style of landscape. Masonry walls and structures are generally more difficult and expensive to install, but they provide immediate screening and may solve other functional problems—especially regarding drainage. They can also be terraced to add varied scale and interest.

As with other functional elements, it is vitally important that constructed elements remain in context with the overall landscape style, in order to keep that all-important unity of design. If you need to partition only a small portion of the site, select screening materials that complement the other plantings and constructed elements.

Privacy walls in front of a house are not as common in North America as they are in the cities of Europe and Asia, but they create private space in an area that would otherwise be unusable by the family.

UNDERSTANDING REGULATIONS

The regulations that will affect your deck or patio design include community design guidelines; restrictions concerning easements, setbacks, and utilities; zoning ordinances; and building codes. All are legal constraints that govern what you can build and how you can build it. They are designed to safeguard the community, promote public safety, and protect the homeowner. Before you move forward with your plans, thoroughly evaluate the demands and constraints of local laws. You may need to obtain a certain permit or attend a hearing if what you request is in conflict with zoning ordinances. The rules of each community vary to some degree; if you have recently moved to a community, do not assume that the rules of your old neighborhood will apply.

Criteria developed by a neighborhood association, historic district, or planned unit development may also govern building activities. If so, you will need to have this organization approve your plans. The review may include the types of materials and the colors to be used in visible elements such as fences, sheds, walls, and shutters. Occasionally, even the choice and location of plant material will need to be reviewed.

Find out what your community has published regarding building regulations. The local building

department is a good place to begin. Some cities have prepared pamphlets that describe in detail the types of drawings and permit applications required in order to make improvements to your property.

Your community may have regulations regarding fences, swimming pools, and structures such as gazebos, breezeways, garages, and decks. Find out about easements and any variances required, and what the set-back requirements are for the front, sides, and rear of your property. The community engineering office may have plat plans and utility and drainage maps available, and they may prescribe certain procedures for working around public utilities. You may need permits for curb cuts (for an element such as a driveway), tree removal, electrical work, plumbing, and other utility connections. In addition, you may be required to submit completed drawings, permit applications, and fees before you can start work.

Legal Restrictions

A certified land survey of your property, if properly prepared, will document most legal restrictions on a drawing of the site. Often these restrictions are also described in the deed to your home. As you prepare the site analysis, as discussed on page 29, carefully include these restrictions on the survey. Some key types of restrictions are described below.

Easements These corridors along or within your property are defined for a specific use by public entities or private individuals. They vary in width from 10 feet to as much as 200 feet. If it is a public easement, you are constrained from building over or otherwise obstructing it. You may be given permission to plant trees or shrubs in the easement or use portions of it on a temporary

basis. Obtain a legal description of the easement in question so you can determine what is permitted. Common examples are street and road rights-of-way and easements for sanitary and storm sewers and for electricity, gas, telephone, and television lines. Utility companies and communities have certain rights regarding easements, often including the right to cross your property to service utilities.

Setbacks These restrictions legally define the location of a structure with respect to the front, sides, and back edges of the property. They are used to determine how far back additions, garages, fences, and walls must be from the property line, especially if footings are involved. Front setbacks are usually 25, 30, or 40 feet. Side-yard and rear-lot setbacks are generally somewhat less. This information is readily available, usually on city or local zoning maps. Know the exact location of your property lines, and record them accurately on your survey. Property lines are not always correctly indicated by existing fences or hedgerows.

Be aware that decks, terraces, and patios are not necessarily subject to the same regulations. A patio is often built directly on the ground and is considered paving. A deck, on the other hand, is usually defined as a structure that must conform to the codes that apply to buildings. A patio may be built next to a property line, for example, provided drainage is not an issue. However, even a few beams built over the patio for shade may be defined as a structure and required to conform to building setback requirements or lot-coverage restrictions. A terraced patio could be defined as either paving or structure, and you would likely be required to hire a structural engineer

Opposite: Large, elevated decks, such as this redwood one, call for building permits and careful attention to building codes and other legal requirements.

Unlike decks, simple patios seldom demand building permits or need to conform to legal requirements.

to design the retaining walls. Depending on the heights of the adjacent levels, railings could be required. Codes are usually very specific about the construction of railings, so check carefully before you begin.

Underground Utilities Throughout your neighborhood and property, there may be underground utilities of which you must be aware. As you plan your design, you must determine the exact location and depth of any underground utilities on your property. Utility companies and communities have hot lines that you are required to call before beginning any construction work that involves digging in the vicinity of such utilities. The

hot-line office, in turn, will send a representative to your home to locate the utilities. In most cases this is a free service.

Zoning Ordinances
These laws describe the uses permitted in a given zone and impose restrictions on development. In some areas zoning ordinances limit the percentage of the lot that can be paved or covered with buildings; they may also restrict building height. If this is the case where you live, you should measure the elements on your property to determine whether you have already reached this limit. Some jurisdictions consider decks and patios to be open landscaped space and others do not.

Building Codes and Permits

Most communities have building codes based on one of the widely used models, such as the Uniform Building Code (UBC) used in most states west of the Mississippi River. You can usually obtain the sections of the code that are applicable to your project from the community engineering office or building department. Building codes set forth standards for beam sizes, footing depths, allowable spans for deck framing, and other construction specifics that you must adhere to. Check also for plumbing and electrical codes if applicable.

Building codes can be boring to read, and they often are so technical that they are difficult to comprehend. You need to be familiar with them, however, in order to understand the level of construction quality your city requires.

Whether you will need a building permit depends on the scope of your design. If the plans call for relatively minor, nonstructural work—such as installing new plants, building a wall less than 3 feet high, or adding a sprinkler system—you probably will not need a permit. You also do not normally need a permit to install or construct a tool shed that occupies 120 square feet or less of floor space. But if you are putting in a deck, patio, driveway, or outdoor lighting—anything that involves structural work or changes in plumbing or electrical wiring—you will probably need a permit. If in doubt, call the community building inspector's office. The staff there can give you advice on how to comply with the codes.

A permit consists of written approval from your municipality, giving you permission to build. Permits protect both you and the community by stipulating the required performance, level of quality, and

methods of installation. Permits must be obtained before construction begins.

To obtain a permit, you'll need to submit plans (usually two sets) to the inspector's office. If the work to be done is extensive, you may be required to submit a final site plan plus specific working drawings, elevations, sections, and details of the electrical system, plumbing, or other components. If the project is very small, a final site plan and a description may suffice. Your plans will be checked and either approved or sent back for changes. You may be asked to modify your plans to conform to local codes, or to demonstrate that you are proficient enough to do the work yourself. The permit may require that you start and end the project within a certain time frame—usually three months to start work and nine additional months to complete it. If you have

Once plans are accepted by your local building department, it is important to follow them in the actual construction.

Opposite: Where an outdoor living area is shared, as in this wooded neighborhood, it is especially important to harmonize your plans with those of your neighbors (see page 56).

not completed the work within the specified period, you will need to obtain a new permit. Failure to apply for a permit may result in serious fines and/or an order to remove the work that has been begun.

Inspections As part of the permit process, the local governing agency will inspect your project at predetermined stages of construction. Don't skip these inspections. If you do, you may be required to tear out new work or have difficulty selling your home.

You must schedule your installation so that you can stop work for inspection. The inspector will tell you at which points during the installation the work should be inspected. If your plans were prepared by an architect or engineer, lay out the work exactly as drawn and execute it per the approved drawings. If changes are made during construction, have the architect or engineer prepare a "change order" and file it with the building department. Do not make structural changes without official approval. Inspectors are especially concerned with foundations, retaining walls, and excavations for utilities. For example, any ditch should be excavated to the specified dimensions shown on the plans, which should meet or exceed local code requirements.

The depth and width of footings and foundations for structures are specified in the UBC. Local codes vary, however, and take precedence over the UBC; therefore, it is very important to confer with a building inspector prior to starting a project.

Electrical Inspection Local building codes rarely require permits for a 12-volt lighting system. However, if you're installing new 120-volt circuits to operate a large low-voltage system, or a new ground fault circuit interrupter (GFCI) receptacle to plug in a transformer, check with the inspector to see if you need a permit. Find out at the same time if local code lists any requirements for low-voltage systems, and if an inspector must come to your site before, during, or after installation or adjustment to your electrical system.

Liabilities

Make sure that you and your contractor(s) have proper liability insurance to protect you against lawsuits from anyone working on the project. Protect yourself from potential liens by withholding a portion of each payment (10% is typical) for at least 45 days after the work is done. This 45-day holdback period should allow time to see that everything is in working order and that no liens have been filed.

Lien laws vary somewhat in different jurisdictions, but the intent is similar. Anyone supplying labor or material for your project has the right to file a lien against your property if he or she is not paid. You pay the contractor, with the assumption that he will pay for materials and subcontract labor. Any unpaid persons have lien rights against the project even though you have paid the contractor for these materials or services. There is a time limit for liens to be filed—usually 45 days after the substantial completion of the work.

Insist that the contractor prove he has used the previous payment to pay for materials and labor for your project by requesting a waiver of lien. This standard legal form, which confirms that subcontractors have been paid by your contractor, can be purchased at office-supply stores. Ensure that all labor and materials have been paid for before you release your final holdback. In

addition to the holdback for liens, it is important to retain the value of any deficiency in the work until it has been completed satisfactorily.

The Good-Neighbor Policy

Another factor critical to the successful installation of a project is that it be pleasing to your neighbors. This is especially true for visible elements, such as fences, walls, overhead structures, elevated decks, and prominent trees. You want to be certain that your project does not have an adverse impact on your neighbors, the neighborhood, and the community. Carefully evaluate the potential repercussions of your design to protect your investment. Your neighbors have legal recourse if your completed project is a visual intrusion.

As a courtesy, and a safeguard, talk to your neighbors about what you are planning to do. Although the changes will be on your property, they may have an impact on a neighbor's home. The removal of significant trees is a common example. Also, find out what is on the other side of the fence. Do not design a quiet sun deck next to the neighbor kids' play area, for example. Be completely candid with those whose opinion may affect the disposition of your plans. Invite them over and carefully map out the project. Do this only after you have done your homework and know what objections to expect and how they may be overcome.

You may even find that a neighbor is interested in splitting some of the cost of improvements that will affect both homes. Especially in a new development, many neighbors will be planning outdoor building projects at the same time. This can be an opportunity for neighborly cooperation in such areas as buying materials, renting equipment, and sharing labor.

DRAWING THE FINAL SITE PLAN

Now that you've isolated the design elements that will combine to make a successful outdoor living area, it's time to put it all down on one sheet of paper. Trace this plan over the base plan, drawing an aerial view of the entire site. You'll later develop more-detailed working drawings for each major project within the scheme. This overview site plan will give an idea of how all the elements interact. Add enough detail to show the brick pattern on a proposed patio or the direction of boards on a new deck.

PROJECT CHECKLIST

Be as thorough and organized as you can. If the project will take more that a few days, use a large calendar to schedule each purchase, phase, delivery, and so on.

❏ Establish the purpose of the project. A statement of purpose might be as simple as, *Create an outdoor living space to extend the enjoyment and use of the property.*

❏ Define the scope of the project. Discuss the project with those who will use it: family members, close friends, and neighbors. Give their comments careful thought. What wishes and considerations can be reasonably included?

❏ Develop a preliminary budget. This is often a chicken-and-egg question. Does the scope of the project depend on the available budget, or is the important thing to determine the needs and then find a way to finance it all? The best approach is to use rough figures to determine probable costs and adjust the wish list accordingly. Perhaps some of the elements in the design can be reserved for future projects. (For

FINAL SITE PLAN AND ELEVATIONS

OVERALL PLAN

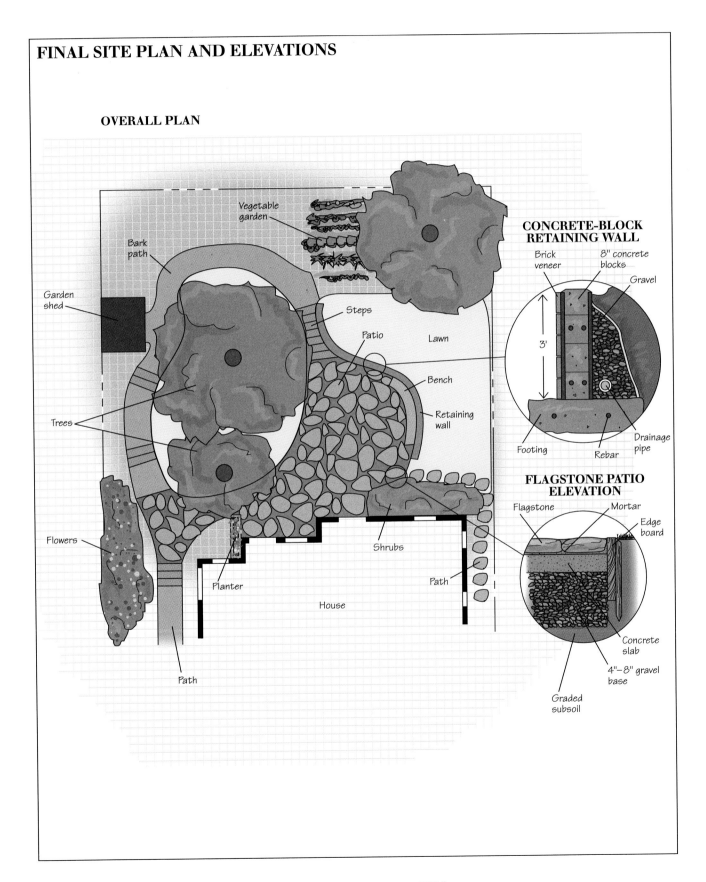

CONCRETE-BLOCK RETAINING WALL

Brick veneer • 8" concrete blocks • Gravel • 3' • Footing • Rebar • Drainage pipe

FLAGSTONE PATIO ELEVATION

Flagstone • Mortar • Edge board • Concrete slab • 4"–8" gravel base • Graded subsoil

Vegetable garden • Bark path • Garden shed • Steps • Patio • Lawn • Bench • Retaining wall • Trees • Flowers • Planter • Shrubs • Path • House • Path

a detailed overview of the steps of planning and budgeting a project, see page 267.)

❑ Check with local authorities. Determine code requirements, location of utility lines, easements affecting the lot, deed restrictions, and all pertinent bylaws. Check to see if any environmental restrictions or limitations apply to your property.

❑ Survey your lot. This site analysis is more informal than it sounds. It simply means observing, measuring, and making notes. Measure everything having to do with the project, including: relative heights (elevations) of all buildings and structures; elevations of the land form itself; the location of all structural elements such as buildings, fences, power poles, walks, and driveways; and details of the buildings, such as windows, doors, and points where utilities enter and leave the building. Also locate structures on adjoining properties and show these on the plan.

Locate all significant shrubs, trees, and vines that might affect the design.

Mark the sun/shade patterns and wind directions.

Note the views, both pleasant and unpleasant.

❑ Prepare preliminary designs. Start with bubble diagrams to record your early thoughts and to establish relationships among elements. Save the bubble diagrams that seem to work best in terms of the initial needs, circulation patterns, site conditions, and budget. Develop the diagram into more-complete design studies until one emerges that best fits all the criteria.

Discuss this preliminary design with a building inspector and the planning department. These de-partments are usually courteous and helpful. Some jurisdictions, however, have policies that prevent staff members from discussing early ideas before plans are fully developed and formally submitted.

❑ Prepare working drawings. If you are going to build a deck or patio yourself and have some experience, sketches may be all you need for working drawings. At the very least, even a small deck structure needs a few dimensions so that the right lengths of lumber can be ordered. Although a concrete patio can be laid out by eye, and the amount of concrete needed can be estimated a few minutes before placing the order, it's best to prepare working drawings as completely as possible. Mistakes on a drawing require only an eraser—and may prevent costly mistakes on the actual construction project.

❑ Permits. Depending on its nature, size, and scope, a project may require a building permit. Apply for and obtain all necessary permits before commencing construction. Penalties for not securing necessary permits can be severe. If permits are required, the working drawings must conform to local requirements.

❑ Prepare an accurate and detailed estimate. Take your working drawings to a couple of building suppliers and ask them to prepare a materials list and a price that includes delivery; or, prepare your own materials list and get unit prices from suppliers so that you can do your own estimate based on actual local unit costs. Either way, compare the prices carefully to be certain that all quotes include the same quantity and type of materials (and services if these are included).

❏ Contact and schedule any contractors you will use. Grading the site, forming and pouring concrete footings, and plumbing and electrical work are all specialty jobs that many homeowners are not equipped to do. Grading usually requires heavy motorized equipment, and installing a lighting system or a gas line to a barbecue grill nearly always requires the services of a licensed professional.

❏ Prepare the site for construction. Carefully transplant any existing plant material that you plan to retain. Provide a clear and convenient area for the delivery of building materials. If not already done in the site analysis, locate underground utilities. Also check again for any underground wiring or plumbing (such as irrigation systems) that may have previously been installed on the site and relocate them if necessary.

❏ Do the major earth moving. If retaining walls are involved or topsoil is needed, the moving of earth may have to be done in two or more stages. Excavate for such underground work as footings, drainage, water supply pipes, and electrical installations.

❏ Complete underground installations. Form and pour footings and foundation walls. Install plumbing for drainage and irrigation, and underground electrical conduit. Construct all required retaining walls, backfilling where appropriate and installing drainage pipes at the same time. Prepare finish grading under proposed decks and patios.

❏ Construct deck and/or patio. Build any supports for later aspects of construction, including footings if required.

❏ Build accessories. Add the final elements, such as screens, fences, benches, barbecue grill, and railings.

❏ Finish electrical and plumbing as required.

❏ Stain or paint.

❏ Clean up and enjoy your new deck or patio.

Stakes and string help create an accurate layout.

DECK & PATIO MATERIALS

Redwood is one of the most popular materials for constructing decks. It is easy to work with, attractive, and long lasting.

Wood, stone, concrete, gravel, brick, metal fasteners, metal reinforcing bars, finishing agents, structural beams made from wood or steel, and composite materials made from plastics are some of the basic materials used in deck and patio construction. With their many permutations, these materials offer a staggering array of possibilities to the designer and the builder. Your choice of materials will depend on a number of considerations, including cost, availability, ease of installation, beauty, and durability. Each material you choose should complement the overall landscape design and be able to withstand the vagaries of climate. Often, a love for a certain material will shape the entire design process. Like the choice of flowers or foliage, the color or texture of a particular material might be the perfect complement to a landscape. Red brick, for example, blends well with most greenery, and most limestone has a basic neutral color that provides a rich background for specimen plants. Some materials, such as glazed tile or painted wood, introduce highlights of their own.

On a more practical level, materials must also be chosen for their ability to solve structural problems. Concrete is a natural choice for patio and deck foundations because it is durable, inexpensive, and can be molded to almost any shape. Some newer materials—steel and plastics in particular—often solve old problems that once had to be designed around. And new developments in fastening systems, such as galvanized deck screws and metal framing connectors, expand the uses of ordinary lumber. Homeowners have never had a greater range of options to choose from.

WOOD FOR OUTDOOR CONSTRUCTION

Choosing the species of wood that's right for your deck has a lot to do with where you live. It's a good idea to choose woods that are native to the region or that grow relatively nearby, because they will be readily available, reasonably priced, and best suited for the weather conditions of the area. Other factors to consider are the strength, workability, and durability of the wood. For tips on selecting and estimating lumber, see page 110.

Redwood

Although redwood is one of the more expensive materials for building decks, it is worth the price. Its straight, fine grain and texture add natural beauty to a deck, and finishes endure longer on redwood than on any other species. For its light weight, redwood is strong and durable and resists warping, yet it is easy to saw and nail. But because it is a particularly soft wood, take care not to dent it when nailing or securing it.

Redwood is available in several grades and lengths. The lower grades, called merchantable, have some loose knots but make excellent decking boards. For highly visible deck components and those that contact the ground, choose grades with all heartwood, which has a particularly attractive grain as well as decay resistance. If you like the look of the rose-colored heartwood but find the price prohibitive, consider combining it with other species. Use the redwood for visible components, such as railings, decking, and benches, and a less expensive species or pressure-treated lumber for the structural members.

Pressure-treated lumber is even more rot-resistant than redwood. Select lumber that is specified for ground contact for locations in contact with the soil.

Cedar and Cypress

For homeowners who want a rustic and aged look for the deck, cedar and cypress are the popular choice. They are denser and stronger than redwood, and their burnt orange hues weather to an attractive gray.

Cedar and cypress are lightweight and durable, with fine, straight grain patterns and few knots. These woods—particularly their heartwood—are resistant to decay, rot, and insect infestation and are easy to saw and nail. Despite their inherent advantages, however, cedar and cypress are not as strong as pressure-treated wood. To add to a deck's load-bearing capacity, you may want to use pressure-treated lumber for the structural components, reserving cedar or cypress for the more visible elements.

Pressure-Treated Lumber

Also called PT lumber, pressure-treated lumber is the most common deck material used today. Like redwood, cedar, and cypress, it resists moisture, insects, and decay, but it is more readily available in most areas and, of course, it is less expensive.

Pressure-treated lumber is medium-grade softwood—usually pine or Douglas fir—treated with preservatives to make the wood resistant to insect infestation, moisture, and decay. The often-visible marks, called incisements, allow a more uniform penetration. They are not defects, so don't worry if you come across many of them. (If you want lumber without the marks, you can order it without incisement.)

To control shrinkage across the grain and to provide a better wearing surface, pressure-treated lumber is often quartersawed. This gives the wood a somewhat rounded appearance and slightly reduces

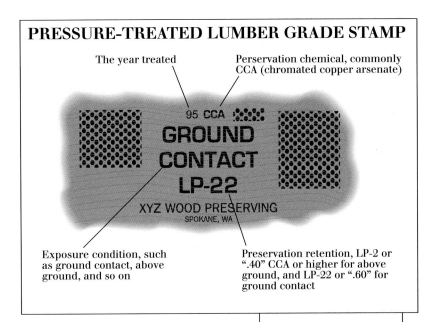

PRESSURE-TREATED LUMBER GRADE STAMP

The year treated

Preservation chemical, commonly CCA (chromated copper arsenate)

95 CCA

GROUND CONTACT LP-22

XYZ WOOD PRESERVING
SPOKANE, WA

Exposure condition, such as ground contact, above ground, and so on

Preservation retention, LP-2 or ".40" CCA or higher for above ground, and LP-22 or ".60" for ground contact

the size of the board; keep this in mind when figuring quantities. Use the quartersawed lumber for decking and railings, since they are exposed to the most wear and tear as well as the sun and rain.

The quality-control identification stamp on pressure-treated lumber indicates the year the wood was treated, the preservation chemical used, the amount of preservation retention, and the exposure condition it can withstand, such as ground contact. Always look for kiln-dried (KD) or kiln-dried-after-treatment (KDAT) pressure-treated lumber to ensure against shrinkage and decay.

Pressure-treated wood is more economical than redwood, cypress, or cedar, but it is more difficult to saw and nail. In fact, you may need to drill pilot holes. Use power tools for sawing and drilling; penetrating the wood with hand tools is too difficult and tiring. Also, avoid rip-cutting (making long cuts with the grain) pressure-treated lumber, as this negates the effectiveness of its chemical treatment. Coat all cuts with wood preservative. The same material used for the original

Using pressure-treated lumber for your projects ensures a long life for garden structures.

pressure treatment is usually available where you purchase the lumber.

Before applying a finish to the deck, wait for the wood's green tint to fade. This will help the paint, stain, or wood preservative adhere.

You may want to ask your supplier about a new treated lumber that uses EPA-registered preservatives. The lumber is protected from rot and decay without the use of arsenic or chromium and it has a water repellent built-in. As it ages, it deepens to a warm brown. But don't let safety concerns deter you from using the traditional pressure-

treated lumber; it makes an ideal, long-lasting, and economical deck material. The pentavalent arsenic used to preserve it is a naturally occurring element that can be found in soil, plants, animals, and even humans. In addition, the preservatives are locked into the wood and cannot migrate or evaporate. As with any wood, however, dust is produced by sawing, sanding, or drilling; the dust from pressure-treated lumber is potentially harmful if inhaled and deserves safety measures. As an extra precaution, avoid using pressure-treated lumber for heavily used surfaces of children's play equipment or for tables where the treated material will be in direct contact with food.

Other Woods

Although redwood, cedar, cypress, and pressure-treated lumber are preferred for deck construction, you may want to use other woods, depending on your taste and budget.

Fir, hemlock, spruce, and pine are inexpensive and will save you money up front, but they are not necessarily the best values. They lack a natural defense against decay and thus require the additional expense and work of applying finishes and preservatives.

Or you may want to include such elegant woods as teak, white oak, yellow cedar, Pacific yew, and sassafras. Keep in mind, however, that they are hard to find, very expensive, and difficult to work with. If you can afford only a small order, consider using one of these woods for an accessory, such as a bench or planter, or for decorative touches, such as newel posts and finials.

Evaluating Structural Lumber

This type of lumber can be made of nearly any species, usually a softwood. Douglas fir and southern yellow pine are the most common, but larch, spruce, hemlock, and other kinds of pine predominate in some regions.

Structural lumber is sold either surfaced or rough-sawn. Surfaced lumber is available in all grades and is used for posts, beams, studs, rafters, and other framing members. Rough-sawn lumber may not be available in every grade, but its coarse, natural texture and somewhat thicker dimensions make it a sensible choice for many outdoor structures. For more information on grades, see page 110.

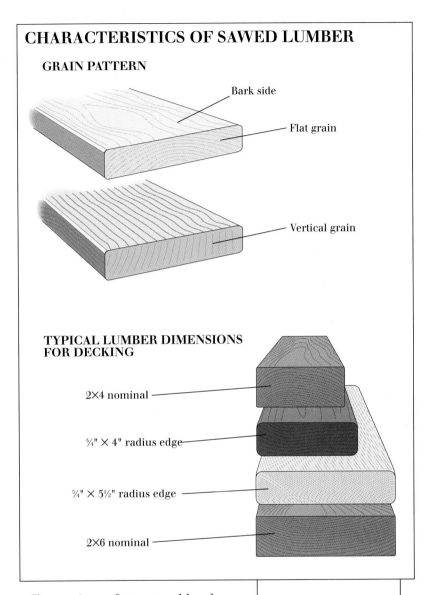

CHARACTERISTICS OF SAWED LUMBER

GRAIN PATTERN

Bark side

Flat grain

Vertical grain

TYPICAL LUMBER DIMENSIONS FOR DECKING

2×4 nominal

¾" × 4" radius edge

¾" × 5½" radius edge

2×6 nominal

Every piece of structural lumber is marked with a grade stamp. This stamp includes the name of the mill where the wood was processed, the initials of the grading agency, the wood species, an indication of whether the wood is unseasoned (S-grn) or kiln-dried (S-dry), and the structural grade of the lumber.

Grades for 2×4s and 4×4s range from utility (low grade), to standard (medium grade), to construction (better grade). There are as many as 10 possible grades for 2×6s and larger, but for practical purposes three will do. In ascending order,

SAFETY

Any construction site has potential dangers, but you and your helpers can prevent accidents with a little know-how and good judgment. Here are some tips for working with tools and materials and for keeping the work site safe.

Personal gear. Your eyes are very vulnerable to contact, dust, and chemical injuries. Always wear safety glasses or goggles when using power tools or when performing any task that could put your eyes as risk, such as spraying wood finisher. Use a dust mask when sawing pressure-treated wood and applying finishes. Unless you are walking on the joists or laying down decking, wear shoes with hard soles that resist nails and other sharp objects.

Power tools and extension cords. When you use power tools while standing on the ground, you're at risk from electrical shock from a malfunctioning tool or cord. To protect yourself, always plug power tools and extension cords into receptacles that have GFCI (ground fault circuit interrupter) protection. You may already have an outdoor GFCI receptacle; if not, look for one in your bathroom and run a cord from it. Otherwise, buy a portable GFCI outlet; you can plug it into an ordinary electrical receptacle (grounded or ungrounded) and plug cords for power tools into it.

Heavy loads. Don't lift heavy objects yourself. Always have a helper ready to assist in carrying heavy and bulky materials and in lifting deck components into place. The greatest risk is lifting and twisting at the same time. You may want to wear around your waist a special support belt, available at most home-improvement centers.

Ladders. Because of the danger of electrical shock, pay attention to overhead power lines when using a ladder. Never stand on the top platform of a stepladder; it is not designed to accommodate loads at its very top. Never climb a ladder higher than a manufacturer recommends, and don't use a ladder with broken parts.

Work site. Clean up the site regularly. Remove all debris to prevent falls and slips. Don't leave tools and supplies lying where someone can trip over them. Be especially careful about how you handle boards with nails and where you place them; remove protruding nails or bend them over so no one will put a nail through a shoe. Cover footing holes and other excavations with sheets of plywood when you leave the job site. Don't use plastic or tarp for this purpose—they cannot support a person's weight. If the holes are too large for plywood, barricade and fence off the area, and post a "Keep Out" or "No Trespassing" sign.

Utilities. Contact your local utility to come to the site and mark any underground television cable, power, telephone, water, and sewer lines, as well as gas lines, before you begin any digging, especially close to property lines. In addition, if you have a septic tank and leach field, mark the location before you begin to dig.

Electrical installations. If you are unfamiliar with electrical wiring, contact a licensed professional to do all installations.

Pressure-treated lumber. Always wear safety glasses and a dust mask when sawing this lumber. After touching it, wash your hands before eating, drinking, or smoking. Dispose of leftover wood and scraps in regular household trash or according to local requirements. Never burn pressure-treated lumber—it produces toxic fumes.

Materials and supplies. Some building supplies, such as preservatives, finishes, and adhesives, are toxic. Read and follow the manufacturer's labels for safe use, storage, and disposal.

Debris. To help protect the environment, follow local regulations or the manufacturer's recommendations when disposing of construction debris, toxic materials, and other trash.

Tool safety. Use the right tool for the job. Keep blades sharp. Always read the owner's manual and understand the manufacturer's instructions before using any power tools. Never use power tools outdoors when it's raining or let a power cord connection lie on damp or wet ground.

Clothing. Wear comfortable, loose-fitting garments. Don't wear clothing or jewelry that could get caught on tools or deck components. If you are wearing loose-fitting long sleeves, roll them up so there's no chance they will be caught by power tools. Wear boots or heavy work shoes during excavation and framing to protect your feet from falling objects and boards with protruding nails. You can wear lighter-weight shoes, if you prefer, during installation of the decking and railings.

Helpers. Instruct your helpers about work safety, including procedures for an emergency. Check your homeowner's policy to be sure that you have adequate coverage if a helper or visitor should be injured during construction.

Contractors. An uninsured contractor is a liability. Always ask for proof of insurance, and don't hire a contractor who does not have proof of coverage for workers and subcontractors.

First-aid kit. Keep a fully stocked kit on the work site.

these are: No. 2 grade lumber, for general-purpose construction; No. 1 grade, for situations in which strength, appearance, and resistance to warping and twisting are considerations; and select structural, where extra strength is critical. As one might expect, the better grades are more expensive. Select structural lumber is usually freer from knots and has a straighter grain than the lower grades. This is generally considered more attractive for exposed construction. As a general rule, choose lower grades for framing lumber that will be covered with siding or other finish material, and higher grades for exposed, exterior work.

In fact, if the framing is to be covered with siding and finished on the interior as well, price steel studs and joists as a cost alternative to lumber-framing members. In some parts of the country, this will result in a substantial savings. Lightweight steel framing is easy to work with and, like lumber framing, can be an excellent do-it-yourself material.

Choosing Finish Lumber

Finish lumber for outdoor construction is nearly always from softwood (evergreen) species. It is usually kiln-dried to control shrinkage and other seasoning defects and is available only in thicknesses of 2 inches or less.

Where finish lumber will be exposed to the weather and simply stained or left unpainted, decay-resistant woods are the best choice. Painted trim and interior finish wood can be of any species.

Different types of finish lumber are graded by different agencies, each with its own rules, so shop around to see what's available in your area.

Plywood

This multipurpose lumber is manufactured by laminating wood veneers into a sandwich, with the grain in alternating layers turned at

STANDARD LUMBER

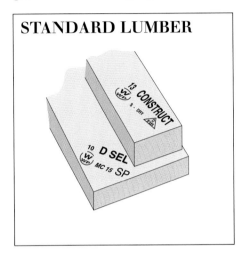

PRESSURE-TREATED LUMBER

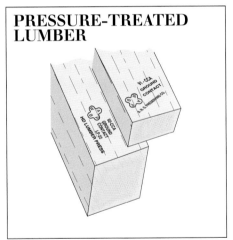

PLYWOOD

90 degrees. This results in a panel with great strength and dimensional stability, ideal for floor and roof sheathing, wall bracing, and siding. The large panel size makes it easy to cover large areas quickly.

Structural plywood is graded on a scale from A to D, with A being the highest grade; each sheet has a two-letter grade mark. The first letter indicates the quality of the front side of the sheet; the second letter refers to the back. C-D interior plywood is commonly used for subfloors and roof sheathing where appearance is not a factor. A-B and B-C plywood panels are better where one side will show, as for the underside of exposed roof decking. Try to buy structural plywood that is marked "interior-exterior glue." This means it will withstand exposure to wet conditions without delaminating.

Plywood siding is rated for continuous outdoor use. It usually comes with a saw-textured face, sometimes with a grooved pattern cut into the surface. Because it's easy to apply and provides excellent lateral bracing, it's a natural for the walls of sheds and gazebos.

Some composite-type panels are also useful in outdoor structures. Oriented strand board, made by fusing large wood chips into a solid sheet, can be substituted for structural plywood of the same thickness. Hardboard siding provides a relatively inexpensive wall covering for painted outbuildings.

Composite panels that replace wood finish materials have reached a very sophisticated level of technological development. Dense, fused materials are available in prefinished surfaces that do not need painting for years. Some have limited warranties that last 15 years or more. The finished surfaces do oxidize a little each year, as any

material will, and so lose a little of their color brightness. This is not really discernible unless you place a piece of unoxidized material next to the faded one, as you might if you needed to repair a damaged piece. Otherwise, these materials will not need maintenance for as long as 25 years. You might think that they would be less expensive than solid wood, but that is not the case. They are more expensive initially, but over time will be less costly than wood you might paint every five years or so.

Of course, the material with lowest maintenance is high-quality wood suited for exterior use and colored to suit with penetrating stains. If the wood is then allowed to weather naturally, no further maintenance is necessary. The surface of wood does oxidize, of course, but it will loose only about ⅛ inch of thickness per century when fully exposed to the weather. It is all a matter of taste; some people feel that unpainted wood structures are a sign of neglect. On the other hand, old redwood barns have silvered over time to an elegant natural patina.

OTHER STRUCTURAL MATERIALS

Your design or site may call for out-of-the-ordinary materials. Although sometimes difficult to find, they can often solve important structural problems and are well worth considering before you begin your working drawings.

Poles
Pole frame structures are wood but are used differently than lumber. Poles have been used by public utilities for decades. They are much more sophisticated now and are pressure treated with chemicals

that will guarantee long, disease-free life. Such poles are usually readily available and can be set directly into the ground, often without a footing. They make great vertical supports for decks on steep hillsides. Used as beams, they will span wide distances and support heavy loads.

Steel

Steel frames compete favorably in cost with wood frames. Steel is an extremely strong and durable material, though it is subject to rust and requires periodic painting. Steel doesn't always require welding, a skill that most homeowners would not bother to learn for a single project. Predrilled steel beams can be easily bolted together, and standard fittings make this a fairly simple task. Although steel is a relatively heavy material, it will span long distances. Compared with wood, steel beams can be more widely spaced, so fewer would be needed; this means fewer footings—a significant savings in cost and labor. Wood decking, such as 2×4s set on edge, can span these distances. Steel will also easily support heavy materials such as concrete or other solid paving materials.

Manufactured Wood Beams

Other materials that are relatively new include a number of types of manufactured lumber for use as long-span beams. These are stronger and more expensive than solid timber beams of the same size. Although used primarily for interior applications, some kinds are suitable for outdoor use. Two types of manufactured beams are readily available. One consists of thin layers glued together in plies, like plywood, to form long, continuous beams of exceptional strength. These beams—called glulams—are usually 1¾ inches thick. For wide

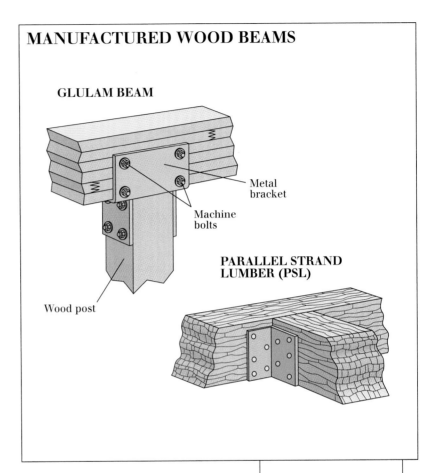

MANUFACTURED WOOD BEAMS

GLULAM BEAM

Metal bracket

Machine bolts

Wood post

PARALLEL STRAND LUMBER (PSL)

spans, two beams can be fastened together to make a composite beam.

Another wood beam product uses totally different technology. First the original timber is physically pulled apart until it consists of long strands of wood fiber. Using resinous plastic glues, the fibers are extruded into beams. This material is available in pressure-treated form for long outdoor life. It is heavier than wood of equivalent size but is two to three times as strong. Suppliers of these products usually provide engineering calculations and assist with preparing shop drawings for structural layouts using their materials.

Plastic

Precolored, timberlike plastic is available for decking and benches. It lasts for many years, is priced

Nails commonly used for deck construction are, from top to bottom and left to right: 8d and 16d galvanized box; 8d, 10d, and 16d galvanized common; 6d, 8d, and 16d galvanized finishing; spiral; 12d stainless steel common; 16d ring shank; 8d galvanized joist hanger; and grommeted spiral.

to handle. They are not as strong as steel but weigh 30 percent less than aluminum and 80 percent less than equivalent steel sizes. Because these materials are glass-fiber reinforced, cut ends must be sealed to prevent the intrusion of moisture.

HARDWARE AND FASTENERS

You have a choice of methods of securing and connecting the various components of a deck, from installing the posts to assembling the railings. Each method described here has its own merits in appearance, strength, and ease of assembly. Some hardware and fasteners, for instance, hold tighter and longer than others, yet they take more time and effort to install. Choose the method you feel comfortable working with. In all cases, choose corrosion-resistant hardware. If you're like most deck builders, you'll use a combination of nails, screws, bolts, and metal fasteners.

Nails

Five basic types of nails are recommended for deck construction—box, common, finishing, spiral shank, and ring shank—all available in various metals and sizes. Spiral-shank or ring-shank nails have the greatest holding power.

The most popular, economical material for nails is hot-dipped galvanized (HDG) steel. These corrosion-resistant nails are coated with rust-resistant zinc and are best used for structures that will be directly exposed to the elements. The nails are easily recognized by their rough gray coating. A common problem with HDG nails is that the coating on the heads may break up when hammered. Some manufacturers double-dip the heads for

about the same as higher-end clear lumber, and is resistant to ultraviolet (UV) rays. It is also resistant to impact damage and scratching and requires almost no maintenance. Plastic building material is comparable with wood in its ability to carry loads, and the surface is much stronger.

Glass-fiber-reinforced plastic beams in traditional steel shapes are also available though quite expensive. Their claim to fame is their strength-to-weight ratio, and their light weight makes them easy

added protection. Avoid nails galvanized by electrolysis rather than hot dipping. They are labeled *EG* (electrogalvanized) and have a very thin zinc coating that wears off easily.

Superior yet costly options to HDG nails are stainless steel and solid aluminum nails. Most homeowners are not attracted to these options because the cost of stainless steel nails is prohibitive, and aluminum nails have less holding power and bend easily under the force of a hammer.

Nails are sized by the unlikely term *penny*, abbreviated with a single *d* (for *denarius*, the ancient Roman coin that was the equivalent of a penny).

If this is your first building project, the number of nails you'll need will surprise you. Be prepared to buy nails in bulk, by the pound. Nails are inexpensive, especially in case lots, so don't be afraid to overbuy. Nothing disrupts a project faster than running out of nails, and you will always find uses for leftovers.

Screws

For superior holding power, screws are better than any type of nails. In addition, they allow for easy disassembly of deck components for repair or replacement. Keep in mind, however, that driving screws takes more time and energy than driving nails, so you might want to reserve them for only those components you may need to remove in the future. Use a power screwdriver with an appropriate bit to speed up the process. As with nails and other fasteners, be sure the screws are hot-dipped galvanized or coated.

Other Fasteners

There are several alternatives to fastening decking boards with nails or screws, including decking clips, metal nailing strips, and deck adhesive (a type of outdoor construction

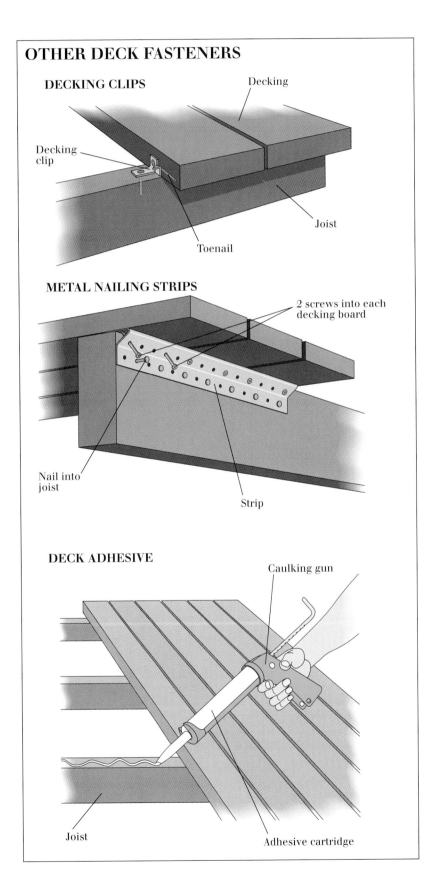

OTHER DECK FASTENERS

DECKING CLIPS

Decking

Decking clip

Joist

Toenail

METAL NAILING STRIPS

2 screws into each decking board

Nail into joist

Strip

DECK ADHESIVE

Caulking gun

Joist

Adhesive cartridge

CONNECTORS USED FOR DECK FRAMING

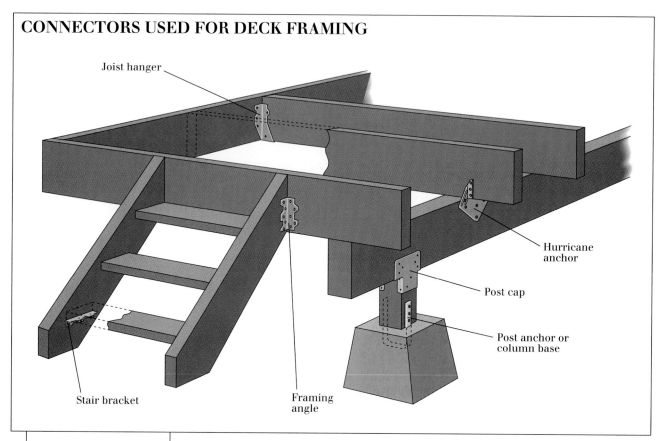

Joist hanger

Hurricane anchor

Post cap

Post anchor or column base

Stair bracket

Framing angle

adhesive). All three systems are intended to fasten the boards with no nail heads or screw heads on the surface. (Also see page 152.)

Decking clips, which are nailed along one edge of a board before it's set in place, secure that edge with small flanges that slip under the previously installed board; the free edge of the board is held in place with traditional toenailing through the side. The clips create uniform spacing between the boards. Some models have teeth or claws to grip the decking.

Metal nailing strips, which are laid on top of joists, are secured with nails into the sides of the joists; screws are then driven up through predrilled holes in the strip into the bottoms of the decking boards. The advantage of this system is that no nails or screws penetrate the tops of the joists,

preventing a pathway for water and eventual rot.

Deck adhesive, applied with a caulking gun, is an invisible method of fastening the decking boards to the joists. Although it makes the decking smooth and attractive, there is one important drawback you should consider: Once the adhesive sets up, it's virtually impossible to remove the decking boards without damaging them and the joists to which they are fastened. It is also difficult to use adhesive to install bowed boards.

Metal Framing Connectors

Framing connectors simplify the assembly of components and they strengthen connections. Building codes may specify that connectors be used to reinforce certain joints, such as the connection between a post and a beam, or between a joist and a ledger. Framing connectors also help prevent wood from splitting when nailed and reduce dents or dimples by acting as a barrier between the wood and hammerhead. The connectors are sized to accommodate standard-dimension wood, some with optional sizes for full-cut (rough) lumber and for built-up members (two 2×4s nailed together, for instance). Be sure that the fasteners are galvanized to prevent rust. Follow manufacturer's recommendations for nailing and bolting; some connections require that full-sized nails, rather than shorter joist-hanger nails, be used, or that all holes have nails. Although strong and practical, most metal framing connectors are unattractive and should be used in exposed areas only when absolutely necessary.

POURED CONCRETE

Poured concrete is the basic patio material. It forms an excellent foundation for most other materials and is a simple, versatile, and economical finished surface, especially for covering large areas. Poured concrete is so fluid that it can be worked into almost any shape and can have a number of interesting surface finishes. These include exposed aggregate, broomed, troweled, travertine, rock salt, smooth, semismooth, stamped, and hand-tooled textures.

Although at first glance concrete seems cold, hard, and institutional looking and, therefore, seems best suited to contemporary patios, it is possible to soften its look to make it suitable for other styles. It can be colored and acid stained to subdue its grayness, and it can be colored and stamped so it looks like tile, cobblestone, or brick (see page 224). It can also be divided into sections with feature strips or bordered with attractive materials that alter its image. Incorporating contrasting materials, such as pavers, bricks, wood dividers, or tiles, into the patio design softens the apparent harshness of concrete and enables you to adapt it to traditional designs. Concrete can also be used to make a contrasting border around other paving materials. And should you eventually tire of a concrete patio, it provides a superb base for a new patio surface of brick, stone, or tile set in mortar. If your budget is initially tight, plan it that way: Prepare the grading and elevations now for an additional patio thickness in a year or so and use a plain concrete base for a temporary surface.

Concrete does have some disadvantages, especially for the do-it-yourselfer. One is that it must be mixed to exact specifications. Another is that it must be poured and finished quickly. Both tasks require technical skill; there is little margin for error in either one, and mistakes are costly. Also, you need one or more helpers, depending on the size of the patio. (For installation techniques, see pages 213 to 230.) Whereas the pouring and finishing go fast, the site preparation—grading, installing the base materials, and building the forms—is tedious but essential. If you don't do it correctly, you risk a buckled or cracked slab. Other disadvantages include a surface that becomes hot and glaring if unshaded, and slippery when wet unless it is textured.

Types of Concrete

Although there are different types of concrete, all are fluid media installed by pouring them into a form. The differences between them depend on two things: the type of portland cement used and the proportions of cement, aggregate, and water used to mix it. Use a concrete made with Type I, IA, II, IIA, III, or IIIA portland cement.

Although it appears to be made of several materials, this sampler is all poured concrete. The different finishes are exposed aggregate (top right and lower left quadrants) and three different stamped patterns.

These are general-purpose portland cements suitable for paving patios and sidewalks. The *A* suffix indicates a portland cement used to make the air-entrained concrete needed in regions subject to freezing weather. If you order concrete ready-mixed, the dealer mixes the right amount in the correct proportions for your climate and use. If you choose to mix it yourself, using bulk dry materials or a dry ready-mixed concrete, you have to make these determinations yourself (see page 218). Follow the manufacturer's instructions exactly.

Concrete Finishes

Applying a decorative surface treatment gives concrete improved traction and a pleasing texture. There are nine finishes from which to choose.

Exposed Aggregate

This is the most popular concrete finish. Its pebbly surface is slightly rugged, naturally colorful, and highly durable.

Troweled Finish

A swirled texture made with a trowel, this finish gives the patio an interesting texture and good traction.

Broomed Finish

This attractive, nonslip texture is created by pulling damp brooms across freshly floated or troweled concrete.

Travertine Finish

This handsome surface resembles travertine marble. It is not recommended for regions with freezing weather.

Rock Salt Finish

This is a slightly pitted, roughened surface created by rolling rock salt (ordinary water-softener salt) into the concrete. It produces excellent traction, but is not recommended for areas with freezing temperatures.

Semismooth Finish

This is a slightly roughened texture produced with a wood float. This surface is recommended when you need good skid resistance and floating is the final finish.

Smooth Finish

Achieve this effect by troweling the floated surface with a metal trowel.

Slippery when wet, it is not recommended for patios and sidewalks.

Stamped-pattern Finish
Geometric designs can be stamped into concrete to make it resemble brick, cobblestone, flagstone, ashlar (veneer stone), or other material. The pattern is scored or pushed into the partially set concrete. You can do this yourself, but a contractor will yield more professional-looking results.

Hand-tooled Finish
This surface is achieved by scoring random patterns in partially set concrete with a tool or stylus, before and after the slab has been floated.

In addition to texturing the surface, you can color concrete to relieve its natural but monotonous gray color (see page 224).

Ordering Concrete
A ready-mix dealer offers the most convenient and economical source of concrete. This company custom mixes concrete according to exact specifications to meet specific conditions and ensure uniform quality.

Concrete is sold by the cubic yard (27 cubic feet), and a supplier will deliver any quantity greater than 1 cubic yard. To determine how many cubic feet of concrete you need, multiply the patio width (in feet) by its length. Multiply that product by its thickness in inches. Divide that product by 12. The result is the cubic footage. Divide that quotient by 27—the number of cubic feet in a cubic yard—to get the number of cubic yards needed. Here's an example using a patio that measures 12 feet wide by 20 feet long

Concrete pumps move concrete from the curb to the pour site much more quickly and with far less effort than moving it with a wheelbarrow.

by 4 inches thick: *12×20 = 240; 240×4 = 960; 960÷12 = 80 cubic feet. 80÷27 = 2.96 cubic yards. 2.96 + .296 (10 percent waste allowance) = 3.25 cubic yards ordered.*

Before placing your order, ask about the cost per cubic yard, the cost of delivery, the "short load" charge for less than a truckload, the amount of time the driver can be on your site before additional charges start, the additional charge (if any) for the driver's time, and the required payment method (cash, check, or charge). Also, tell the dealer how many cubic yards of concrete you want and that it's for a patio. If you live where the ground freezes in the winter, be sure to specify that you want air-entrained concrete.

When ordering, specify a 5-sack mix with ¾-inch aggregate (the number of sacks of portland cement

per yard of concrete, and the maximum size of the gravel). Tell the dealer the distance from the work site to the nearest parking place for the concrete truck. Most trucks have chutes that can reach as far as 16 feet. If the truck cannot reach the patio, you should also arrange for a pump truck—either through the dealer or on your own. Tell the dealer which pumping service you are using, so they can coordinate their deliveries. Also, verify that the hose on the pump truck can accommodate ¾-inch aggregate, which requires a 4-inch-diameter hose. If not, order ⅜-inch pea gravel instead, which can be pumped through a 3-inch-diameter hose.

If you plan to mix the concrete yourself, which is cost-effective only for very small jobs, decide whether you want to use bulk ingredients or a dry ready-mixed

Bricks come in many textures. Select one that is functional and gives the effect you want.

concrete. You buy bulk ingredients based on square footage. If you plan to use dry ready-mixed concrete, an 80-pound bag yields ⅔ cubic foot of concrete. Figure your patio's cubic feet using the formula given above and divide by 0.66. Using the 10-percent safety factor and the example above, this formula means that you would need 133.33 bags of ready-mix. This would be a very expensive quantity of concrete to buy in ready-to-mix bags. For instructions on mixing concrete yourself, see page 218.

BRICK

Brick is the old standby—the most adaptable, attractive, and popular patio paving material. It is timeless and evokes nostalgic warmth. Its beautifully textured surface comes in a wide range of colors, from yellow ochre to chocolate brown, so it ranges from earthy to refined in style. In addition, the dimensional (modular) shape of brick allows it to be laid in an infinite number of interesting patterns. It can be used to build walls and other structures, such as columns, as well as for a border material. All these qualities make it suitable for use with most architectural styles, traditional to contemporary.

Brick offers the do-it-yourself patio builder many advantages. It is fairly simple to install, especially in a bed of sand, and its size makes it easy to handle. Brick is durable and requires little maintenance. It is widely available and, if a delivery is not feasible, it can be transported in small quantities.

Brick does have drawbacks. It is more expensive than most other paving materials and looks

Used brick is often more expensive than new bricks, but it can sometimes be reclaimed from an old wall or patio.

A sampling of brick: building brick, including cored and oversized; dark red paving brick; glazed facing brick (partially concealed); yellow firebrick; manufactured "used" brick; and gray concrete paving units.

awkward if not laid in a precise pattern. Occasionally, some bricks heave and have to be reset. Also, brick can become slick with moss in humid or heavily shaded areas. Otherwise, a brick patio requires little maintenance except occasionally weeding the joints and refilling them with sand.

Methods of Installation

Once you establish your rhythm, brick goes down with ease, and it is satisfying to watch the surface develop beneath your hands. Brick is laid by four methods. The most common is brick-in-sand, an easy paving technique that also produces a low-upkeep patio. It is not a permanent installation and may be subject to uneven settlement. Installing brick in dry mortar locks the bricks more firmly in place. However, this method still lacks a stable foundation. The third alternative is laying brick on a thin (½-inch) sand base over a 4-inch concrete slab for long-term stability and the more informal appearance of brick on sand. For a permanent

installation, brick is laid in mortar over a concrete-slab foundation.

Types of Brick

You face a bewildering array of choices—more than 10,000 potential combinations of sizes, shapes, colors, and textures—when you shop for brick. Start winnowing down the selection with this fact: Common brick, face brick, and paving brick are best for paving patios.

Common Brick Also called building brick or standard brick, common brick is not uniform in shape or color. These imperfections give it a natural appearance that is ideal for patios. It is the least expensive kind of brick.

There are three types of common brick: sand-mold, wire-cut, and clinker. Sand-mold brick is slightly larger on one side and has rounded edges and a smooth texture. It is easy to clean. Wire-cut brick is square cut. It has sharp edges, a rough texture, and a slightly pitted face. Clinker brick has the flashed patches and rough surface caused by overburning.

These common types can be new or used. Used bricks are salvaged from old buildings. Their rustic appearance makes an attractive informal patio. Experts recommend not using common bricks more than 30 to 40 years old to pave a patio in regions with freezing weather, however. They are too porous to stand up under such conditions.

Used bricks are expensive because they must be cleaned and are in high demand. In response to this popularity, manufacturers make new "used" bricks by tumbling them to chip their edges and splashing them with mortar and paint.

Common bricks come graded according to their ability to withstand cold weather. Only two grades are acceptable for use on patios.

❑ SW (severe weathering) brick. This type is suitable for patios in all climates, including areas with subzero winters. It is the most expensive common brick.

❑ MW (moderate weathering) brick. This is suitable for patios in areas with subfreezing, but not subzero, weather. It is less expensive than SW common brick.

Face Brick Face brick is used to face buildings and walls. Available new or used, it is uniform in size, shape, and color and has a smooth, defect-free surface. It is the best-quality brick and also the most expensive. Face brick is not stronger than common brick, but the extra care with which it is manufactured makes it more weather-resistant. Its smooth surface also makes it more slippery when wet.

Paving Brick Composed of special clays and fired at higher temperatures for longer periods, paving brick is stronger than common brick, which is why it typically is half the thickness of standard brick. Designed and sized for mortarless installation, it is ideal for building brick-on-sand patios.

How Brick Is Sized

Bricks come in modular 4-inch increments, so they fit together regardless of how they are placed. This makes them easy to lay in a pattern.

Typically, standard modular bricks are used for patios, although other sizes are available. These

STANDARD BRICK DIMENSIONS

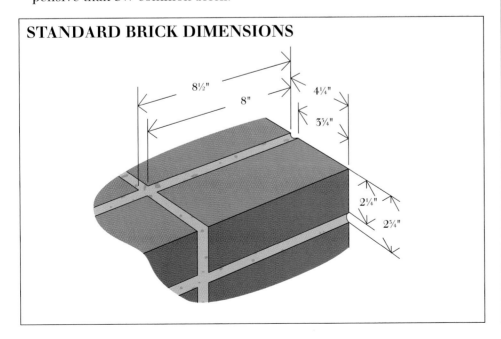

Brick patterns can be simple or complex, as shown here. Select a style that coordinates well with the patio surroundings or any adjacent brick walls or paths.

as much as ½ inch from standard dimensions.

Paving brick is an exception to this rule. It is referred to by its exact dimension—4 by 8 inches—because it is designed for mortarless installation. Do not confuse paving brick with brick pavers, which are actually concrete pavers.

Brick Colors and Textures

Brick comes in a wide range of warm, earthen colors. Most bricks get their color from the mineral oxides in the clay from which they are made. These oxides turn their natural color when fired. Bricks made from mixtures of different clays end up with blends of pleasing colors. Some bricks are colored with ceramic glazes. Don't use glazed bricks on patios because they are slippery when they get wet.

Brick finishes, or textures, range from smooth to rough. Choose a texture like a sand finish that provides good traction and a comfortable walking surface. It doesn't become slippery when wet and it produces little glare.

Brick Patterns

Once you've chosen a brick, select the pattern, called a bond, that you want to use. As you make this decision, consider the following points.

❑ What type of joint will you use—an open joint that has some space between the bricks, or a closed joint that tightly butts the bricks together? Open joints become a part of the pattern; butt joints produce a smooth, uniform appearance. Keep in mind that the natural size variations in common bricks make it difficult to execute some patterns with butt joints. Open joints let you adjust for these differences. If a butt joint is essential, use a mortarless paving brick.

standard bricks have a stated measurement of 4 by 8 by 2⅔ inches. This may be the brick's nominal measurement, however, which includes the thickness of an average mortar joint. You need to know the brick's *exact* dimensions when planning a patio. Ask the dealer if the stated size is the nominal size or the actual size of the brick. Do not try to determine the size by taking a brick off a pile and measuring it with a ruler. It's common for individual bricks in a run to vary

BRICK PAVING PATTERNS

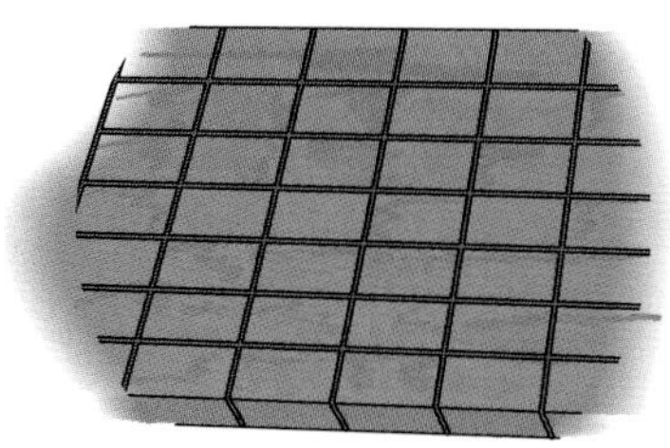

Jack-on-jack

Running bond

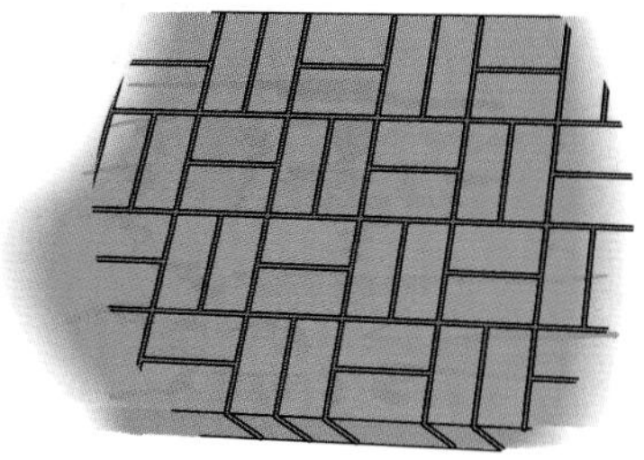

Basket weave

Half-basket weave

Herringbone, 90°

Herringbone, 45°

Pinwheel

Pinwheel with concrete dividers

Grid pattern

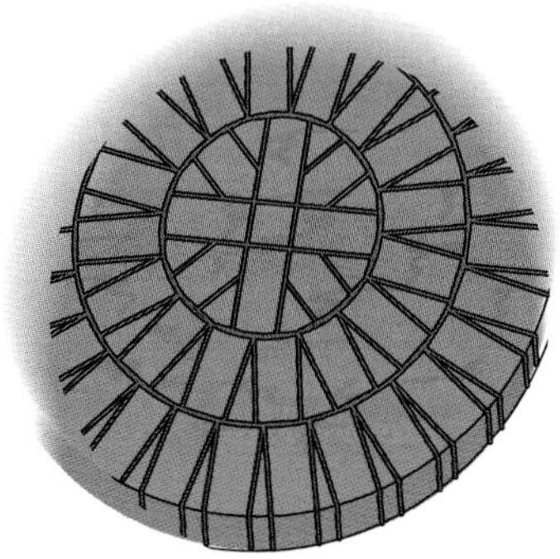

Whorled

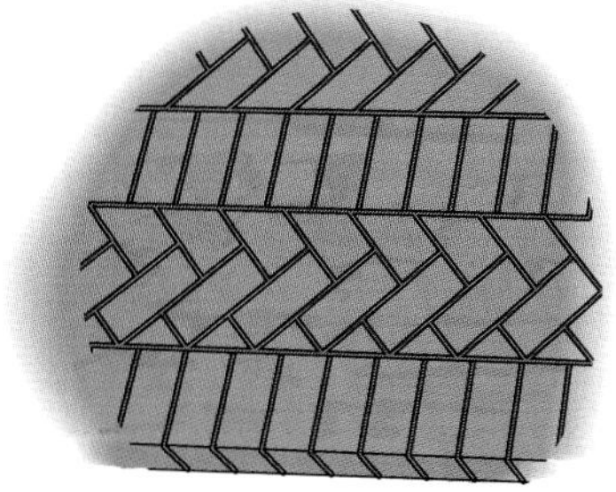

Herringbone and soldiers

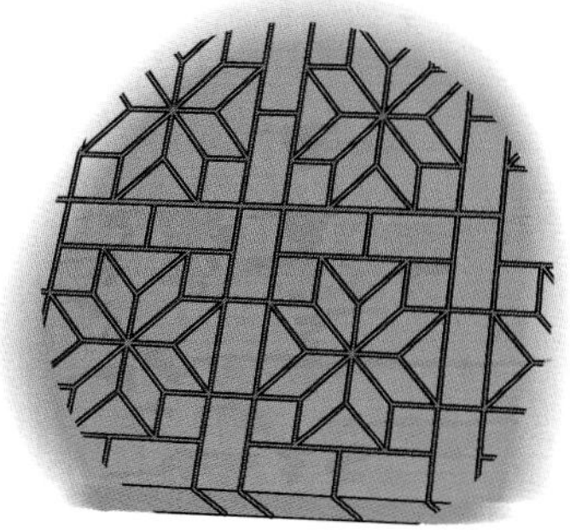

Mediterranean

PATIO EDGING OPTIONS

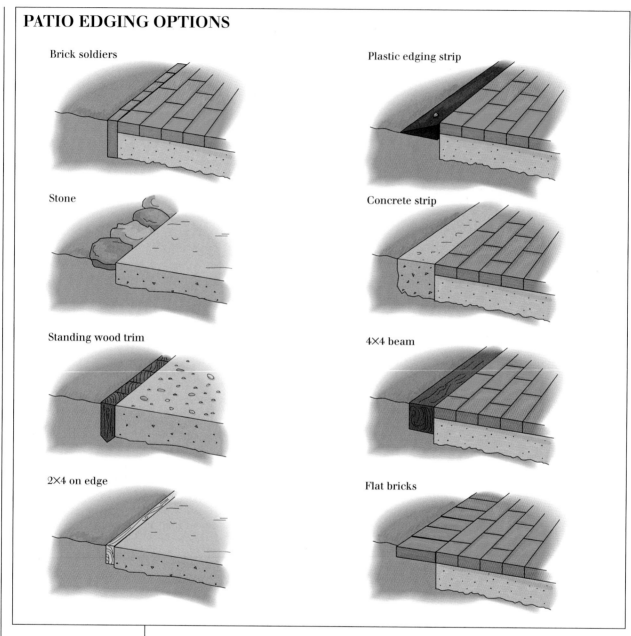

Brick soldiers

Plastic edging strip

Stone

Concrete strip

Standing wood trim

4×4 beam

2×4 on edge

Flat bricks

❏ How difficult is the pattern to lay? Intricate patterns require a lot of brick cutting as well as technical precision in laying.

❏ How will the pattern look on the patio? Easy patterns such as jack-on-jack and running bond become monotonous on large areas. Intricate patterns like Mediterranean look confusing on a small patio.

Use variety to put interest into the patio pattern. Some effective ways to do this include changing the direction of a bond, combining patterns, mixing or alternating brick colors within a pattern, adding a decorative border, or incorporating feature strips of another material, such as wood or concrete. Test your design by laying it out on graph paper or by laying out cardboard "bricks" on the ground.

Ordering Brick

Landscape- and building-supply companies and brickyards have the best selection of bricks. If you want used brick, try salvage yards.

To order bricks, first determine the square footage of the patio. For a rectangular patio, multiply the length by the width. For a circular patio, multiply the square footage of the radius (one-half the diameter) by 3.1416 (pi). For irregular shapes, draw the patio on graph paper, each square representing 1 square foot. Count all the squares and half-squares inside the patio border. To estimate the number of bricks you need, allow 5 bricks per square foot of patio surface, and then add 5 percent to the total to allow for waste. Have the brick dealer recalculate the total to ensure accuracy.

Bricks are sold individually or in blocks of 100 or 500 units. A block of 500 bricks weighs 1 ton. You need a sturdy truck or trailer to haul that load. Ask the dealer what it costs to have the bricks delivered. This fee is not included in the brick price. The expense of having bricks delivered on a pallet is far less than the cost of the damage done by dumping them off a truck.

INTERLOCKING CONCRETE PAVERS

The ideal do-it-yourself paving material, interlocking concrete pavers are manufactured expressly for use in paving patios and walks. They have evolved into a sophisticated product available in an endless variety of shapes, sizes, colors, and textures. The shapes include circles, squares, rectangles, pentagons, hexagons, octagons, and puzzle shapes. They butt or interlock together to make broad, unbroken patio surfaces. Depending on the shape, they make excellent substitutes for more expensive brick, tile, and stone paving materials. The size, shape, and color of each paver or pattern of pavers

Attractive and inexpensive, interlocking concrete pavers come in a number of patterns and are quick and easy to install.

These interlocking pavers have been combined with brick and natural rock to create an interesting pattern. It can be very pleasing to break up the expanse of a patio with rock, as shown here, or with spontaneous eruptions of plants.

determines the mood created. There's a mood for every architectural style. Pavers are inexpensive compared with other patio paving materials, and they are durable and stable. One disadvantage of pavers is that they tend to look institutional and lack the subtle, random color variations that add richness to some types of brick. A downside of some colored pavers is that they have shallow pigment; over time, bare concrete shows through worn and damaged areas. Buy pavers that are permeated with color throughout.

Installing Pavers

Concrete pavers are designed for mortarless installation in a sand bed. This makes them an ideal do-

it-yourself material. No mortar is needed because the pavers tightly abut one another to form a rigid surface. Their interlocking or interconnecting shapes give them such stability that the surface remains intact, even under stress and heavy loads. Pavers with beveled or chamfered edges are even more stable. They roll rather than crack when subjected to freezing weather.

Types of Concrete Pavers

Pavers are made from extremely dense concrete that is pressure-formed into various shapes. The shapes and colors distinguish one type of paver from another. They range from simple stepping-stones to brick pavers (so called because they look like real bricks) to large geometric shapes that look like hand-cut stone. There are even turf-retaining pavers, which have holes in which to plant ground covers or grass. They provide a means to include green space in large expanses of paving. Although pavers are significantly less expensive than real bricks, stones, and tiles, there is a wide variation in price among pavers. The cost of a specific paver depends on its size, thickness, and texture. You can cast your own pavers using forms and other materials supplied in a kit, but they won't be as strong as commercial pressure-formed pavers.

Paver Characteristics

Pavers vary in size as much as in shape. They run from 1½ inches to 3⅛ inches thick. Pavers up to 2½ inches thick work well on patios. Thicker units, designed for paving streets and driveways, also work, but you are paying for excess strength. There is a broad choice of colors too, including grays and off-whites, but the majority classify as earth tones.

Paver Patterns

Because a paver's shape creates the pattern on a patio, choose it carefully. Pay particular attention to its scale in proportion to the patio size. The pattern created by small pavers becomes too busy or gets lost on a large patio. Likewise, the pattern created by large pavers dwarfs a small patio.

Their modularity makes it possible to lay pavers, especially rectangular ones, in the same basic patterns in which you lay bricks. The most effective patterns are running bond, basket weave, half-basket weave, pinwheel, and herringbone (see page 81). Take care that the pattern doesn't become too busy. Use wood feature strips or other contrasting material to relieve the monotony of large expanses of simple rectangular pavers.

Ordering Pavers

Pavers are sold by building-supply outlets, home centers, nurseries, landscape-supply dealers, and paver manufacturers. Whereas the first three sell pavers by the individual piece, landscape-supply dealers and manufacturers sell them by the square foot. This is the preferred way to buy them. Use the methods outlined for ordering brick (see page 83) to figure your patio's square footage. If your chosen paver is the size of standard brick, multiply the square footage by 5 and add 5 percent for waste to get the amount you need. However, if your paver has a more intricate pattern and different size, ask the dealer to calculate the amount you need. Pavers come packaged in full cubes, or bands, sufficient to pave 16 lineal feet. The dealer will convert the square footage of your patio to lineal feet and then round off to the next highest band. Ask for an additional 5 percent to cover waste.

STONE

Another material available as pieces that can be amalgamated into a whole is stone. Stone includes many choices, including cobblestone (usually granite blocks), flagstone, slate, and marble. Even broken pieces of concrete from demolished sidewalks or patios can be used in rubble patterns fit together like jigsaw puzzles. The important consideration is that at least one face, the one you walk on, is relatively flat and smooth. *Relatively* is the operative word here, as surfaces that are too smooth tend to be slippery.

Most stone materials are available in the shape and relative size of brick or tile. The range is vast,

Perhaps the most natural-appearing landscaping material, stone comes in irregular shapes and sizes that can be difficult to fit together well. It is easy to work into a retaining wall, however, because the soil behind supports most of the weight, making careful fitting less important.

so a trip to a stoneyard or two is a must. If you select a cut pattern, ask the supplier to help you determine the exact amount you'll need for your patio design and size. For more information on obtaining stone, see page 253.

Cut stone is almost always laid on a concrete base, and the joints are mortared. The exception to this general rule is thick-cut cobblestone, which is often laid on a soil or sand base and the tight-fitted joints filled with sand.

Stone is the oldest and most rugged of all the paving materials. It is natural, beautiful, colorful, and plentiful. If you use a stone indigenous to your region, you can't go wrong in terms of style. Few areas of the country are without wonderful native stone, ideal for making a handsome patio. The only requirement is that it can be cut into flat pieces—dimensional tiles for formal patio floors, and flagstones or cobblestones for informal patios. Stone, like brick, has the added advantage of being suitable for constructing walls.

Methods of Installation

Technically, stone is the only material that can be laid directly on stable soil without first grading a base. Simply remove the turf under the stone and drop it in place. Like bricks and concrete pavers, however, stone works best when laid in sand, dry mortar, or wet mortar. The irregular thickness of stone means it must be seated in at least 2 inches of sand. Use the instructions for installing a brick-in-sand patio (page 203) as a guide to installing a flagstone or cobblestone patio.

Types of Stone

Three styles of stone are used for paving patios: cut stone, flagstone, and cobblestone. These names do not identify a type of stone; rather,

they describe its shape. Cut stone refers to machine-cut materials such as slate or marble, though limestone and sandstone are sometimes machine-cut as well. Flagstones are flat, thin, and irregularly shaped; cobblestones are smaller and roughly rounded. Of the three, flagstones are far more common on patios.

Native limestone and sandstone are the most common flagstones.

Above: Flagstone, with its rough surface, fits comfortably into informal gardens.
Opposite: With mortar to fill the gaps, natural stone is a fairly forgiving construction material.

water freezes and thaws. Conversely, dense stones don't absorb water and hence become slippery when wet. Most natural stones tend to be rough and uneven, which makes for a poor surface for outdoor furniture and a difficult one to keep clean. Finally, stone is expensive. It costs 5 to 10 times as much as brick or concrete, partly because it's so heavy; shipping all that weight long distances is exorbitant. Using indigenous or native stone helps minimize that cost because it is mined locally. If you can buy directly from the quarry, stone can be a competitive paving material.

In response to the demand for stone, many quarries now cut the dense stones, such as slate, into rectangular and square tiles with relatively even faces, making them easier to ship, handle, and install.

Stone Sizes and Colors

Flagstone comes cut in standard sizes, or uncut in irregular shapes. Cut flagstones are sized in modular 4-inch increments so they can be fit together in interesting patterns. Irregular flagstones get their beauty from their random shapes. They must be laid out carefully, however, to avoid creating a chaotic, patchwork look. Flagstones range from ½ inch to 2 inches thick. These thicknesses work well on residential patios. Don't try to use ashlar—stone cut to veneer walls and buildings—because it is too thick.

Stone Patterns

Lay cut flagstones in one size to make a uniform pattern or in multiple sizes to make a random but regular pattern. Irregular and semiregular flagstones are far more difficult to lay out successfully. If you plan to lay them in a sand bed, make trial layouts until you get the look you want; then install permanently.

Cut flagstone has just the right balance of formality and irregularity to add a pleasing texture to this formal landscape.

These sedimentary rocks split easily along their sediment lines, making ideal paving stones. Other common paving stones include granite, bluestone, basalt, and other igneous rocks. Formed from molten magna, igneous rocks are heavy, hard, extremely durable, and handsomely colored. They make excellent patio pavers. Slate is another popular paving stone. A dense, fine-grained metamorphic rock, the result of centuries of complex physical forces, it makes an attractive, durable patio surface.

Flagstones do have some disadvantages. Sandstone and limestone are porous, so they absorb water and continue to break up as the

Ordering Stone

Purchase stone from a landscape stone dealer. Professional landscape contractors buy it by the ton, but you can buy it by the square foot if you prefer. For reference, 1 ton of flagstone covers 80 to 120 square feet of patio surface. Use the method outlined for ordering brick (page 83) to determine your patio's square footage. For ordering stone for a wall, see page 254.

Another Option

Gathering your own stone is a viable alternative if native stone is available in your area. Streambeds, highway cuts, and open fields may offer opportunities for gathering (also see page 254). Picking up and transporting stone is heavy work; always wear gloves and lift only what you can carry comfortably. Be sure you have appropriate permission for stone gathering.

UNGLAZED TILE

Handsome, colorful ceramic tiles make attractive patio surfaces that are ideal for warm climates. They create a uniformly patterned surface and have the advantage of a wider choice of colors than other materials. There are four basic types of unglazed outdoor tile: patio tiles, quarry tiles, pavers, and synthetic stones. Some people consider adobe to be another type of unglazed tile, although it is sun dried and not fired in a kiln.

Patio, or terra-cotta, tiles are molded, fired ceramic tiles; their earthy colors and irregular shapes and surfaces create a peasant mood. Quarry tiles are molded, fired ceramic tiles that look like quarried stone. Pavers, too, are molded and fired, and come in bigger sizes for paving large areas. Paver styles range from rustic and

The unglazed tile of this patio contrasts attractively with the glazed tile of the fountain.

Tile, because of its relative weakness, must be supported by a rigid mortar foundation. Because it absorbs water, which can freeze and expand in cold weather, cracking the tile, it is unsuitable in climates with very cold winters.

informal, such as the familiar Mexican pavers, to crisp and modern. Synthetic stones are lightweight, fired ceramic tiles that resemble such rock as granite and sandstone; they are similar in composition to the veneer stones used to face walls. All these tiles come in earthen colors and work well on southwestern and southern California–style patios.

Use only unglazed ceramic tiles for a patio surface. Glazed tiles are slippery, even when dry, and they're deadly when wet. It's best to use unglazed tiles that also have some texture. Better yet, for the surest, safest traction, use unglazed, textured tiles specified for outdoor use.

Methods of Installation

All ceramic tiles must be set in mortar on a concrete slab that is sound and absolutely level. True ceramic tiles don't work in a sand bed. Although ceramic tile is recommended for warm climates, it can be installed in cold climates that do freeze, but only according to a set of exact standards established by the Tile Council of America. These regulations are so complicated that they prohibit do-it-yourself installation in such climates.

Ceramic-Tile Characteristics

The ceramic tiles most commonly used for patios are patio (terracotta) tiles, quarry tiles, pavers, and synthetic stones. Synthetic stones are ceramic tiles that look like granite, quarry tile, slate, even marble. They are being manufactured in response to the increasing popularity of natural stone. These tiles come in warm, earthen colors and natural, neutral tones. They measure 6 inches square or larger; 12 inches square is the most popular size. Note that these are nominal measurements that allow for a ½-inch-wide grout line.

Because they are square, it is harder to lay ceramic tiles in patterns like those achieved with brick. Instead, rely on contrasting grout lines and the natural beauty of the tile to achieve an interesting patio surface, or use tile for borders and feature strips for patios paved with other materials.

Ordering Tile

Today, many ceramic-tile suppliers sell to do-it-yourselfers. That was not always the case—for decades they refused to sell to anyone but professional installers. Now that you have access to such dealers, the supply of tile from which you can choose is greatly expanded. So is the technical help to which you have access. Purchase tile by the square foot, using the method outlined for ordering brick (page 83) to determine the square footage. Because most tiles are 6 by 6 inches or 12 by 12 inches, figuring the exact number of tile you need isn't complicated.

WOOD PAVING

Although wood is most often thought of as a decking material, it can be laid on grade as a patio pavement. It's available in round slices that look like stepping-stones, square blocks that look like old bricks, decking squares that look like parquet tiles, and decking boards. Slices and blocks usually are embedded in the earth. Squares and boards are mounted on low frames built directly on grade. The naturalness and warmth of wood make it an ideal paving material for all types of informal patios, traditional and contemporary. It is also an excellent border and divider material.

Wood is the least permanent of all the paving materials, even if it's pressure treated and of a rot- and insect-resistant species such as heart redwood, cedar, and cypress. These factors slow the decaying process but they do not stop it. Even optimal wood species require regular sealing against water and UV-ray damage. Still, wood has a special beauty that makes it a desirable patio material. It's easy to work with, comfortable to walk on, nonslip, and readily available in modular sizes. Unfortunately, it is no longer inexpensive.

Woodlike products have recently been developed for outdoor decking that are manufactured from recycled plastics; some are composites made from a blend of wood fibers and plastic resins. This alternative material comes in dimensioned boards, just like ordinary lumber. These boards can be sawn, fastened, and finished like lumber. The advantages of this material are that it is dimensionally stable, it is more durable than wood—a particular advantage for patios that hug the ground—and it is made from recycled materials. On the negative

side, it lacks the grain pattern of natural wood and is no less expensive. Also, cut ends of most such materials must be sealed with a compatible resin, or the fibers will absorb moisture that can be very destructive.

Methods of Installation

Installation choices range from setting wood rounds or wood paving blocks in a gravel or sand bed to constructing a deck surface on

Wood paving modules, such as these, make attractive stepping-stones and patio surfaces. These match the small bridge, carrying its lines beyond the stream.

grade using 2×4 or 2×6 planks nailed to 4×4 wood sleepers. Pre-built modular deck sections also can be set on grade. Use the instructions for installing a brick-in-sand patio (page 203).

Ordering Wood

Purchase wood from a home center, building-supply outlet, or lumberyard. Use the instructions for ordering brick (page 83) to determine the square footage. Use that figure to determine how much lumber or how many rounds or blocks you need. Be sure to specify an all-heart grade of lumber if you are using a durable species such as redwood, cedar, or cypress; the boards should contain no sapwood, which rots easily.

An edging of slate contrasts gently with the paving-block patio.

EDGING MATERIALS

Except where a patio abuts walls, planters, and steps, it requires an edging to keep loose-laid materials in place and to keep grass, plants, and soil where they belong. Edgings also serve a decorative function by providing clean, crisp borders and, where contrasting materials are used, adding interesting design effects.

The most common do-it-yourself edging materials are brick, wood, stone, concrete, and plastic strips. When selecting an edging, also consider such aspects as contrast (to emphasize lines and shapes or to relieve large expanses of paving material), maintenance (some lawn trimmers require a straight edge),

safety (smooth versus jagged edges), durability, and ease of installation. To help you evaluate the options, see pages 238 to 241, which summarize the various installation methods for the many edging materials.

COSTS

Home-improvement veterans will warn you that projects nearly always go over budget. It is easy to overlook needed items when putting together the budget. For a detailed overview of the steps of planning and budgeting a project, see page 267. Some project upgrades will hardly affect the budget—a desirable brick style or color may add only $100 to the job cost. But add to that the decision to buy a larger tree for more shade, or an additional foot of fence height for a greater degree of privacy, and the original budget is soon left in the dust. Here is a checklist that will help anticipate *all* your costs—including the hidden ones that so unexpectedly add up.

Materials Estimating Checklist

When preparing estimates it is important to consider all the factors that will establish the final costs.

❏ Paperwork and legalities
❏ Drafting materials for plans
❏ Cost of building permits and other fees
❏ Grading and site preparation
❏ Removing excess material from the site or importing needed material
❏ Transplanting existing plant material
❏ Moving or rerouting existing utilities
❏ Excavating for footings
❏ Drainage pipe installation

❏ Digging trenches for underground drainage or installation of utilities, such as plumbing, electrical, or irrigation
❏ Drainage pipe material and gravel
❏ Foundations and footings (concrete)
❏ Retaining-wall footings
❏ Footings for deck supports
❏ Footings for any buildings that are part of the project
❏ Forming lumber
❏ Form boards for patio edges and exposed foundations or concrete walls
❏ Framing lumber (note that deck-framing materials should be pressure treated for long life
❏ Base material
❏ Gravel or concrete base under patio paving
❏ Finished-surface material
❏ Wood decking or patio paving
❏ Stain or sealers
❏ Overhead structures
❏ Electrical and plumbing
❏ Landscaping
❏ Miscellaneous hardware
❏ Fencing, railings, built-in benches, planters
❏ Contingency

An expensive installation, such as this one, can be built in stages to spread the financial burden over several years. You might build the lower sitting area first, paving it temporarily with gravel. Later, the brick walls and paving could be added, then the deck and planters.

DECK DESIGN & CONSTRUCTION

Wood deck construction is similar to house construction. Many of the same materials and techniques are used, but decks are usually much simpler to build, bringing them within the skill level of most amateur carpenters.

Once you have a final site plan, you are ready to develop working drawings for building the deck. With careful planning, the project will be an enjoyable and rewarding experience. This chapter presents step-by-step instructions for selecting materials and building a deck. Some of the steps include variations on certain tasks. Depending on the deck design, site requirements, local codes, and personal experience, you may prefer an alternative method, or even choose to alter the order of the steps. If you plan to hire a contractor to do all or part of the work, this chapter will give you an understanding of the construction process, so you will be able to communicate clearly your needs and concerns.

THE ELEMENTS OF A DECK

The many variations concerning joist spacing, beam spans, and post sizes can be confusing. Keep in mind some basic rules about solid deck construction: It should have no spring in the flooring and no sugges-

tion of sway. You must also be able to lean against a railing with complete confidence. Decks are built from the ground up with several key elements joined together to make a firm, lasting structure. The following terms are common to the construction and landscaping trades.

ELEMENTS OF A DECK

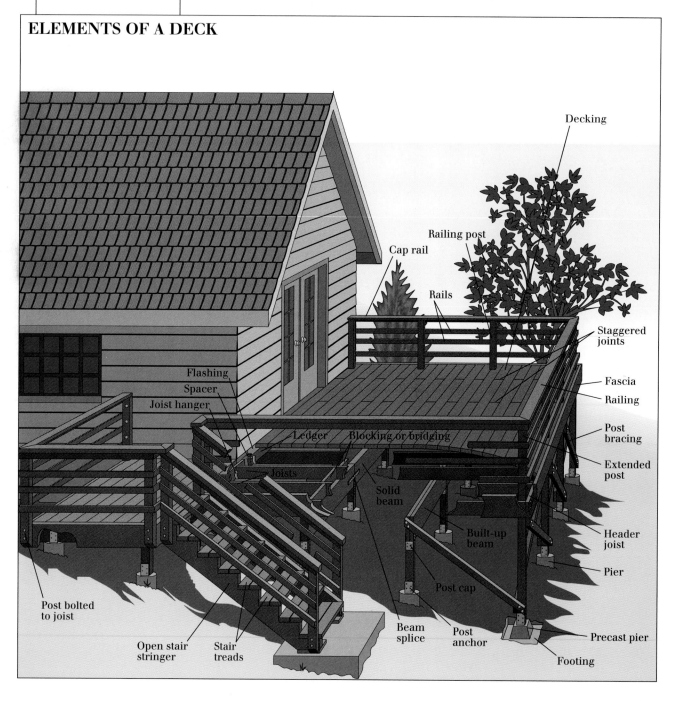

Footings

Footings support the entire deck and keep it from shifting or sinking into the ground. A footing is usually poured concrete 12 inches or more square and 6 to 8 inches thick. It must sit on firm, undisturbed soil or reach at least 6 inches below the frost line. In cold climates this could be as much as 4 feet below the surface. Not all decks need footings. Provided the ground is flat, well drained, and never freezes, a deck can be built right on 4×4s laid on the surface, if the wood has been pressure treated with a preservative. Some local codes even permit putting piers a few inches into the ground to support posts or beams.

Piers

Piers extend the footings, rising several inches above ground to keep the posts or beams clear of soil and ground splash. Like the footing, a pier carries and distributes the weight of the deck. Piers can be replaced with pressure-treated posts seated directly on the footings.

Posts

These are the thick uprights bearing the weight of the deck and transmitting it evenly to the piers and footings. Posts are commonly 4×4s but can be larger, depending on the structural needs of the deck. And depending on the design, posts can either support a beam or extend past it to form railing posts or other structures such as benches.

Beams

Beams rest on top of the posts or are bolted to them. The heavier the beam, the greater distance it can span, which means fewer posts to put up. Also note that if the plans call for a 4×6 beam, you can make one by nailing or bolting together three 2×6s.

Joists

Usually 2×6s (though often 2×8s or even 2×10s are used in snow country), joists are the connection between the beam and the ledger on the side of the house that supports the decking. Joists are normally spaced 16, 24, 32, or even 48 inches apart, depending on the type of decking. When using 2-by decking boards, try not to exceed 32 inches

This post sits on a pier, which is made of a concrete block with a piece of redwood set in its top to receive the nails. The pier is set into a poured concrete footing, which is mostly below ground level.

for joist spacing; 24-inch joist spacing makes a much firmer deck. When using 1-by decking, don't exceed 16-inch spacing.

Decking

The hardest-working and most visible part of the deck, decking can be a number of 2-bys of ¾-inch lumber. How you plan to lay it out and pattern it will determine how you build the support structure. Decking material should not exceed 6 inches in width because wider boards have a strong tendency to cup and trap water.

Ledger

Normally the same width as the joists, the ledger is bolted to the side of the house and supports one end of the joists. Ledgers must be placed so that when the decking is fastened in place, there will still be a 1-inch clearance below any existing or planned doorway. This prevents rain from running over the door sill.

DRAWING WORKING PLANS

A clear, concise, and detailed set of plans is invaluable for ordering supplies, scheduling the work, and keeping the construction steps in proper sequence. Plans also enable you to modify the design to fit your budget, schedule, and available materials well before construction begins. After all, it's much easier and less costly to make adjustments on paper.

The process of drawing the plans will also help you break down large tasks into smaller, more manageable ones. This puts the entire project in perspective by showing what each phase entails. With this information, you can choose which tasks to do yourself and which to contract out to a professional.

Make several copies of the working drawings—one or two sets for yourself, one for the local building department to review before issuing a permit, and, if hiring professionals, one for each contractor you ask to place bids.

Take a copy of the drawings with you when buying materials. Suppliers are usually willing to help you check your calculations or figure the quantities you need.

Drawings to Include in the Plans

A basic set of plans includes all, or most, of the following drawings. Some of the views, or details, may be combined into one drawing. Check with the local building department to see which ones are required for a permit.

❏ A *final site plan* is an overhead view that shows the deck's position in relationship to the house and yard and how all the elements interact. It details the known facts, showing patterns and shapes, including the direction of the decking boards. You can include present or future landscaping on this layout as well. When adding trees, be sure to consider their future growth. Always draw an arrow indicating north for easy identification.

❏ The *general layout drawing* is an overhead view that shows the decking pattern, exact dimensions, plus the location of any built-in or portable features. You can include present or future landscaping on this layout, or draw a separate landscape layout.

❏ *Elevation drawings* show the deck from each side, as if you are standing directly in front and level with the side being viewed. They should include details of footings and dimensions of the various structural elements.

SAMPLE DECK PLANS

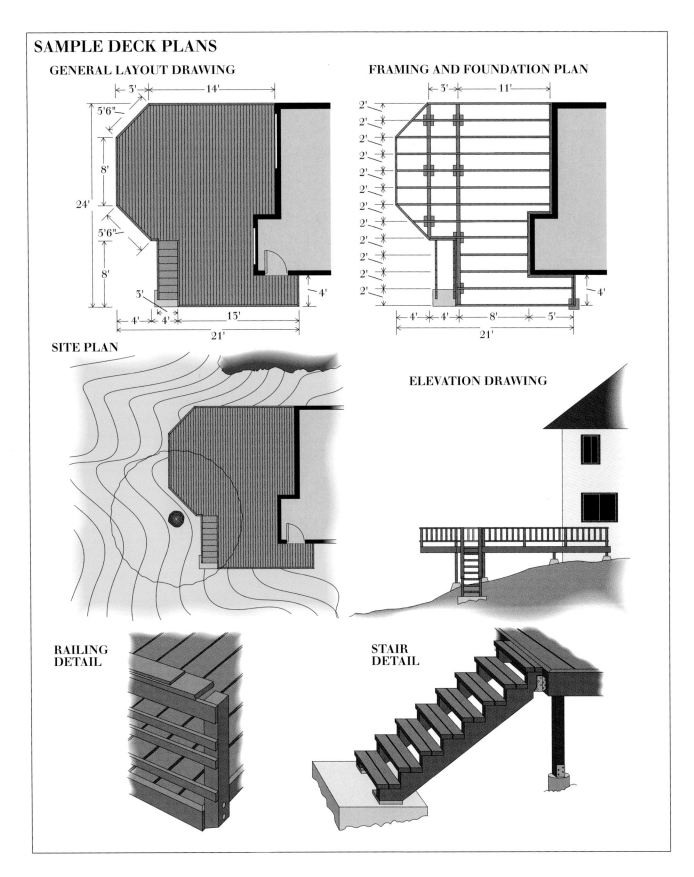

GENERAL LAYOUT DRAWING

FRAMING AND FOUNDATION PLAN

SITE PLAN

ELEVATION DRAWING

RAILING DETAIL

STAIR DETAIL

❑ *Foundation and pier drawings* indicate the position of the posts. This helps to eliminate the possibility of forgetting to compensate for the ledger when measuring for post locations.

❑ The *substructure, or framing, plan* shows placement and construction details for the ledger, posts, beams, joists, and bracing. The framing plan and the foundation and pier drawings are often combined.

❑ *Detail drawings* for railings, stairs, built-ins, and other extras should be drawn separately and include the methods of attachment.

If future deck additions or accessories are planned, include them in your initial plans. For instance, if a spa or extremely heavy amenity is to be added later, include the necessary structural elements with the plans now, so you will have the details for roughing-in the plumbing and electrical during construction.

DESIGNING THE STRUCTURAL SYSTEM

The structural requirements for most decks can be calculated using tables based on typical building-code requirements. These requirements are designed to ensure the deck's structural integrity and they greatly influence its design and construction. If you have any special considerations, such as heavy snow loads, wind loads, or earthquake bracing for a high deck, consult the local building department or a design professional experienced in deck planning.

Once you've established the overall shape and dimensions of the deck, you can work backward to plan the framing system. Start with the decking, which usually runs parallel to the house. Then plan the joist layout by determining the size and spacing of the joists, based on the distance they must span. Then

BASIC DECK DIMENSIONS

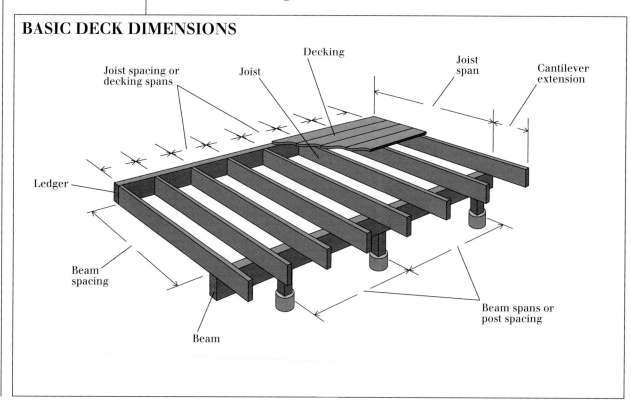

Decking

Joist spacing or decking spans

Joist

Joist span

Cantilever extension

Ledger

Beam spacing

Beam

Beam spans or post spacing

plan the ledger and beam (or beams) that will support the joists. Finally, plan the posts and footings for supporting the beams.

As you plan the structure, you may need to revise the size, spacing, or spans of certain members. This is normal. For instance, you may choose a joist size that requires the beam and posts to be located where it will be difficult to excavate for footings, such as directly over a buried pipe. By changing the joists to a larger size, or placing them closer together, you may be able to move the beam out far enough to avoid the obstruction. The size and number of structural members are based on the capacity of the lumber to span certain distances and carry certain loads. You could calculate each individual board based on standard load formulas, but the accompanying tables give you a quicker way to figure minimum lumber sizes and maximum spacing and spans of the deck members. Keep in mind that these recommendations are minimums—you can always choose larger sizes of lumber to increase the strength and stability of the deck. Be sure to check local codes for any other requirements that may apply.

Follow these steps to plan the deck structure.

Step 1: Be Aware of Actual Lumber Sizes

To begin, you need to understand how lumber is sized, or dimensioned. Two terms are used to indicate size: *nominal* and *actual.* You will find that most lumber charts use nominal sizes.

Nominal size refers to the dimensions of lumber before it is kiln- or air-dried and planed, or "dressed." Actual size refers to the dimensions after drying and planing. Table 1 (above) shows the difference between nominal and actual sizes.

TABLE 1: NOMINAL AND ACTUAL DIMENSIONS OF LUMBER

Nominal Size	Actual Size*
1 × 2"	¾ × 1½"
1 × 3"	¾ × 2½"
1 × 4"	¾ × 3½"
1 × 6"	¾ × 5½"
1 × 8"	¾ × 7¼"
1 × 10"	¾ × 9¼"
1 × 12"	¾ × 11¼"
5/4 × 6"	1¼ × 5½"
2 × 2"	1½ × 1½"
2 × 3"	1½ × 2½""
2 × 4"	1½ × 3½"
2 × 6"	1½ × 5½"
2 × 8"	1½ × 7¼"
2 × 10"	1½ × 9¼"
2 × 12"	1½ × 11¼"
4 × 4"	3½ × 3½""
4 × 6"	3½ × 5½"
4 × 8"	3½ × 7¼"
4 × 10"	3½ × 9¼"
4 × 12"	3½ × 11¼"
6 × 6"	5½ × 5½"
6 × 8"	5½ × 7¼"
8 × 8"	7¼ × 7¼"

*Dimensions may vary. Always measure.

Here are examples of why it's critical to be aware of the actual size of lumber:

Example 1: As a money-saving method, or because not enough 4X4 posts are available, you decide to fasten two 2X4s face-to-face. Table 1 shows why this will not do.

A nominal 4X4 has actual dimensions of 3½ inches by 3½ inches. A nominal 2X4 has actual dimensions of 1½ inches by 3½ inches. Two nominal 2X4s fastened face-to-face, therefore, will be 3½ inches wide at one face of the post but only 3 inches wide on the side. These dimensions would affect the strength and load-bearing capacity of the deck drastically.

Redwood decking can be laid on joists as far as 28 inches apart. This decking is being installed with decking clips, small L-shaped brackets that are nailed to one edge of a board before it is put in place. The clip slides under the previous board, holding down that edge. The free edge is toenailed, as shown here.

Decking clips, which are hidden from view, eliminate the need for nails being driven through the surface of the deck and possibly marring the surface with unsightly nail heads. They are also more secure than surface nails, which sometimes work loose as the deck alternately swells and shrinks with the weather. Decking clips are further described on page 152.

Example 2: Let's say the decking plans call for twenty 2×12s placed edge-to-edge. When you get to the lumberyard, there are only fifteen 2×12s, so you decide to get ten 2×6s to make up the difference. However, by consulting Table 1, you can see that this won't work. A nominal 2×12 actually measures 11¼ inches across. Twenty planks placed edge-to-edge equal 225 inches. A nominal 2×6 is 5½ inches across. Combining ten 2×6s with fifteen 2×12s makes a total of only 223¾ inches—about 1¼ inches shorter than necessary to cover the deck.

Step 2: Consider Variations in Softwood Strength

Each species of wood has its own level of strength, which is measured as the ability to resist bending. Strength varies considerably among different species. Softwoods are categorized in one of three groups. Group A is the strongest category, Group B has a middle strength rating, and Group C has the lowest strength rating. If you change to lumber with a lower strength rating after the plans are completed, you must refigure spans and sizes. Table 2 (at right) shows the strengths of some common softwoods.

Step 3: Establish the Decking Board Sizes and Spans

The decking attaches to the joists to form the surface on which you walk; decking boards transfer the load to the joists. The size and strength of the decking determine how far it can span. This distance becomes the maximum joist spacing, no matter what size joists are used.

Table 3 (at right) shows how close together the joists should be, depending on the species of decking boards used. The stronger the board,

the wider the joist span can be. Do not exceed the span listed; this is neither recommended nor permitted by code.

To use Table 3, match up the species group with the nominal thickness of the decking. For example, nominal 2×6 planks laid flat, using wood species Group B, would have a maximum span between joists of 36 inches on center. Note that with the weaker wood species, using the maximum figures in the table can create an unwanted springy effect. With these species, position the joists closer together than indicated in Table 3 to give the deck a more solid feel.

TABLE 2: STRENGTH GROUPINGS OF COMMON SOFTWOODS*

Group A	Cypress, Douglas fir, West Coast hemlock, western larch, southern yellow pine
Group B	Western red cedar, white fir, eastern hemlock, lodgepole pine, Norway pine, Ponderosa pine, sugar pine, northern white pine, redwood (clear, all heart), eastern spruce, Sitka spruce
Group C	Northern white cedar, southern white cedar, balsam fir, redwood (construction heart or better)

*Assumes #2 grade or better.

TABLE 3: RECOMMENDED MAXIMUM SPANS FOR DECKING BOARDS*

	Species Group		
	A	**B**	**C**
Laid Flat **			
Nominal 1" boards	16"	14"	12"
⁵⁄₄" pressure-treated boards	24"	16"	—
Nominal 2×3	28"	24"	20"
Nominal 2×4	32"	28"	20"
Nominal 2×6	42"	36"	28"
Laid on Edge			
2×3	48"	40"	32"
2×4	72"	60"	48"

*Spans are based on the use of construction grade lumber or better (select structural, appearance, #1, or #2).
**These spans are based on the assumption that more than one floorboard carries normal loads. If concentrated loads are a rule, reduce spans accordingly.

TABLE 4: MAXIMUM JOIST SPANS (BEAM SPACING)*

Joist Size	Species Group		
	A	B	C
12" Joist Spacing			
2×6	10'6"	10'0"	9'0"
2×8	14'0"	12'6"	11'0"
2×10	17'6"	15'8"	13'10"
2×12	21'0"	19'4"	17'6"
16" Joist Spacing			
2×6	9'7"	8'6"	7'7"
2×8	12'6"	11'0"	10'0"
2×10	16'2"	14'4"	13'0"
2×12	19'0"	18'6"	16'0"
24" Joist Spacing			
2×6	8'6"	7'4"	6'8"
2×8	11'2"	9'9"	8'7"
2×10	14'0"	12'6"	11'0"
2×12	16'6"	16'0"	13'6"
32" Joist Spacing			
2×6	7'6"	6'9"	6'0"
2×8	10'0"	9'1"	8'2"
2×10	12'10"	11'8"	10'8"
2×12	14'6"	14'0"	12'6"

*Joists are on edge. Spans are center-to-center distances between beams or ledger and beam. Loads are based on 40 psf deck live load plus 10 psf dead load. Assumes a grade equivalent to #2 or better (#2 medium-grain southern pine).

Step 4: Determine the Joist Sizes and Spans

Once you've figured how far apart the joists can be, based on the species of wood you will use for the decking, use Table 4 at left to figure their maximum span—that is, how far apart the beams can be laid—according to their dimension and species. The joist span is measured on center, with the joist installed on edge. For example, using nominal 2×6 lumber for joists in wood species Group B with 24-inch joist spacing, the maximum joist span, or beam spacing, would be 7 feet 4 inches.

Step 5: Determine the Beam Sizes and Spans

One or more beams, along with the ledger, support the joists. The size of each beam is determined by balancing two variables: the joist span (distance between beams, or ledger and beam) and the distance between the posts that support the

Blocking—the boards between the joists—adds rigidity to the joists. The spans in the table above assume the use of blocking at 8- to 10-foot intervals.

TABLE 5: MAXIMUM BEAM SPANS (POST SPACINGS) FOR DECKS*

Species Group	Beam Size	Beam Spacing (Joist Span), in Feet								
		4	5	6	7	8	9	10	11	12
A	4×6	6'	6'	6'						
	3×8	8'	8'	7'	6'	6'	6'			
	4×8	10'	9'	8'	7'	7'	6'	6'	6'	
	3×10	11'	10'	9'	8'	8'	7'	7'	6'	6'
	4×10	12'	11'	10'	9'	9'	8'	8'	7'	7'
	3×12	12'	11'	10'	9'	9'	8'	8'	8'	
	4×12	12'	12'	11'	10'	10'	9'	9'		
	6×10	12'	11'	10'	10'	9'	9'	9'		
B	4×6	6'	6'							
	3×8	7'	7'	6'	6'					
	4×8	9'	8'	7'	7'	6'				
	3×10	10'	9'	8'	7'	7'	6'	6'	6'	6'
	4×10	11'	10'	9'	8'	8'	7'	7'	7'	6'
	3×12	12'	11'	10'	9'	8'	8'	7'	7'	7'
	4×12	12'	11'	10'	10'	9'	9'	8'	8'	
	6×10	12'	11'	10'	10'	9'	9'	9'		
C	4×6	6'								
	3×8	7'	6'							
	4×8	8'	7'	6'	6'					
	3×10	9'	8'	7'	6'	6'	6'	6'		
	4×10	10'	9'	8'	8'	7'	7'	6'	6'	6'
	3×12	11'	10'	9'	8'	7'	7'	7'	6'	6'
	4×12	12'	11'	10'	9'	9'	8'	8'	7'	7'
	6×10	12'	11'	10'	9'	9'	8'	8'		

*Beams are on edge. Spans are center-to-center distances between posts or supports. Loads based on 40 psf deck live load plus 10 psf dead load. Assumes a grade equivalent to #2 or better (#2 medium-grain southern pine).

beam. Generally, it's best to make the beams as large as possible to reduce the number of posts and footings. The posts and footings, however, must not be so far apart that each one bears a load greater than the bearing capacity of the soil itself (for most soils, it is 2,000 pounds per square foot).

To calculate the minimum number of footings (posts) required to support the deck: (1) calculate the deck area in square feet by multiplying length by width; (2) multiply one half of the span between the beam and ledger times the length of the deck; (3) subtract this figure from the total deck area; (4) multiply the remaining area of the deck by 50 pounds per square foot (the load); (5) divide the total load by the bearing capacity of the soil (assume 2,000 pounds per square foot). The answer is the number of footings required, if each one covers 1 square foot.

For example, a deck measuring 16 by 20 feet would have a total area of 320 square feet. If the distance between the ledger and beam is 12 feet, the area of the deck supported by the ledger would be one half of that span (6 feet) multiplied by the length of the deck (20 feet), or 120 square feet. The beam, then, would be supporting 200 square feet (320 minus 120). At 50 pounds per square foot (psf), the load on the beam would be 10,000 pounds. Assuming that the soil could bear 2,000 pounds per square foot, the beam would require five footings if each one were 12 inches square (1 square foot). If the footings were 16 inches square (2 square feet), only three would be required.

Post height can vary, especially on steep terrain. Measure the height from the top of the pier to the beam, or to the top rail if the post will support the railing.

Step 6: Determine the Post Sizes and Spacing

The posts support the beams. The overall load and the height of the deck determine the size of the posts. To figure the load, multiply the beam spacing (joist span) by the post spacing (beam span). If the result falls between two numbers on the chart, use the higher of the two.

TABLE 6: MAXIMUM POST HEIGHTS FOR DECKS*

Species Group	Post Size	Load Area (Beam Spacing × Post Spacing) in Square Feet									
		36	48	60	72	84	96	108	120	132	144
A	4×4	Up to 12' high			Up to 10' high			Up to 8' high			
	4×6	Up to 12' high							Up to 10' high		
	6×6	Up to 12' high									
B	4×4	Up to 12' high		Up to 10' high			Up to 8' high				
	4×6	Up to 12' high				Up to 10' high					
	6×6	Up to 12' high									
C	4×4	To 12'	Up to 10' high		Up to 8' high		Up to 6' high				
	4×6	Up to 12' high		Up to 10' high			Up to 8' high				
	6×6	Up to 12' high									

*Loads based on 40 psf deck live load plus 10 psf dead load. Grade is #2 and better for 4 × 4 posts and #1 and better for larger sizes. Group A: Douglas fir (north), larch, and southern pine. Group B: Hem fir and Douglas fir (south). Group C: Western pine, western cedar, redwood, and spruce.

Example: If the beams are spaced 8'6" OC and the posts are spaced 11'6", then the load area is 98 square feet. Calculate post heights based on next larger area: 108.

PLANNING STAIRS AND RAILINGS

Although it is best to plan stairs and railings after the rest of the deck is designed, do not consider them mere afterthoughts. Railings, especially, can dominate the appearance of a deck, and both elements have very important safety functions. Both have strict code requirements that dictate much of their design.

Stairs

Stairs consist of treads, risers, and stringers. Risers are optional, provided the area under the stairs is attractively maintained. Stairs must be strong enough to carry substantial loads. To do this effectively and safely, the treads must have the same dimensions throughout, as must the risers; and all steps, except the first, must be the same height.

Check building codes for stair requirements in your area. The stringers are usually made of 2×12s. If you use a ratio of a 6-inch riser to a 12-inch tread, the stairs can be made completely from 2×6s, using one for the riser and two for the tread. However, decks and other outdoor structures lend themselves to more spacious and leisurely

Top: Stairs can be complex and high, as shown here, or simple. If the deck is low, make the stairs wide for easy access and a feeling of generosity. Narrower stairs are safer for higher elevations because a hand rail is always within reach.
Bottom: Railings (see page 109) add a pleasant sense of enclosure.

BASIC STAIR DIMENSIONS

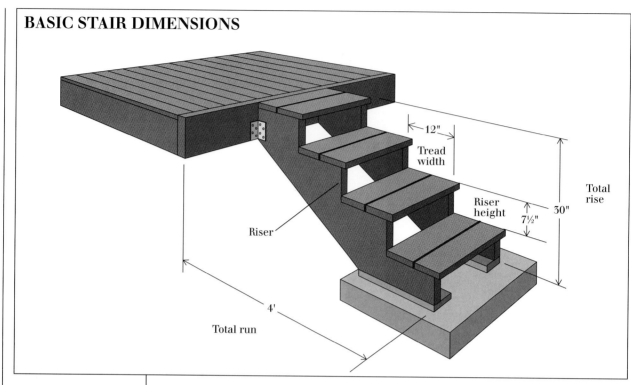

RISER AND TREAD PROPORTIONS

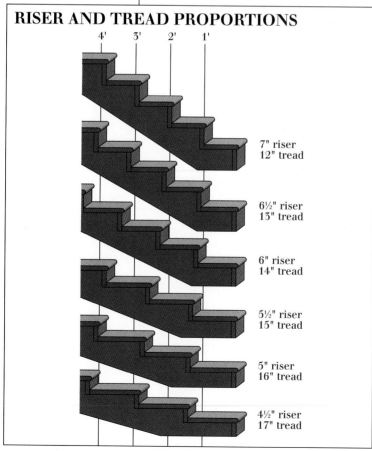

7" riser
12" tread

6½" riser
13" tread

6" riser
14" tread

5½" riser
15" tread

5" riser
16" tread

4½" riser
17" tread

dimensions. Although most codes require that stairs have a maximum riser height and minimum tread width of 7½ inches and 11 inches, respectively, there is no reason why the stairs cannot have less of an incline—a 6-inch riser and 14-inch tread, for instance, or a 5½-inch rise and 15-inch tread. Such dimensions have a more luxurious feeling, conducive to lingering and relaxing. They are also safer.

When the stairs are assembled, the leading edge of the tread should overlap the riser below by ½ inch to create a shadow line, which helps define the steps. The upper ends of the stringers should be attached to the deck header with joist hangers. The lower ends of the stringers can be placed on concrete, bricks, or pressure-treated lumber specified for ground contact. Never rest the lower ends of the stringers on bare ground. It is unstable, and the wood will absorb ground moisture, leading to rot and insect infestation.

BASIC RAILING DIMENSIONS

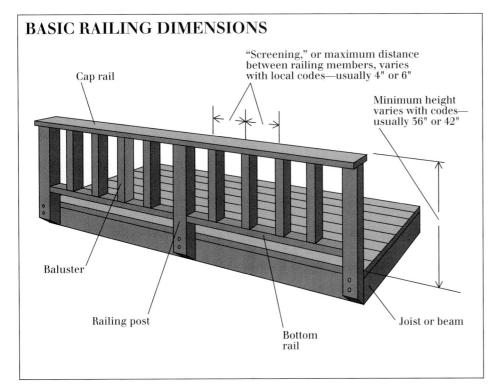

Cap rail

"Screening," or maximum distance between railing members, varies with local codes—usually 4" or 6"

Minimum height varies with codes—usually 36" or 42"

Baluster

Railing post

Bottom rail

Joist or beam

Railings can be made from a wide variety of materials and in many forms. Be sure they meet code requirements.

An alternative to wood steps is to use prefabricated concrete steps, or build forms and pour concrete ones. Another alternative is a ramp for garden carts, wheelchairs, or tricycles.

Railings

All raised decks should be protected by railings for safety. Railings can also enhance appearance. Railings can support flower boxes or be part of a built-in bench system. They can be plain or ornate, open or solid, basic or custom-made.

Many types of materials can be used to fill in the area between the top rail and the deck. The possibilities include redwood lattice, wood spindles, vertical or horizontal wood strips, sheets of clear rigid plastic, wrought iron, rope, cable, or canvas.

Local codes require railings for stairs when there are a certain number of steps in a set. The railing is typically 30 to 33 inches above the step. If the deck is elevated, the

railing is typically 36 to 42 inches above the deck surface. The railing must be able to resist a horizontal force of at least 15 pounds per lineal foot. For child safety, the maximum distance between railing members is 6 inches for most local codes (4 inches for some).

SELECTING AND ESTIMATING LUMBER

The bewildering variety of wood species used for building is further complicated because all lumber is classified into a number of different grades. Furthermore, the grading differs among wood species. The nice thing about building a wood deck is that you really can't go wrong with almost any type or grade. However, some are better than others for specific purposes.

Because of their availability in the western United States, redwood and cedar are the top choices for decking material. These same woods, along with cypress in the East and South, are popular for decks because of their natural resistance to decay brought on by moisture. Other woods, such as Douglas fir, hemlock, spruce, and pine, also make excellent decks and are usually considerably less expensive than redwood or cedar. Your final choice of decking will of course be influenced by your budget. If the microclimate is dry, don't be overly concerned if your budget allows only pine for the decking material. Given proper finishing and care, a pine deck can last many years. For more information on specific wood species, see page 62.

After deciding on the species of wood, the next consideration is how much you'll need. Because the support structure will involve large-dimension, expensive lumber, draw it in detail on the work-ing drawings and then count it up piece by piece. If you have some beams that are 8 feet long and some 12 feet long, don't hastily decide to order all 12-foot lengths—the waste would be costly. Instead, make a detailed list of how many pieces of each length you need. Count up all the connectors or joist hangers the plans call for. Count posts individually and note the lengths, allowing for grading variations in the site.

In calculating the amount of decking lumber, first figure the square footage of the deck by multiplying length by width. With this information, almost any lumberyard can quickly calculate how much decking lumber you need based on board feet.

Estimate the lumber involved in a post-to-post section, including top and bottom rails and balusters. When you set out to buy the lumber, it will be very much worth your while to shop around. Prices of lumber vary considerably. A little comparative shopping could save you hundreds of dollars.

Wood comes in a variety of grades (see pages 62 to 68).

BUYING THE LUMBER

The staff of the local lumberyard is one of your best resources for information about materials. They probably sell a great deal of lumber for decks and can tell you the best type of wood for your area, considering the climate and the availability of different wood species. As a do-it-yourselfer organizing a project of significant size, don't be shy about asking for a contractor's discount when ordering the lumber. It can mean savings of 5 to 10 percent.

Before going to the lumberyard, keep in mind that lumber is sold in 2-foot increments. These lengths

LUMBER DEFECTS

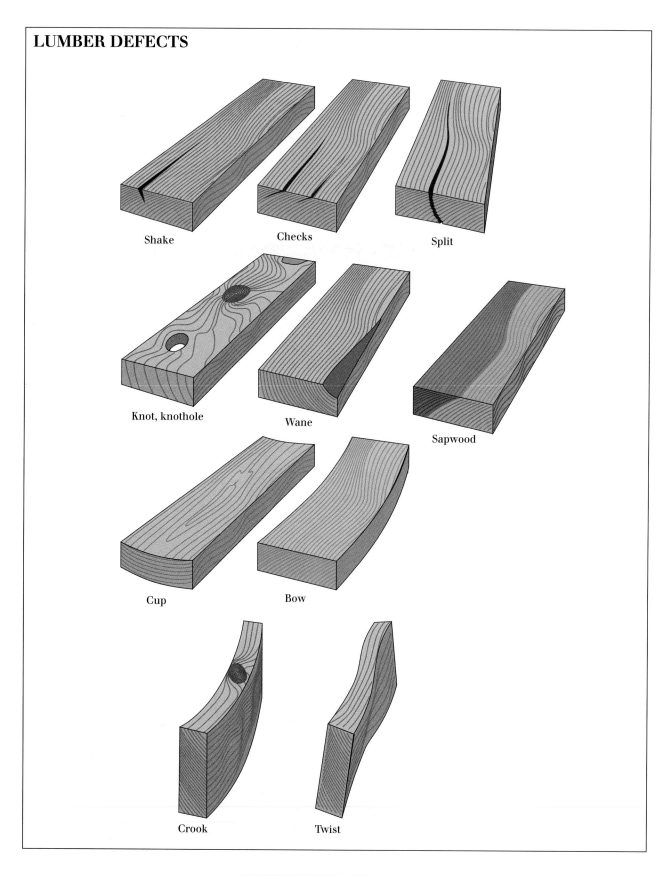

Shake

Checks

Split

Knot, knothole

Wane

Sapwood

Cup

Bow

Crook

Twist

usually range from 6 to 20 feet. Boards longer than 20 feet often have to be specially ordered, and you would probably find them too unwieldy for easy handling. If for some reason your deck comes out 15 feet long, you will have to buy 16-foot lengths and trim off the extra foot. In which case, consider changing the design to a 14- or 16-foot deck.

Theoretically, you should also be able to buy lumber that is surfaced only on one side (S1S), which would be cheaper. In most cases, however, this would require a special order with plenty of advance notice. Wood is commonly available either S4S (surfaced four sides) or rough. The cheaper rough wood is suitable for the support structure unless it is highly visible. Sometimes, of course, it is desirable even for highly visible uses, such as retaining walls. If you use rough lumber, be sure to wear protective gloves to prevent splinters. (Always wear gloves when working with pressure-treated lumber.)

Wood Grain and Defects

Grain direction is determined when raw timbers are processed at the mill. Vertical grain lines are parallel and run lengthwise. A flat-grain pattern has wavy grain lines, giving the lumber a marbled look. For decking, look for a vertical grain pattern because it is stronger and more attractive (and also more expensive). For joists and beams, flat-grain lumber is strongest.

Lumber grades and prices are influenced by the overall condition of the wood. Natural defects and those that occur during processing, such as splits and gouges, affect strength and workability. A better grade is more costly but generates little waste, whereas a less expensive grade requires more work and generally produces more waste:

Loose knots must be cut around, warped or twisted boards must be straightened, and pitch pockets and bark wane along the edge disfigure the natural beauty of the wood.

Inspecting the Lumber

At some lumberyards, you can choose all your wood, particularly if you are hauling it yourself. Other dealers insist that it be taken as it comes from the pile unless you are willing to pay a premium for selecting the specific pieces you want.

When buying lumber, choose and inspect each piece yourself whenever possible. You can expect slight variations in quality within a shipment, but be sure the lot is what you want. Most lumber today is second-growth and fast-growth wood, which is often not as dense and durable as first-growth, or virgin, lumber.

Sawmills cut every log in a manner designed to get the maximum amount of lumber out of it. Some cuts are better than others because they have fewer knots or are less likely to warp. Boards for construction and decking are generally flat-grain cuts, where the end grain is parallel to the face of the board, or cross-grain, with the end grain at an angle up to 45 degrees to the face. Vertical-grain lumber is cut with the grain at a right angle to the face, a higher grade usually reserved for finishing wood.

Note that there is a bark side and pith side to all lumber. In laying down the decking boards, try to keep the bark side up; otherwise the grain on the top side of the board separates, causing splinters and accelerating deterioration.

Wood also comes green or dried. Air- or kiln-dried wood is considerably more expensive and normally not worth the extra cost. The lumber you purchase for a deck, once nailed in place, will season itself.

TIPS FOR BUYING, ORDERING, AND STORING MATERIALS

Now that you've figured out your materials, do you buy them as needed or all at once? If you buy as you go, you will spend a lot of time making trips to suppliers, but you won't have to store large quantities of materials or invest a considerable sum of money up front. If you carefully broke the large tasks into small ones when you set up the budget, you already know just what you need and when you'll need it.

Buying all the materials at once has advantages, however. You'll save time on the shopping, and you can save money too. Some suppliers offer volume discounts and free delivery for large orders.

Before you leave the store, inspect the materials closely for damage. Pay attention to the manufacturer's labels—they provide valuable information about the product's uses, coverages, and shelf life. Safety information on the label protects you. Follow it. Read the cautions regarding handling, storage, and proper disposal of leftovers.

Avoid special-order items, especially if you're new to construction. Generally, these items are more expensive. If you want to use special-order items, however, plan ahead. Obtain cost estimates and the lead time for ordering. Once you place the order, check regularly on its status. Have a contingency plan in case the item is delayed or not available.

Transporting large, heavy lumber and materials is a major concern. It is dangerous to load up your car with long or bulky materials. Unless you have access to a truck with a sturdy lumber rack, make arrangements for delivery. Some suppliers may charge a nominal fee,

The lumber for this deck is green, so the spaces between boards are small; the green lumber will shrink slightly as it seasons, opening the gaps. Easier to cut and nail than dried lumber, green lumber is also less easily split by nails.

If you install green lumber, however, do not space the decking widely; use an 8-penny (8d) nail as a spacer. The green lumber will shrink as it cures, noticeably increasing the gap.

In selecting lumber, keep an eye out for checks, cracks across the grain, and shakes—cracks that run with the grain. These not only weaken the board but make it unsightly. They can also cause dangerous splinters. When you are framing, avoid large knots at the edge of a joist. In any case, never place a large edge knot in a downward position. Edge knots seriously weaken the lumber. Also try to avoid lumber that is bowed, cupped, twisted, or crooked at one end.

but many offer free delivery of large orders.

Finally, when loading and unloading heavy or bulky items, don't attempt to do it alone; it is easy to damage the material or yourself. As the materials are unloaded, organize and stack them carefully. Be aware that theft of material and tools from construction sites is very common.

Storage

Prior to delivery, choose the storage area. Select a secure location for lumber, supplies, and tools. It could be a garage, locked shed, or even the yard, but it must be easily accessible from the work site.

Choose a storage site that is high and dry. Cover the materials with plastic, whether indoors or out, to protect them from dirt as well as the elements. To keep lumber from warping, stack it on a perfectly level platform or with stickers (lath or 1×2s) between levels. Don't let the lumber sag or lean against a wall; it may warp permanently. Lumber of higher quality than construction grade cannot be exposed to the sun.

Be sure to store toxic substances, such as stain and adhesives, in a locked cabinet or shed.

Devise a way to keep nails, screws, bolts, and other hardware organized. Empty paint cans or coffee cans are ideal for nails and screws—label each one clearly.

Don't let supplies and lumber become "ankle busters"—left where you can trip over them while you're working. Store and organize them in one area in a way that gives you easy, clear access.

THE RIGHT TOOLS FOR THE JOB

Deck building doesn't require a lot of tools, just the right ones. An assortment of a few common

---

HIRING HELP

In some cases, your plans may require a contractor. It will cost you more money, but the job will likely be done faster and perhaps better. The professional doesn't have to do the entire deck—you can hire out only the footings installation, or building a tricky part of the substructure or some elaborate railings. Experienced carpenters who advertise their services in the newspaper can often be hired by the hour or the day. Once they finish the part that requires professional skills, you can carry on with the rest.

Before you hire someone to assist you, be sure to inspect other projects they have done. Decks are built with heavy individual elements with structural qualities, much like the framing in your house; and on decks, framing and finish carpentry must be combined. As a result, a competent framing contractor may not be precise enough for finished deck work. Hammer marks in substructure framing members are inconsequential, but they are highly visible on a deck floor. Some of the most skilled carpenters in the business specialize in outdoor landscape construction that the average builder might approach with a heavy, clumsy hand.

---

hand and power tools is all you will need, and you probably have many of them in your workshop already. Most of the tools are inexpensive and easy to find, but you may want to rent or borrow any you don't have.

Site Layout
- ❏ Tape measure (1 inch by 25 feet) for general measuring
- ❏ Tape measure (100 feet) for laying out large deck site
- ❏ Sledgehammer for driving stakes
- ❏ Nylon string (mason's twine) for laying out string lines
- ❏ Hydro level for establishing level marks on the site
- ❏ Carpenter's level for aligning posts vertically and for general leveling
- ❏ Torpedo level for aligning forms, piers, and brackets
- ❏ Plumb bob for laying out site and positioning components

Excavation and Concrete Work
- ❏ Garden spade for preparing site
- ❏ Garden rake for preparing site
- ❏ Posthole digger or power auger for digging footing holes

BASIC TOOLS FOR BUILDING A DECK

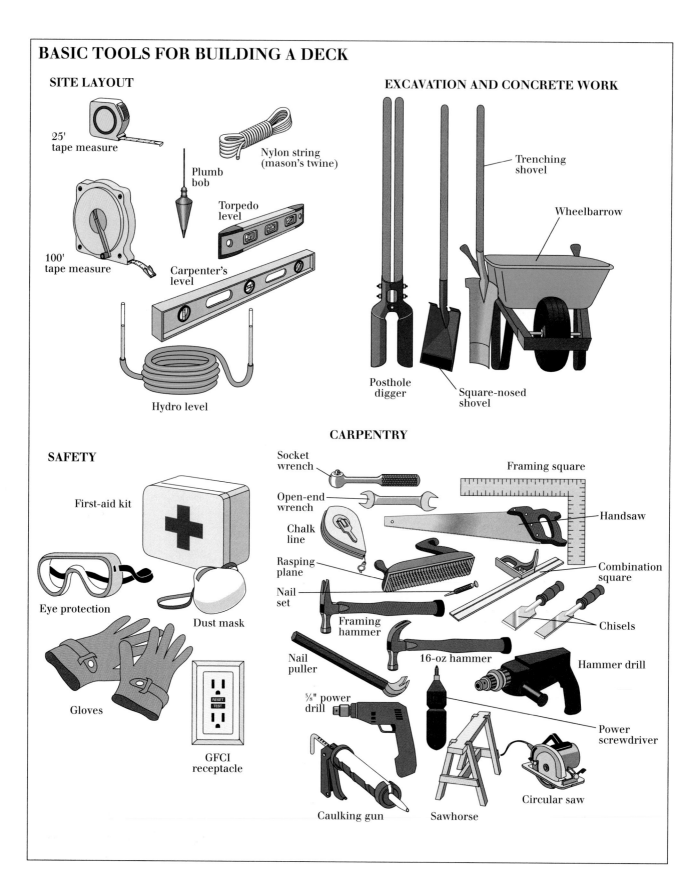

SITE LAYOUT

25'
tape measure

Nylon string
(mason's twine)

Plumb
bob

Torpedo
level

100'
tape measure

Carpenter's
level

Hydro level

EXCAVATION AND CONCRETE WORK

Trenching
shovel

Wheelbarrow

Posthole
digger

Square-nosed
shovel

SAFETY

First-aid kit

Eye protection

Dust mask

Gloves

GFCI
receptacle

CARPENTRY

Socket
wrench

Open-end
wrench

Chalk
line

Rasping
plane

Nail
set

Framing
hammer

Nail
puller

³⁄₈" power
drill

Caulking gun

Sawhorse

Framing square

Handsaw

Combination
square

Chisels

16-oz hammer

Hammer drill

Power
screwdriver

Circular saw

❑ Square-sided shovel for squaring hole edges

❑ Trenching shovel for widening footing area at bottom of deep hole

❑ Wheelbarrow for moving materials and mixing concrete

❑ Hacksaw, or metal cutoff blade for circular saw, for cutting reinforcing steel

❑ Buckets (5 gallon) for measuring concrete ingredients and cleaning tools

Carpentry

❑ Combination square for marking crosscuts

❑ Framing square for marking crosscuts, squaring corners, and laying out stringers for stairs

❑ Chalk line for marking straight lines and for an extra plumb bob

❑ Handsaw (crosscut) or power circular saw

❑ Hammer (20 ounce, smooth face) for framing

❑ Hammer (16 ounce) for finish trim

❑ Nail puller (cat's-paw) or pry bar

❑ Nail set (⁵⁄₃₂ to ¼ inch) for driving nail heads below the wood surface

❑ Chisels (¾ or 1 inch, and 1½ inch) for notching and prying

❑ Rasping plane or power sander for smoothing edges

❑ Power drill (⅜ inch, cordless or conventional) for drilling pilot holes and holes for carriage bolts and other hardware

❑ Power screwdriver with Phillips head, square-drive, or hexagonal bit for driving decking screws

❑ Hammer drill for drilling into concrete or masonry (if necessary)

❑ Wrenches (open-end, adjustable, or socket) for assembling deck components with lag screws, carriage bolts, or machine bolts

❑ Caulking gun for applying caulk and adhesives

❑ Sawhorses (sturdy) for supporting lumber to be cut

❑ Brushes, rollers, or garden sprayer, as needed, for applying finish

Safety Equipment

❑ GFCI-protected receptacle, or portable GFCI, for plugging in power tools and extension cords

❑ Flags, ribbons, or rags for flagging dangerous obstacles, such as steel stakes or low concrete piers that will be left exposed while you are not working

❑ Eye protection (goggles or safety glasses)

❑ Gloves, especially for working with concrete and pressure-treated lumber

❑ Dust mask

❑ Hard hat for anyone working below others

❑ First-aid kit with tweezers

A carpenter's level can be used alone or, as shown here, with a straight board to check the level of broad areas.

SITE PREPARATION AND LAYOUT

Preparing the site is the first step in the construction process. The amount of work involved depends on the extent of the alterations you must make to your house, as well as the condition of the site itself. Once the site is cleared, graded, and ready, you can install the ledger and lay out string lines for the post locations.

Step 1: Prepare the Site

Begin by measuring and marking off the overall deck area and the approximate location of the posts, using stakes and string. At this stage you can use rough estimates, unless there are specific obstacles or underground conditions that you are concerned about. If so, see step 3 on page 126 for techniques for laying out an accurate string perimeter, which will aid you in pinpointing critical locations on the site. If you aren't certain about property-line locations, easements,

setbacks, or other site legalities, hire a surveyor to verify them. Now is the time to buy that "ounce of prevention."

Part of site preparation is making any necessary repairs or alterations to the house. These include painting siding or trim that the deck will cover; adjusting gutters and relocating downspouts out of the way of the ledger and to rechannel water away from the ground below the deck; removing any attached structures, such as a porch or stairs, that are in the way of the deck; and removing, relocating, or installing doors and windows as necessary. Complete as much of this work as possible before deck construction begins. If the plans include a new door, however, wait to install it until after the deck is built.

If the deck site is covered by an existing patio, so long as it slopes away from the house you can simply build over it. You will have to break holes through the patio to excavate for the deck footings, but leaving the rest of it in place makes

Construction of a deck begins with marking the perimeter with a string line. The initial setting can be rough, but before construction begins it should be adjusted for as much accuracy as possible.

it easier to control weeds, clutter, dust, and moisture. If the patio slopes toward the house or interferes with the design and structure of the deck, break it up and remove the pieces. You may find uses for the broken concrete in your garden, such as for a retaining wall, or someone else may be able to use it, in which case they should haul it away for free.

Grading Take a careful look at the deck site. Does the ground slope away from the house? Are there minor rises, dips, and other irregularities? It may be necessary to smooth and slope, or grade, the site in order to improve surface drainage. This may be a matter of simply moving soil from one area to another with a shovel and wheelbarrow, or it may involve bringing in or removing large amounts of earth. If the site requires extensive excavation, you should consider hiring a contractor who can complete the work quickly and efficiently. If it's a major job, this is well worth the price.

If you tackle the job yourself, you may want to rent a minitractor with a front loader. Try to avoid the areas where the footings or posts will be located. Disturbed soil is less stable and may allow the posts or concrete to shift. If you have to add fill to those areas, plan to excavate the footing holes proportionately deeper. Likewise, if you are building the deck on a filled site, consult a soils engineer, landscape architect, or experienced contractor.

Providing Drainage You'll also need to evaluate the site for adequate drainage. Poor drainage causes standing water, which accelerates wood decay and tends to become a breeding ground for mosquitoes and other insects. Proper drainage helps stabilize the soil and prevents erosion, which can

plug up drains, destroy your topsoil, and cause the deck to shift.

To control water runoff, you can provide surface drainage to divert water around the deck area. To control standing water, you will need to build a subsurface drainage system that will channel the water away from the deck and disperse it properly—away from other structures as well as away from a neighbor's property.

For subsurface drainage, start by determining the direction in which you want the runoff to go, then locate the nearest low point on your

Small tractors like this one can be rented by the day. They not only make earth-moving tasks go much more quickly and easily, but they are also fun to operate. The rental agency will give you any instruction you need.

property where water can be dispersed. Keep in mind that you can't drain water onto adjoining properties. If you have no appropriate spot, you may need to divert the water into a dry well—a hole 4 feet in diameter and 4 to 6 feet deep, filled with rocks and gravel.

If you do have a suitable low point, create a drainage ditch by digging a 12- to 14-inch-deep trench that runs from the deck site to the low point. The ditch should slope ⅛ inch per foot, or 1 inch every 8 feet. Spread a 1-inch bed of gravel or crushed rock in the trench. Cut or piece together, as necessary, 4-inch-diameter drainage pipe—either rigid polyvinyl chloride (PVC) or acrylonitrile-butadiene-styrene (ABS) pipe, or flexible polyethylene tubing—with one or two rows of holes along one side. Place the pipe on the gravel in the trench, with the holes toward the bottom but not pointing straight

INSTALLING DRAINAGE

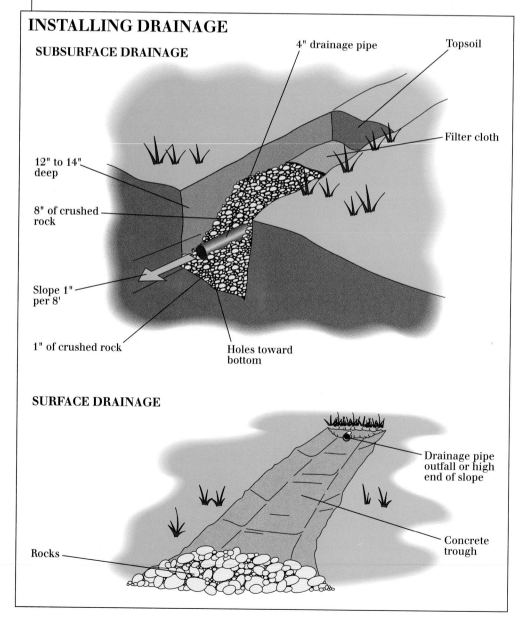

SUBSURFACE DRAINAGE

4" drainage pipe

Topsoil

Filter cloth

12" to 14" deep

8" of crushed rock

Slope 1" per 8'

1" of crushed rock

Holes toward bottom

SURFACE DRAINAGE

Drainage pipe outfall or high end of slope

Concrete trough

Rocks

down (skewed approximately 30 degrees). Cover the pipe with an additional 8 inches of gravel. To prevent dirt from clogging the gravel and pipe, cover the gravel with a layer of filter cloth. This water-permeable barrier holds the soil in place yet allows water to filter through. Finish by filling the trench with soil to match the existing grade.

If you anticipate a large amount of runoff, form a gravel or concrete trough at the exit point of the drainage pipe to further disperse the water, sloping it 1 inch for every 8 feet.

Controlling Weeds and Grass To prevent weeds, grass, and other vegetation from growing under the deck, clear the area and cover it with a weed-blocking fabric, which blocks sunlight and, unlike polyethylene sheeting, allows moisture to pass through into the ground rather than accumulate in puddles. Use as large a piece as possible to minimize seams, which will eventually stretch out of place.

Cover the fabric with about an inch of sand or small gravel. Use heavy rocks to hold the fabric in place while you do this. When you must walk over the covered area, do so carefully to prevent tears. If the area under the deck will be visible, you may want to spread a layer of mulch over the sand or gravel to give it a more finished appearance. Some weed seeds will sprout, but the seedlings will be easy to remove.

Step 2: Install the Ledger
The ledger is the major structural component that connects the deck to the house. It supports up to half of the deck load, so selecting the board, providing moisture protection, and attaching it securely to the house are all critical tasks. Although you can install the ledger

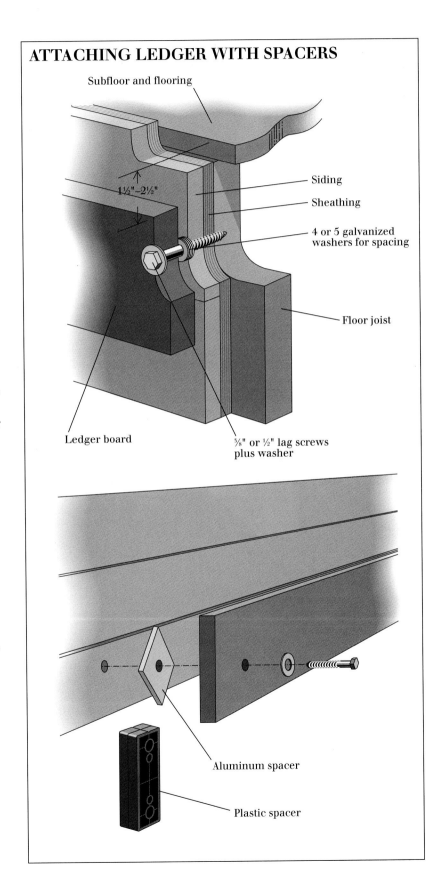

ATTACHING LEDGER WITH SPACERS

Subfloor and flooring

1½"–2½"

Siding

Sheathing

4 or 5 galvanized washers for spacing

Floor joist

Ledger board

⅜" or ½" lag screws plus washer

Aluminum spacer

Plastic spacer

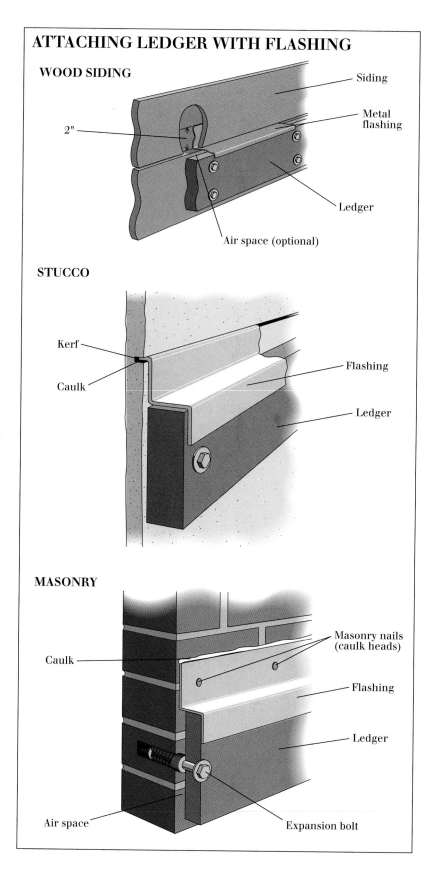

ATTACHING LEDGER WITH FLASHING

WOOD SIDING

Siding

Metal flashing

2"

Ledger

Air space (optional)

STUCCO

Kerf

Caulk

Flashing

Ledger

MASONRY

Masonry nails (caulk heads)

Caulk

Flashing

Ledger

Air space

Expansion bolt

after the footings are in, installing it before layout makes layout easier and more accurate. *Note:* This step applies only if the deck is attached to the house. If you are building a stand-alone deck, proceed to step 3 (page 126).

Selecting and Measuring the Ledger When buying lumber for the deck, hand-select one piece specifically for the ledger board. It must be straight, and its top edge should be free of knots. Select the piece from pressure-treated lumber or all-heart construction-grade lumber of a durable species. Most ledgers are one size wider than the joists (a 2×8 ledger for 2×6 joists, for instance) or slightly thicker than the joists (unsurfaced lumber for the ledger, surfaced for the joists). Check the local building code for precise requirements.

The length of the ledger depends on how the end joists are attached. If you use joist hangers, make the board at least 3 inches longer than the outside-of-joist-to-outside-of-joist framing dimension. If you bolt the two outside joists against the ends of the ledger, shorten the board by the width of the joists. After cutting the ledger to length, apply preservative to the cut end.

Preventing Trapped Moisture The back of the ledger must be protected from moisture and rot. For most areas and for most types of siding, the easiest and most reliable way to prevent moisture from being trapped is to provide a ½-inch air space between the ledger and the house, using galvanized washers, aluminum or plastic spacers, or other rust-resistant spacers. Do not use wood for spacers.

If the deck will be subjected to constant moisture (on the shady side of a house in a humid climate, for instance), or if the siding is a material that retains moisture (such as brick), protect the ledger with metal flashing. Cut the flashing to the length of the ledger and secure it to the house wall. For horizontal board siding, loosen the board above the ledger, tuck the flashing under the siding at least 2 inches, and bend the flashing down over the ledger. For a stucco wall, cut a groove, or kerf, in the wall, using a circular saw with a masonry blade. Then run a bead of caulk into the groove, tuck the top edge of the flashing into it, and bend the flashing down on top of the ledger. In this case, do not nail or screw the flashing; it will be held in place by the first decking board. For masonry, secure the flashing with masonry nails. First run a bead of silicone caulk behind the flashing. Then bend the flashing over the ledger, run another bead of caulk along the top edge of the flashing, and caulk the nail heads.

Positioning and Attaching the Ledger Mark a level line on the house wall for the top of the ledger. Position this line 1½ to 2½ inches below the house floor level to make the deck surface even with the interior floor—allowing for the thickness of the decking boards—and to keep rainwater and melted snow from seeping under doors.

There are three ways to make the ledger level: Use a long level to scribe a series of straight lines linked to each other; with a helper, hold a long straightedge in place with a level on top and scribe along it; or use a hydro level or carpenter's level to establish two level end points for the line and snap a chalk line between them.

The method of fastening the ledger to the house depends on the house structure, the type of siding material, and the method you will use to prevent moisture from getting trapped behind the ledger.

Wood-Frame Wall With Siding
Attach the ledger with carriage bolts or lag screws, and malleable washers (heavy washers that distribute pressure better than ordinary cut washers). The bolts or lag screws must be at least ⅜ inch in diameter and must connect to the framing behind the siding. Lag screws should penetrate the framing according to local code requirements (typically, 3 inches). If you have access beneath the house, use carriage bolts or machine bolts, and nuts.

First, using a tape measure and square, lay out the bolt hole locations on the ledger. Locate two

BOLTING LEDGER TO WALL

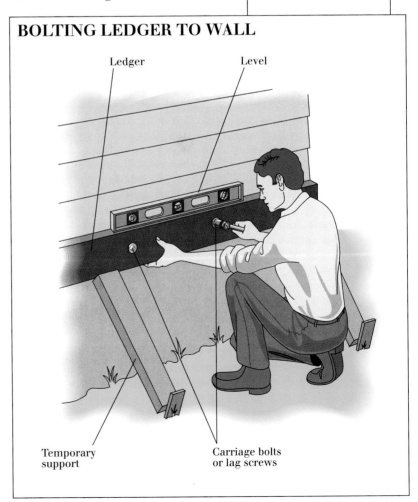

Ledger

Level

Temporary support

Carriage bolts or lag screws

LAYING OUT BOLT LOCATIONS

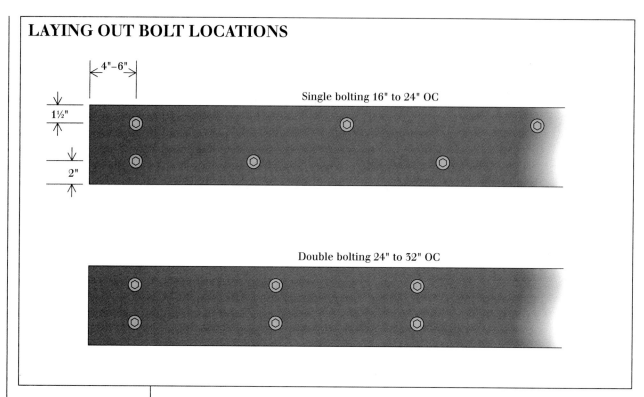

bolts one above the other, 4 to 6 inches from each end of the board; then place single bolts every 16 to 24 inches, staggered top and bottom, or double bolts every 24 to 32 inches. (If the deck is at a height other than floor level, mark the hole locations where they will align with the wall studs.) Position the bolts at least 2 inches from the bottom edge of the ledger and 1½ inches from its top edge. Drill the holes with a bit ⅛ inch larger than the diameter of the bolts you will use.

To drill holes into the house wall, position the ledger temporarily with bracing or with 16d duplex nails. Using the holes in the ledger as guides, drill pilot holes for lag screws through the siding and into the framing. Drill through the siding and sheathing with the same bit you used for the ledger holes; then drill into the framing, just far enough for the lag screw tip to reach, with a smaller-sized bit (¼-inch bit for ⅜-inch lag screws,

⁵⁄₁₆-inch bit for ½-inch screws). If you are using carriage bolts, drill the bolt holes all the way through the floor joist or blocking, using the same-diameter bit as for the ledger.

To secure the ledger, first pull it from the wall and dab silicone caulk into each pilot hole in the wall. With the ledger standing on edge, slide the bolts or lag screws, with washers, through the holes in the ledger; then slip on the spacers, position the board, and tighten the bolts.

To drill holes into a stucco wall, transfer the hole locations from the ledger onto the wall with a pencil. Remove the ledger. Using a masonry bit, drill only through the stucco. Then change to wood bits to drill shank holes through the sheathing and narrower pilot holes into the framing. Dab silicone caulk into the holes. Slip the lag screws, washers, and spacers onto the ledger, position the board, and tighten the screws. If flashing is required, saw the kerf into the stucco before bolting the ledger in place.

For vinyl or aluminum siding, or for board siding where you want to install metal flashing, you'll need to remove some of the siding before installing the ledger. First mark cut lines on the wall where the ledger will go. (Add space at both ends for end joists that go outside the ledger.) Use snips to cut aluminum or vinyl siding, taking small "bites" to keep the cut straight and even.

You can also cut aluminum or vinyl with several passes of a utility knife against a straightedge, and unlock panels at a joint with a zip tool.

To cut away wood siding, use a circular saw with the blade depth set at only the thickness of the siding; then use a compass saw or chisel to finish the cutout. Cut a 5- or 6-inch-wide piece of aluminum flashing to the length of the cutout, slide the flashing under the siding to a snug fit, and bend the flashing

REMOVING VINYL OR ALUMINUM SIDING

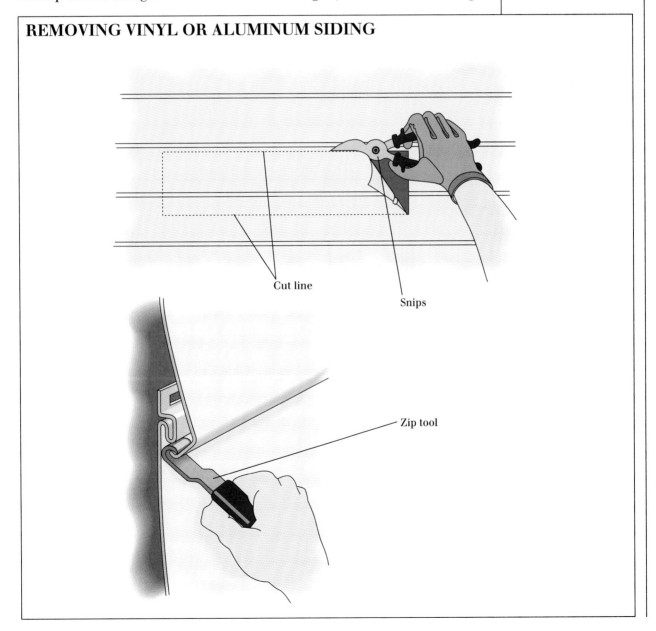

Cut line

Snips

Zip tool

up to make room for the ledger. Install the ledger. Then, using a woodblock and a hammer, bend the flashing down over the front edge of the ledger.

Masonry, Brick, or Concrete Wall
To attach the ledger to brick, masonry, or concrete, use masonry expansion bolts or lead shields with lag screws. For these materials, the holes in the wall are drilled first, followed by the holes in the ledger. To begin, using the level layout line for reference, measure and mark the positions of the anchors on the wall: two holes every 24 inches. Using a hammer drill and masonry bit, drill these holes. To cool the bit and agitate dust out of the hole, squirt window-cleaning fluid into the hole occasionally. Drive the lead shields or anchors into the holes. Be aware that the masonry exteriors of many houses are simply a veneer of stone or brick over wood framing. Don't attach a deck ledger to masonry veneer; drill through the veneer and into the structural framing behind it. This might require a long lag screw (at least 12 inches or more); you cannot rely on masonry veneer for lateral strength.

To mark the hole locations on the ledger, brace the board in position on the wall and hammer the face of the board so that the anchors protruding from the wall make indentations on the back. Take down the ledger and drill the holes at these marks. Insert the lag screws through the holes (with malleable washers), slide the spacers onto them, and screw them into the anchors.

Step 3: Lay Out Post Locations

There are two reasons for an accurate deck layout. First, it ensures that the four corners of a basic rectangular deck will each be exactly 90 degrees. Second, it ensures that the posts are placed accurately, so the footings, beams, joists, and decking will be in proper position. The best way to square the deck and align the posts is to lay out temporary string lines that indicate the post locations. Although you could lay out string lines to delineate the deck platform itself, and take measurements from those lines for the location of the posts and footings, it simplifies construction to lay out lines for only the posts. Other measurements, such as for footing excavations or beam lengths, can be taken from them.

The starting point for a layout is the ledger. If the ledger is not in place and you don't plan to install it until after pouring the concrete footings, lay out the top line of the ledger on the house to use as a reference for laying out post locations (see page 123). Be sure to allow for the thickness of the ledger, as well as for any spacers, when measuring and marking for the layout. For a stand-alone deck, batter boards take the place of the ledger.

Building Batter Boards Note on your plans where the outside edges of the two outside posts are located in relation to the ledger—that is, whether they are flush with the outside edge of the ledger or set in a few inches. Drive a 6d nail into the top of the ledger at each of these locations and tie the end of a string to each one. Use nylon mason's twine, not cotton string.

Measure from the ledger, across what will be the width of the deck, to the farthest posts. With a helper, and using a framing square placed against the ledger to keep the strings perpendicular to the ledger, stretch each string 2 to 3 feet beyond that point. There you will need to set up temporary braces to support string lines as you align

BUILDING BATTER BOARDS

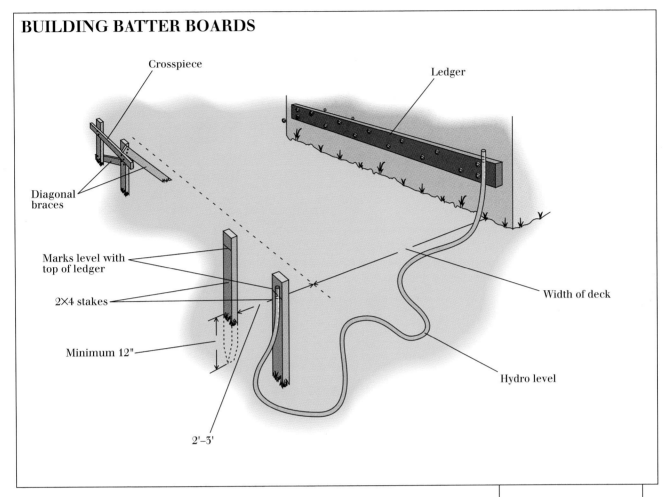

Crosspiece

Ledger

Diagonal braces

Marks level with top of ledger

2×4 stakes

Width of deck

Minimum 12"

Hydro level

2'–3'

and adjust them. You may be able to nail a 2×4 crosspiece to a nearby fence, wall, or other structure. If not, create batter boards: Cut a pair of 2×4 stakes long enough so that when they are pounded into the ground they'll be at least as high as the ledger. Sharpen the ends and drive them into the ground 12 inches, parallel with the ledger and 2 to 3 feet apart.

Using a hydro level, a long straightedge with a carpenter's level, or a line level, mark on each stake (or fence or wall) the point that is exactly level with the top of the ledger. With 16d duplex nails, nail a 3- to 4-foot 2×4 crosspiece to the stakes (or fence or wall) so the top is even with the marks, attaching it to the sides of the stakes fac-

ing away from the ledger. Brace the stakes diagonally with a 1-by piece of scrap lumber. Stretch out each string line again and drive a 6d nail into the top of each crosspiece where the line crosses over it. Tie the strings to the nails.

Next build batter boards for a third string line that will cross the first two at right angles on a line marking the outside edges of the posts. With a line level, check to be sure this line is level with the other two. If there are additional rows of posts parallel to this one, lay out a string line for each row.

Note: Where batter boards for a high deck are not feasible and there are no high structures convenient enough for attaching string lines, move the layout grid closer to

LAYOUT FOR A DECK

SQUARING STRING LINES

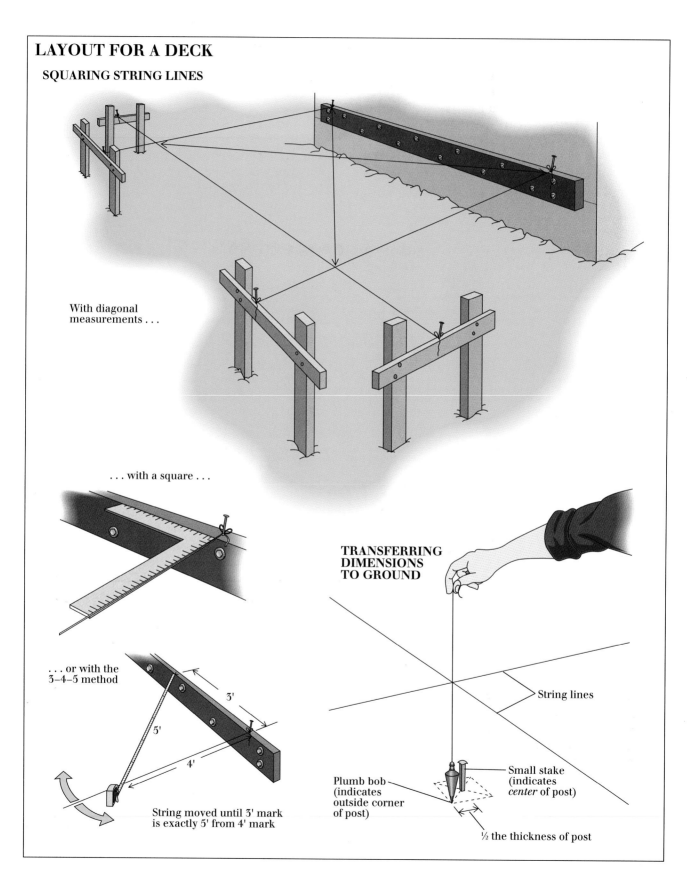

With diagonal measurements . . .

. . . with a square . . .

. . . or with the 3–4–5 method

3'

5'

4'

String moved until 3' mark is exactly 5' from 4' mark

TRANSFERRING DIMENSIONS TO GROUND

String lines

Plumb bob (indicates outside corner of post)

Small stake (indicates *center* of post)

½ the thickness of post

the ground. Make sure that it is level and that the corners under the ledger are aligned plumb with the marks for the ledger.

Squaring the String Lines Once the string lines are in place, you must adjust them so they are absolutely square to each other and to the ledger, forming a perfect right angle at each intersection. There are two ways to do this. One way, for a simple rectangular deck, is to measure the diagonals (the distances between opposite corners). The two measurements should be equal; adjust the string lines until they are, moving the nails on the batter boards to the final position.

Another way to establish square corners is with the 3–4–5 triangle method. Multiples of 3, 4, and 5, such as 6–8–10, 9–12–15, and so on, can be used in increments of feet or yards. To form the triangle with these three numbers, measure 3 feet from the corner along one line and 4 feet along the other line; then measure the distance between the two points. It should be 5 feet. If not, pivot one of the lines until the measurement is precisely 5 feet.

With the string lines level and square, transfer the post positions from the plans to the ground. Keep in mind that the string lines indicate the outside faces of posts. Using a plumb bob and tape measure, find where the center of each post will be, and drive a small stake in the ground at that point.

FOOTINGS AND PIERS

Most foundations for deck posts consist of a buried concrete footing that supports a concrete pier, although some deck posts are buried directly in the ground. Whichever type you build, you will have to dig

Using either the method of equal diagonals or the 3–4–5 triangle method described on this page, make the deck lines completely square.

DIGGING HOLES

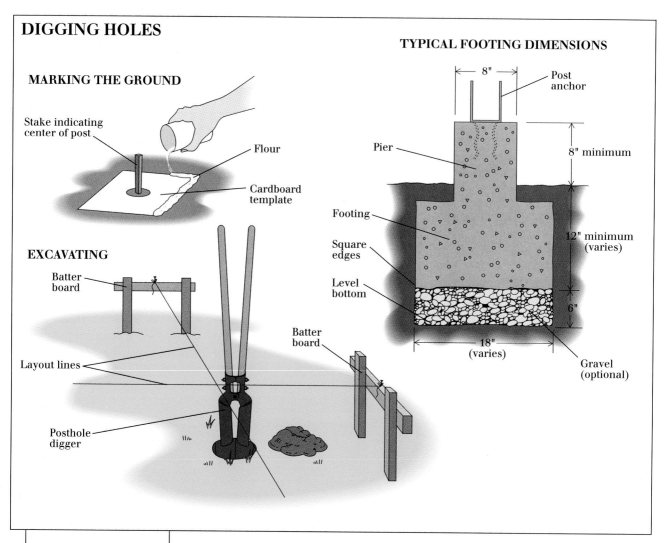

MARKING THE GROUND

Stake indicating center of post

Flour

Cardboard template

EXCAVATING

Batter board

Layout lines

Batter board

Posthole digger

TYPICAL FOOTING DIMENSIONS

8"

Post anchor

Pier

8" minimum

Footing

Square edges

Level bottom

12" minimum (varies)

6"

18" (varies)

Gravel (optional)

holes for the footings, and mix and pour some concrete.

Step 4: Dig the Holes

The depth of the footing holes depends on local soil conditions and the frost line in your area. Typically, the minimum depth in areas with mild climates is 12 inches on flat sites, 18 inches on slopes. In areas with cold climates, dig the holes deep enough so the footings sit below the frost line on a 6-inch bed of gravel. Verify the required depth and width of footings with the local building department, and consult local utility companies about any digging restrictions, especially near property lines.

For shallow footings (18 inches or less), excavate the hole to the same width as the footings, which usually vary from 12 to 18 inches square. For deeper excavations, make the width of the hole the same as the minimum diameter for the pier; then enlarge the bottom of the hole to the required footing width. If the soil is not stable enough to hold this bell-bottom shape, excavate a wider hole and build a form for the pier with a fiber forming tube (see page 132).

To begin, mark an outline on the ground for each hole, using the layout stakes as guides. A quick way to make outlines is to cut a cardboard

PIER AND POST OPTIONS

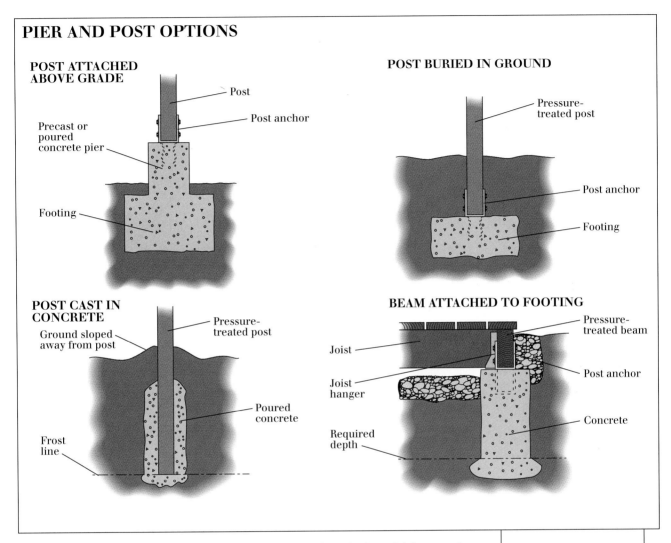

POST ATTACHED ABOVE GRADE

Post

Post anchor

Precast or poured concrete pier

Footing

POST BURIED IN GROUND

Pressure-treated post

Post anchor

Footing

POST CAST IN CONCRETE

Ground sloped away from post

Pressure-treated post

Poured concrete

Frost line

BEAM ATTACHED TO FOOTING

Pressure-treated beam

Joist

Post anchor

Joist hanger

Concrete

Required depth

template to the size of the footing excavations, with a small hole in the exact center. Lay the template on the ground so the hole fits over the layout stake, and sprinkle flour around the perimeter. Be sure the stakes represent the center of each post, not an edge. If the template is a square, be sure to align its edges parallel to the layout lines. Remove the layout lines temporarily for digging.

To excavate for the footings, use a posthole digger. Unlike a shovel, it removes dirt without disturbing the surrounding area and leaves smoothly shaved holes with firm sides. Use a square-sided shovel for squaring the sides and shaping the

bottom of the hole, which must be level and form right-angles where the sides meet the bottom. For a large job, hire a professional, or consider renting a power auger. The auger resembles a huge power drill; it is gasoline powered and is best operated by two people.

In the process of digging, you'll come across rocks and roots. Have handy a pry bar and a wrecking bar to break up rocks, and an ax or a pruning saw to cut away roots. Place all excavated dirt (it will be a sizable amount) far enough away so it will not interfere with construction. If any batter boards are disturbed, restring the layout lines

CALCULATING VOLUME OF FOOTING AND PIER

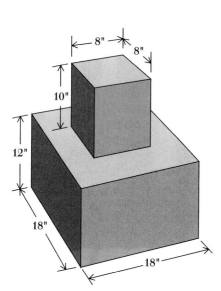

For straight-sided shapes, multiply length times width times height of each shape and add total of shapes together:

$$8 \times 8 \times 10 = 640$$
$$+ \ 12 \times 18 \times 18 = \underline{2,592}$$
$$3,232$$

Then divide by 1,728 to get cubic feet:

$$3,232 \div 1,728 = 1.87$$

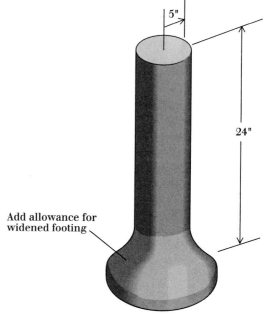

Add allowance for widened footing

For circular shapes, use pi (π) times radius (r) squared times depth of hole, then divide by 1,728:

$$\pi = 3.1416 \quad r = 5" \quad r^2 = 25"$$
$$3.1416 \times 25 = \ 78.5$$
$$\times \quad \underline{24}$$
$$1,885 \div 1,728 = \ 1.09$$
$$+ \ \underline{.10} \ (for \ footing)$$
$$1.19 \ cu \ ft$$

immediately and check for square by measuring diagonals.

Step 5: Mix and Pour the Concrete

The simplest foundation is made by setting a precast pier in a poured concrete footing; but if footings are deeper than 12 inches, or if you want to customize the appearance of the piers or tie the footing and pier together with reinforcing bars (rebar), you should cast the piers and footings as one unit.

Whether you use precast piers or pour your own, you will need to mix and pour some concrete for the footings. If you estimate that you will need more than ½ yard (14 cubic feet, or 10 wheelbarrows) of concrete, you may want to order a delivery of ready-mixed concrete

(see page 75). Be sure to have the holes and any forms or rebars inspected by the local building inspector before you pour the concrete.

Pouring the Footings and Piers

The easiest way to form piers is with fiber forming tubes, available from most concrete suppliers and many lumberyards. (You can also nail together four-sided forms made from scrap lumber; reinforce the forms for large piers by wrapping them tightly with wire.) Tubes come in various diameters; most deck piers require 8-inch tubes. The top of each tube should be 8 inches above grade and the bottom will be 12 inches (or the thickness of the footing) above the bottom of the hole. Estimate the height of all the piers and buy a tube long enough for the total, plus an extra foot or two.

MIXING CONCRETE

PROPORTIONING MATERIALS

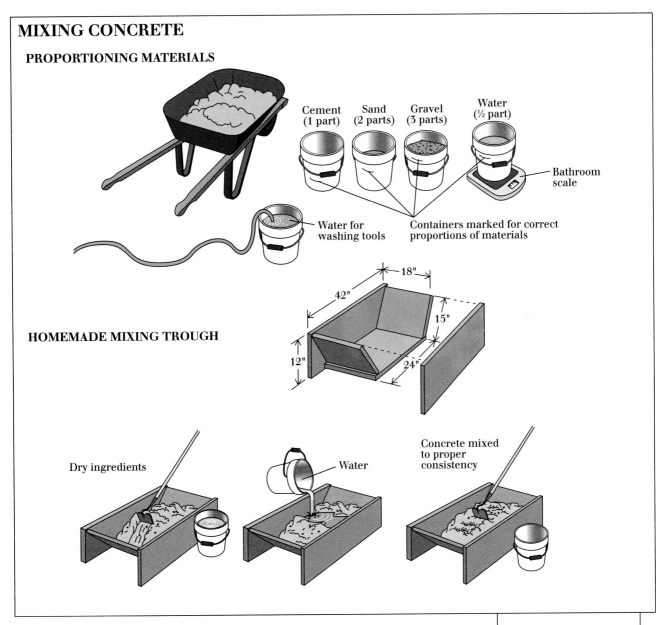

Cement (1 part) Sand (2 parts) Gravel (3 parts) Water (½ part)

Bathroom scale

Water for washing tools

Containers marked for correct proportions of materials

HOMEMADE MIXING TROUGH

18"
42"
15"
12"
24"

Dry ingredients

Water

Concrete mixed to proper consistency

With a handsaw or circular saw, cut the tube for each pier to length. Position the cut section of the tube between two 1×3s (or scrap lumber) cut long enough to bridge across the hole. Keep the bottom edges of the boards 8 inches below the top of the tube (12 inches if the site is sloped). Nail the tube to each board with a 1-inch roofing nail from inside the tube, or with an 8d duplex nail through the boards into the tube, angling it upward. Restring the lay-out lines and, with a plumb bob and tape measure, position each tube so it is centered exactly where its post will be centered. Then nail one end of a short 1×2 (or scrap) to the top edge of the tube and, with a torpedo level, adjust the tube so it is plumb. Then nail the bottom of the 1×2 to one of the supporting boards to create a diagonal brace that holds the tube plumb. Secure the ends of the supporting boards with stakes driven into the ground or with weights,

POURING PIERS WITH FOOTINGS

BUILDING FORMS

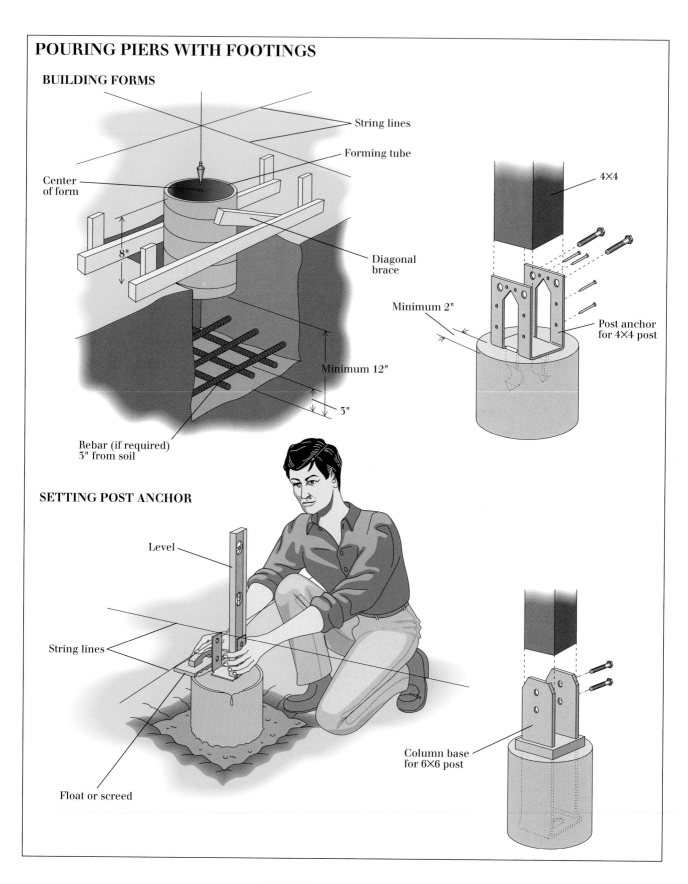

String lines

Forming tube

Center of form

8"

Diagonal brace

Minimum 12"

3"

Rebar (if required) 3" from soil

4×4

Minimum 2"

Post anchor for 4×4 post

SETTING POST ANCHOR

Level

String lines

Float or screed

Column base for 6×6 post

such as bricks or concrete blocks. Cut one or two pieces of ½-inch (No. 4) rebar 6 to 8 inches longer than the tube and set them beside the hole so they will be handy for placing in the wet concrete. Finally, remove the string lines and call for an inspection, if required. *Note:* If rebar is required in the footing, wire together a grid with three or four bars crossing in each direction and set it in the bottom of the hole on 3-inch "dobies" (square concrete blocks). No steel should be within 3 inches of the soil.

To pour each footing, first remove loose dirt from the bottom of the footing hole, or tamp it solid with a 2×4. Place about 6 inches of gravel in the bottom of the hole and tamp it. Mix enough concrete for only one footing and pier. Place enough concrete in the hole to fill it slightly higher than the bottom of the tube, then consolidate the concrete by jabbing a piece of rebar or other rod up and down in it. Then fill the pier form, consolidating the concrete by using a rod and by tapping the side of the form with a hammer. Strike off, or level, the concrete at the top of the pier, using a wood float or scrap of wood as a screed. Wait a few minutes for the concrete to set up, then insert the rebars vertically into the center of the pier until the top ends are 1 inch below the surface of the concrete.

Next, while the concrete is still fresh, restring the layout lines. Using the layout lines, a plumb bob, and a tape measure, ascertain the position for a metal post anchor and embed it in the top of each pier. (Be sure to orient all brackets in the same direction.) Place a level on all sides of the anchor to check for plumb, being careful not to disturb the concrete. Carefully adjust the anchor as needed, jiggling it slightly so the concrete will consol-idate around the embedded flanges. Repeat the process for each footing and pier.

For safety, mark each bracket with a bright ribbon or other warning, or cover it with an inverted box or bucket. If necessary, fence off the site to prevent someone from tripping over the brackets and getting injured.

For maximum strength, leave the pier forms in place and undisturbed for at least five days so the concrete will cure fully. Moisture is needed for hydration, the chemical process by which cement mixed with water hardens; removing the forms too soon allows moisture to evaporate.

Pouring Footings for Use With Precast Piers There are several styles of precast piers available, but for most deck posts the type with a metal post anchor built into it is best. In a few situations—for instance, where a low profile or quick connections are required—other types may be more suitable.

Excavate the footing holes to the required depth, allowing for an additional 6 inches of gravel. To set a pier, first place the gravel in the bottom of the footing hole and tamp it firm. Mix only enough concrete for one footing and pour it into the hole, then strike off the top of the footing just below grade with a wood float or scrap of 2×4. Wait a few minutes, or until the concrete begins to set up.

In the meantime, soak the precast pier with water from a garden hose or in a bucket. Restring the layout lines and, using a plumb bob and tape measure, position the pier over the footing so the post anchor will be centered on the footing. Take into consideration the direction in which you want the bolts and brackets to align; they should all be turned in the same direction.

POURING FOOTINGS FOR PRECAST PIERS

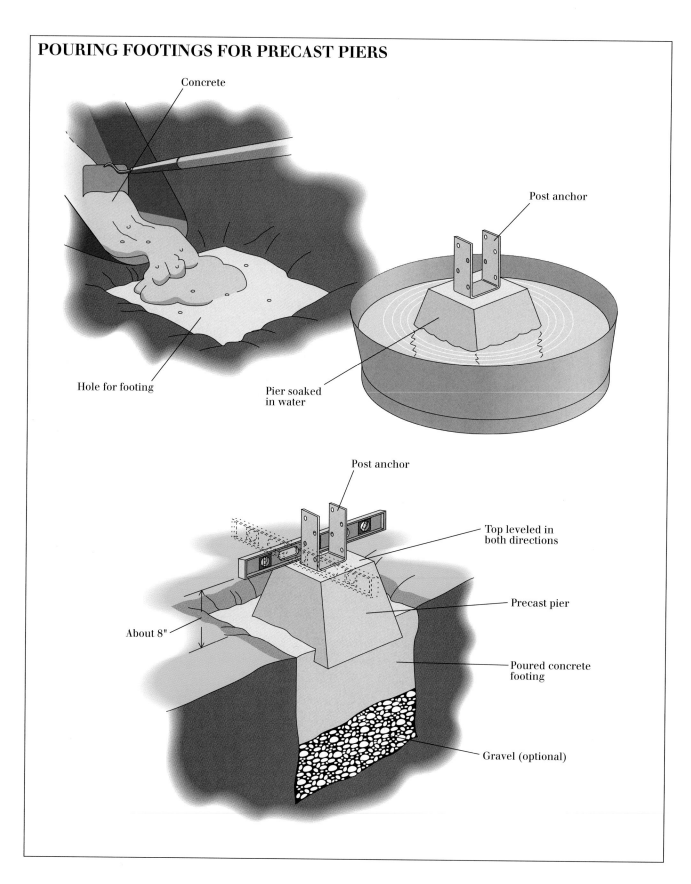

Concrete

Hole for footing

Post anchor

Pier soaked
in water

Post anchor

Top leveled in
both directions

About 8"

Precast pier

Poured concrete
footing

Gravel (optional)

Push the pier slightly into the footing, so that the top is at least 8 inches above grade, and check that it is level in all directions. Repeat the process for each footing and pier. Give the concrete five days to cure properly before continuing with the post installation.

FRAMING THE DECK

The framework that supports the decking consists of posts, beams, joists, and related blocking or bracing. The sequence and techniques that are described on the following pages assume a one-directional decking pattern parallel with the house wall; if you plan to install decking in a parquet, herringbone, or other decorative pattern, see page 149 for alternate joist layouts.

Step 6: Install the Posts

This is one of those tasks where the rule of thumb to "measure twice, cut once" certainly applies. It also takes two people, so line up an assistant before you begin.

Refer to your plans to determine the height of the posts in relation to the beams and ledger. Cut the posts approximately 6 to 12 inches longer than needed. If the design calls for extended posts that reach up to the railing, don't cut the posts. Just mark them for placement of the beams.

Start with one of the outermost posts, and have an assistant hold it in position in the post anchor. Check for plumb on two adjacent sides with a carpenter's level. Make a mark on the post level with the top of the ledger. There are several ways to do this: with a layout string line, if the lines are level; with a line level suspended from a string; with a hydro level; or with a long straightedge with a carpenter's level placed on it. The mark on the post indicates the height of the

post, plus the joist depth, plus the beam depth, plus clearance for any hardware that will come between the top of the post and the beam.

Take down the post. From the mark on the post, subtract the total of the joist depth, beam depth, and hardware clearance. Mark this point on all four sides of the post. Assuming that the post will not extend all the way to the railing, cut it to length. If it will extend to the

These posts are installed on cast concrete that combines the footing and the pier in a single unit.

INSTALLING POSTS

MARKING POST

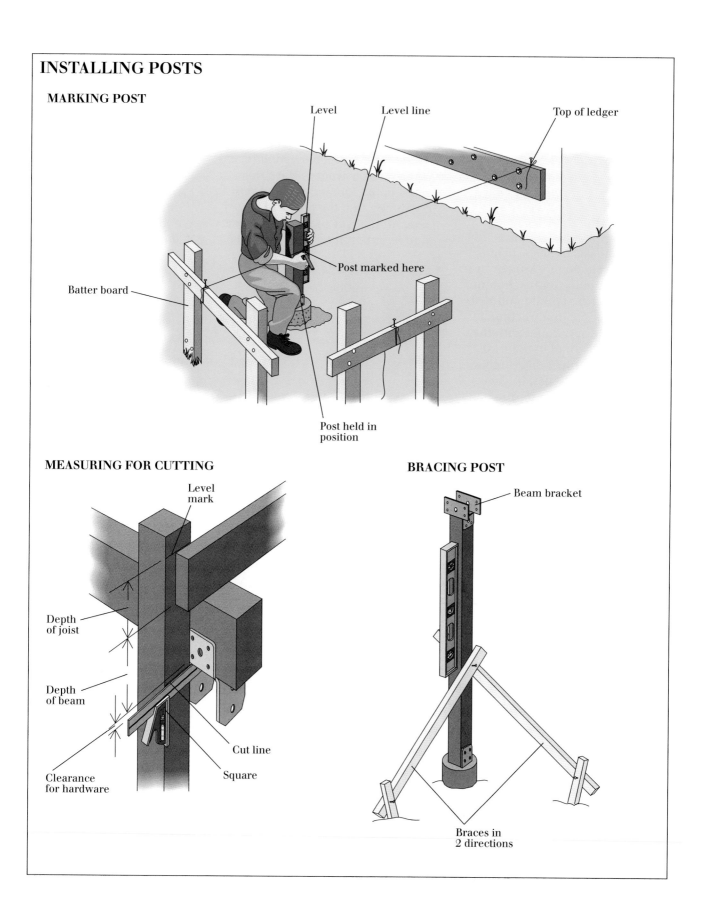

Level

Level line

Top of ledger

Post marked here

Batter board

Post held in
position

MEASURING FOR CUTTING

Level
mark

Depth
of joist

Depth
of beam

Clearance
for hardware

Cut line

Square

BRACING POST

Beam bracket

Braces in
2 directions

railing, wait to trim it to the exact length until after the deck structure is built and the decking is installed. Dip all cut ends into a clear wood preservative. If the top of the post will be hard to reach after it is erected, attach the beam-connecting hardware to the post now. *Note:* If the plans call for a header or beam bolted to the sides of the posts instead of attached to the top, or if joists will be attached to the beam with hangers instead of resting on top of it, alter the dimensions accordingly.

Fasten the post securely to the post anchor with screws, bolts, or hot-dipped galvanized (HDG) nails, then add temporary bracing made of scrap lumber nailed to two adjacent sides of the post and fixed to a stake in the ground. The bracing keeps the post secure and plumb until the beams are installed.

Next, measure, cut, and erect the post on the adjacent corner. To mark the cut lines of any posts positioned between these corner posts, stretch a chalk line between them and snap it against the other posts.

For a stand-alone deck, measure the post height according to the plans, subtracting the thickness of the joists, beam, and hardware, as necessary. Cut one post to length, install it, and add the temporary bracing. Measure all of the other posts from this post, using a line level, hydro level, or long straightedge and carpenter's level to mark the proper height.

Step 7: Install the Beams
The beams carry the weight of the joists, decking, accessories, and people, and transfer it to the posts. When you are working with the beams, be sure the crown, where

TYPES OF BEAMS

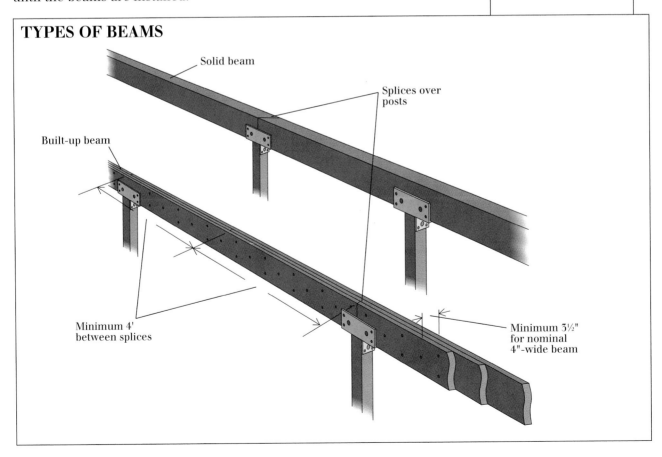

Solid beam

Splices over posts

Built-up beam

Minimum 4' between splices

Minimum 3½" for nominal 4"-wide beam

the grain curves, faces up. This way, the weight of the deck will straighten it out.

Solid Versus Built-up Because beams are major load-bearing components of the deck, they must be sized carefully. Generally, solid lumber (such as 4-by or 6-by lumber) should be your first choice—because it will shorten construction time considerably and because a solid piece of lumber won't collect rot-causing moisture or debris, as built-up beams can.

Solid lumber in long lengths is costly, however, and you may not find it readily available. Also consider that its weight makes it slightly more difficult to handle if you are moving lumber by hand to a remote deck location.

In sizing built-up, or laminated, beams, note that two 2-bys nailed together do not create a 4-by beam, and they cannot span the same distance. Two 2×10s, for example, do not make a 4×10, because their combined thickness is only 3 inches (*1½ inches + 1½ inches*), not the 3½-inch width of a 4×10. To bridge a span requiring a 4×10, use three 2×10s nailed together. (For a table of nominal versus actual lumber sizes, see page 101.)

Making Built-up Beams To make built-up beams, select the size lumber you'll need in lengths you feel comfortable handling. Always use pressure-treated lumber. To construct the beams, first plan where any end splices will fall. It's important that end-to-end splices of outside members be located over posts, not in midspan. Splices should also be spaced so that none is within 4 feet of any other.

Cut each board square and to length and apply preservative to the cut ends. Lay the pieces in position and fasten them together, face-to-face, with galvanized bolts, lag screws, or 12d HDG nails, spaced about 3 inches apart and staggered top and bottom. For added strength, reinforce all outside splices with post caps, metal-strap bracing, or cleats. The lumber may be crooked; in order to keep the pieces in straight alignment as you nail or bolt them together, stretch a string along one edge of the bottom piece to check for straightness.

Attaching Beams to Posts The easiest and strongest way to attach beams to posts is with metal post caps or column caps. Be sure to buy the proper size—the nominal size is usually for surfaced lumber; unsurfaced (full-cut) lumber or built-up beams require different sizes of brackets. As an alternate method, you can bolt T-straps or wood cleats to the sides of the connection, or sandwich a built-up post between the outer members of a built-up beam. Whichever method you choose, be sure to install the beam with its crown facing up so the weight of the deck will straighten the bow.

If you're not using post caps or similar metal connectors, you will need a temporary guide to help position the beams on top of the posts. Nail a cleat on one side of each post so it extends a few inches above the top of the post. This guide will act as a backstop when you line up and place the beams.

Before installing a beam, cut it to the exact length. Center a splice over the top of a post. If the ends of a beam will be exposed, give them a more finished appearance by shaping them. A simple technique is to chamfer the bottom edges (cut them off at a 45-degree angle). You could also round the edges with a saber saw and some sanding. If you feel especially creative, you might

CONNECTING BEAM TO POST

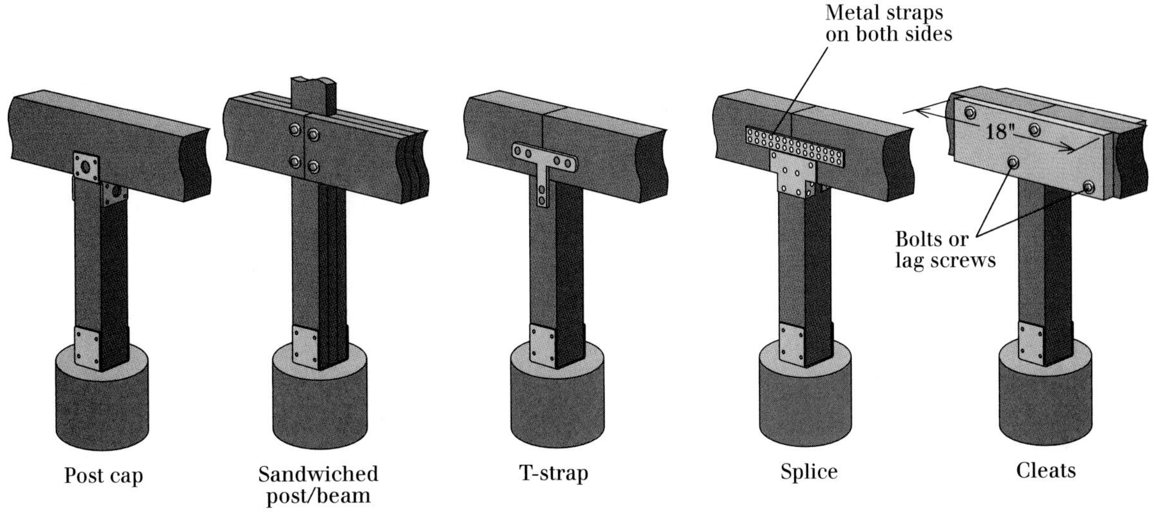

Metal straps
on both sides

18"

Bolts or
lag screws

| Post cap | Sandwiched post/beam | T-strap | Splice | Cleats |

LIFTING AND POSITIONING BEAM IN POST CAP

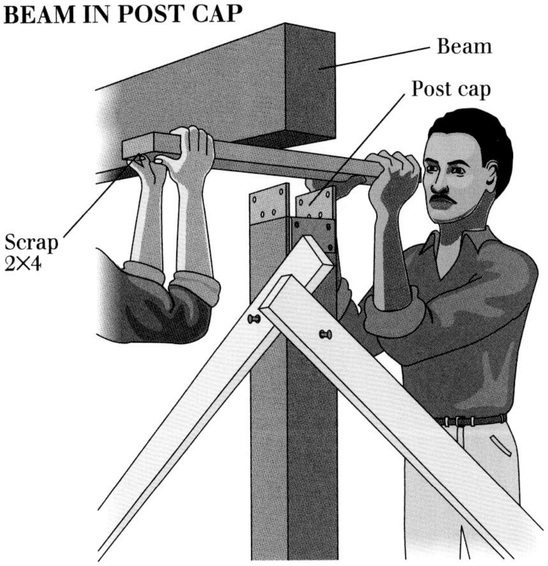

Beam

Post cap

Scrap
2×4

POSITIONING BEAM ON POST WITHOUT CAP

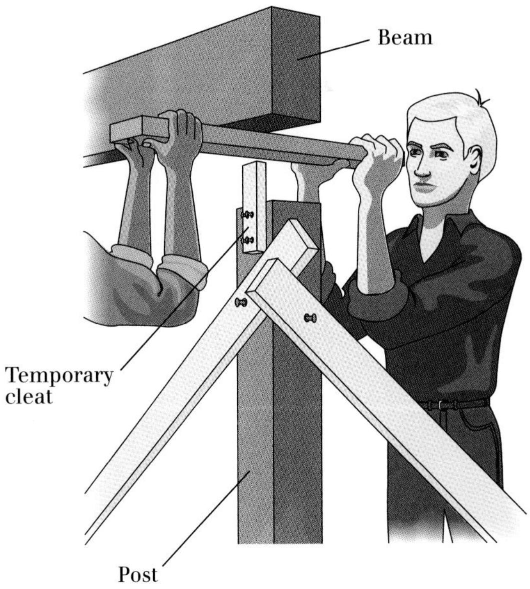

Beam

Temporary
cleat

Post

try carving a whale head, giant thumb, gargoyle, or other whimsical shape.

Get help installing the beams—don't attempt to lift them by yourself. Relatively lightweight beams can be easily lifted, positioned,

and secured by two people, but heavier beams definitely call for more helpers.

Here's a simple technique for easy and safe lifting: Select a beam and move it to the installation location. Place a short length (2 to

BRACING POSTS

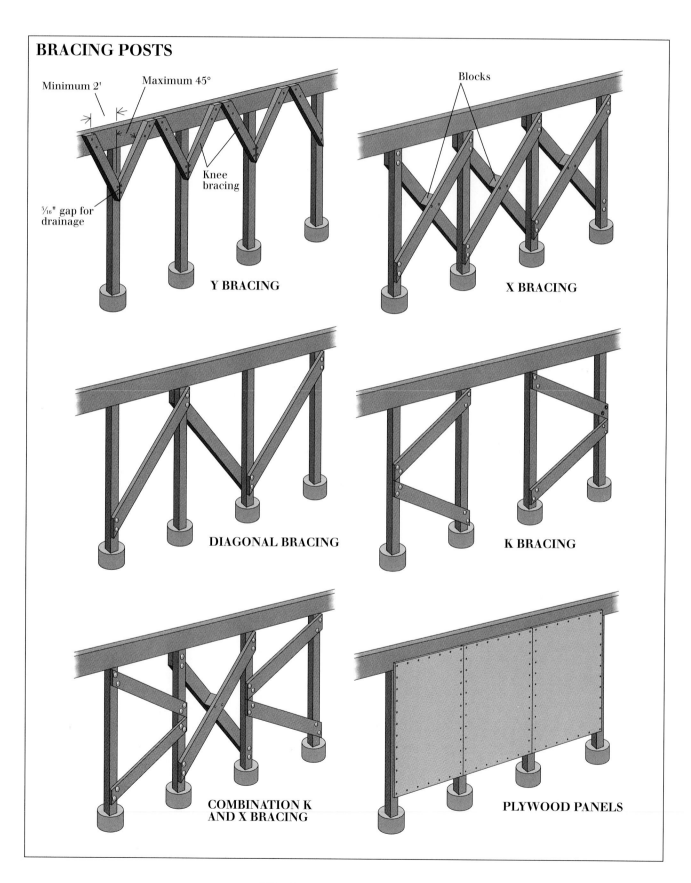

Minimum 2'

Maximum 45°

Blocks

Knee bracing

³⁄₁₆" gap for drainage

Y BRACING

X BRACING

DIAGONAL BRACING

K BRACING

COMBINATION K AND X BRACING

PLYWOOD PANELS

3 feet) of 2×4 lumber under one end of the beam and at right angles to it. With a helper, use the 2×4 to lift that end and place it on top of the post. Drive a nail through the post cap or connector, or the temporary guide, and into the beam. Lift and secure the other end of the beam in the same way. Check the beam and posts for level and plumb and adjust the beam as necessary.

Remove the nail from the connector or guide and permanently attach the beam to the posts with carriage bolts or machine bolts. Drill holes through the beams and posts for each bolt, using a bit ⅛ inch larger than the diameter of the bolt. Depending on the thickness of the lumber, you may need an extralong drill bit or shaft extension, or you may need to drill from both sides. Use the holes in the metal brackets as guides. After drilling, run the bolts through the holes and secure the beam. If a bolt won't go through a hole because drilling from opposite sides of the beam was not in perfect alignment, bend the bolt slightly by whacking it with a sledgehammer. Nails or lag screws can also be used to fasten the beams to the posts.

Step 8: Install Permanent Bracing

Bracing requirements are specified by local building codes. Typically, decks with posts higher than 5 feet and decks that may be subjected to high winds, earthquakes, snow loads, or shifting soil must be braced, but all decks benefit from some permanent bracing.

Permanent bracing can be attached to just the posts or to the posts and beams. Use 2×4s for bracing distances that are less than 8 feet; use 2×6s for longer distances. Attach the bracing with carriage bolts or lag screws. Where the ends of the braces abut, leave a little space so the joint will not trap water.

Step 9: Install the Joists

Joists, which distribute the weight of the decking boards evenly over the beams and ledger, are cut from 2-by lumber. The joist size (width) is determined by the joist span (distance between beams or between ledger and beam), the joist spacing (distance between joist centers), and the species and grade of lumber used.

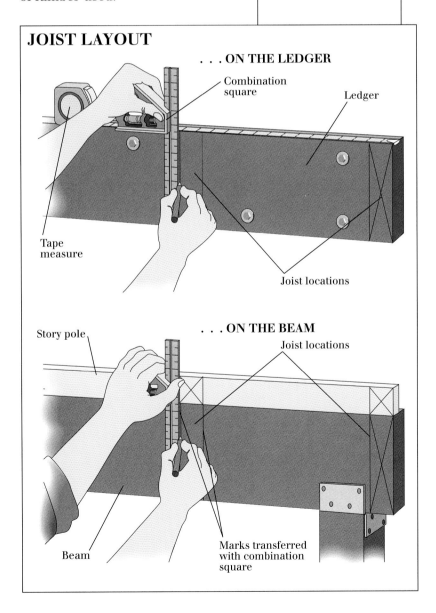

JOIST LAYOUT

. . . ON THE LEDGER

Combination square

Ledger

Tape measure

Joist locations

. . . ON THE BEAM

Story pole

Joist locations

Beam

Marks transferred with combination square

MEASURING FOR JOIST LENGTH

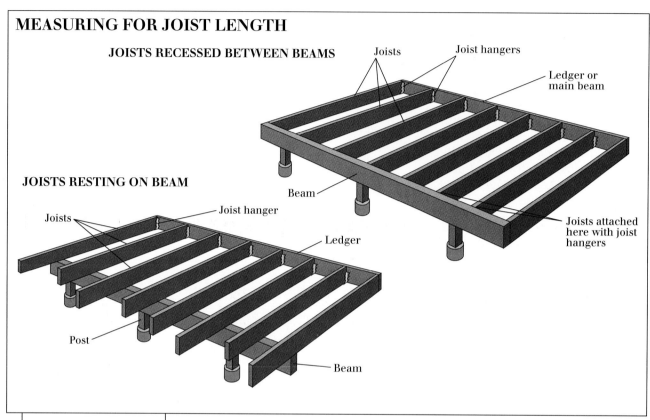

JOISTS RECESSED BETWEEN BEAMS

Joists

Joist hangers

Ledger or main beam

Beam

Joists attached here with joist hangers

JOISTS RESTING ON BEAM

Joists

Joist hanger

Ledger

Post

Beam

LAPPING AND SPLICING JOISTS

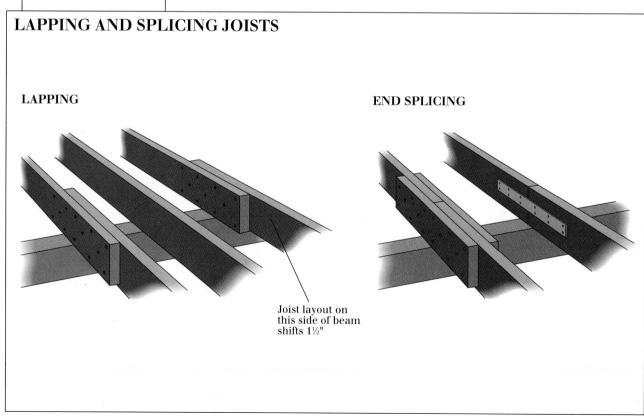

LAPPING

END SPLICING

Joist layout on this side of beam shifts 1½"

Laying Out the Joists To mark the joist positions on the ledger and beams, use a pencil, a combination square, and a tape measure or story pole (a long scrap of lumber used as a measuring template).

First locate and mark the positions of the two outside joists on the ledger. Place an *x* on the side of each mark where the joist itself goes, so there will be no confusion about whether a mark refers to the inside or outside edge of a joist. Refer to the plans for the spacing of the remaining joists, then measure and mark their positions on the board. Draw a vertical line through each mark, using a combination square or a level to keep it straight and plumb. Remember that the joist spacing doesn't refer to the distance between joists, but to the distance between the joist centers (or left edges or right edges).

If your tape measure doesn't have 16-inch increments highlighted, here's an easy way to transfer these marks to each beam: Lay a story pole on top of the ledger and, with a combination square, transfer the joist marks from the ledger to the face of the story pole. Then, using the layout string lines to align the end of the story pole, lay the story pole on the beam and transfer the marks. Using a combination square, draw a line at each mark across the top of the beam. Place an *x* next to the line to mark the side on which the joist will go.

If you will be lapping joists over a beam because they are not long enough to span the entire width of the deck, allow for the jog when marking the joist positions—the joist layout on one side of the beam will be offset 1½ inches from the joist layout on the other side (see opposite page).

Cutting the Joists Joist lumber should be properly dried and straight and should have few imperfections, such as loose knots. Sight each piece carefully and determine the crown (the edge that bows upward at the middle), then mark the joist with an arrow so the crown will be facing up when the joist is installed. If the joists will rest on top of the beams, trim the outside ends after you install all the joists. If you are installing the joists by attaching both ends to the ledger and/or beams with joist hangers, measure the joist spans between the beams, allow for ⅛-inch clearance at each end of each joist, and cut all the joists before installing them. Using metal joist hangers allows as much as ½-inch discrepancy between joist lengths, so if the distance between beams does not vary more than that, you can cut all the joists to the same length. If there is greater variation, measure and cut each joist individually. If you are using pressure-treated lumber, apply preservative to the cut ends.

When Joists Are Too Short If joist lumber is not available in the lengths you need, you will have to join the shorter pieces of lumber by splicing them or by lapping them over a beam. Laps should extend 6 to 12 inches beyond each side of the beam. The overlap method is easier, but remember to allow for the jog when marking the joist positions on the ledger or main beam.

There are two ways to splice a joist: with a metal strap, or by sandwiching the ends between short (18- to 24-inch) pieces of joist lumber. Sandwiching provides greater strength.

There are two rules for placing overlaps and splices. First, stagger their placement; don't position the splice or overlap at the same location on each joist. Second, place the splice or lap over a beam. This will require a little planning as you measure and cut.

Installing the Joists First, attach the joist hangers to the ledger at each *x*. To position each one at the right height, insert a scrap piece of joist lumber in it and align the top edge of the scrap with the top of the ledger. Nail only one side of each hanger into position, using HDG joist-hanger nails. If the joists will be attached to the facing beam with joist hangers, attach hangers to the beam in the same way.

Install the two outside joists first. If you are attaching them to the ends of the ledger rather than hanging them with joist hangers, drill two pilot holes through the end of each joist. Nail each joist to the ledger with two 16d HDG spiral-shank nails, then strengthen the corner with an angle bracket nailed on the inside with HDG joist-hanger nails. Secure the other end of the joist to the facing beam in the same manner, if the beam is the same height as the ledger, or by

INSTALLING JOISTS

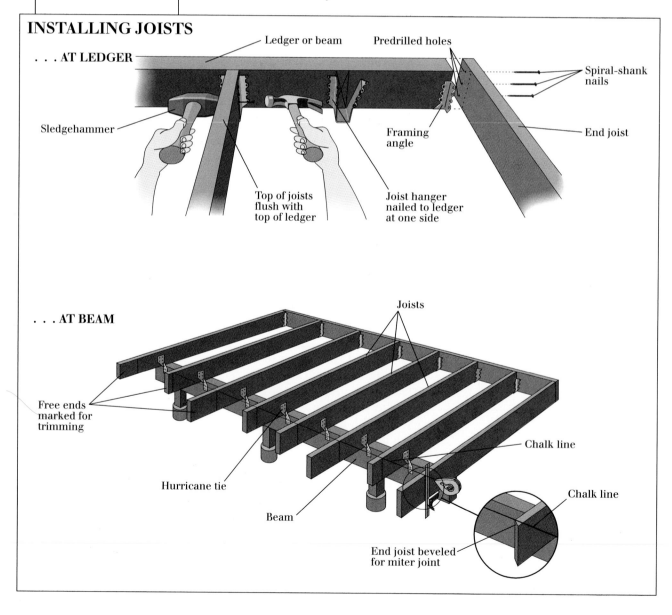

. . . AT LEDGER

Ledger or beam

Predrilled holes

Spiral-shank nails

Sledgehammer

Framing angle

End joist

Top of joists flush with top of ledger

Joist hanger nailed to ledger at one side

. . . AT BEAM

Joists

Free ends marked for trimming

Chalk line

Hurricane tie

Beam

Chalk line

End joist beveled for miter joint

resting the joist on top of the beam and toenailing it with three 8d HDG common nails.

Install each inside joist, one at a time, by sliding the end into the hanger so there is at least ⅛-inch clearance at the end. Squeeze the unattached side of the joist hanger closed and nail it to the ledger. Then nail the hanger to the joist; when nailing the second side, hold a sledgehammer against the hanger on the opposite side to prevent nails from coming loose. Attach the other end of the joist before installing the next joist. If the joist rests on top of the facing beam, toenail it to the beam with three 8d HDG common nails, or with a metal hurricane tie attached to the face of the beam and the side of the joist. If you use the toenailing method, set the nails far enough from the ends of the joist to prevent splitting.

Installing the Header Joist If the joists extend beyond the outside beam (are cantilevered), you must stabilize the open joist ends by covering them with a header joist. Do this the same day the joists are installed, or their ends may warp. First, trim the joists to length. To do this, measure and mark the required width of the deck along each of the two outside joists. Subtract 1½ inches from these marks (the thickness of the header) and snap a chalk line between the new marks across the tops of the joists. With a square, transfer the chalk mark to the face of each joist. Cut them with a circular saw and apply wood preservative to the ends. Cut the header joist to length. Predrill both ends of the header to prevent splitting. Start at one end of the header and, with a helper holding the other end, attach the header to each joist with three 16d HDG box or spiral-shank nails, or use galva-

nized decking screws. *Note:* If you want to make miter joints at the corners, leave the two outside joists 1½ inches longer than the inside joists and cut 45-degree bevels on the ends of the header joist and the outside joists.

Stabilizing the Joists Bracing between the joists adds strength and rigidity to the entire deck structure. It prevents joists from rolling over, twisting, and flexing, and stops those noticeable squeaks and creaks when you walk on the deck. There are two methods of bracing joists: blocking and bridging. Blocking, which is the easiest method, uses short pieces of joist lumber that fit snugly between the joists. Bridging is more difficult and is not often used on decks. It consists of two pieces that crisscross

JOIST BLOCKING AND BRIDGING

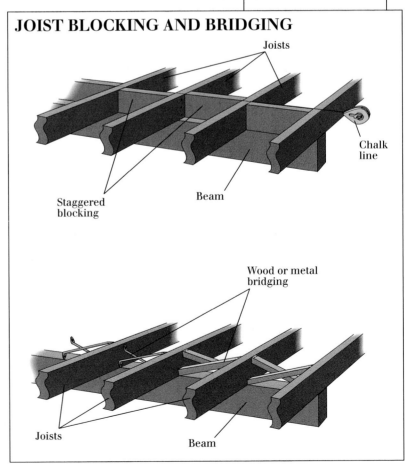

Joists

Chalk line

Staggered blocking

Beam

Wood or metal bridging

Joists

Beam

between the joists; if you use wood bridging, you must cut the ends at precise angles. You might want to look for galvanized metal bridging at a local home center. It is sold for specific joist spacing and it is also economical.

Generally, blocking or bridging is required between joists wherever they rest on beams and at least every 8 feet along spans, but be sure to check local codes for the required spacing.

To lay out the blocking or bridging, start at the outermost beam. For blocking over beams, locate the centerline of the beam and mark it on top of the two outside joists. Snap a chalk line across the rest of the joists between the two marks. Then, using a combination or framing square, transfer the chalk mark onto the face of each joist. Mark other rows of blocking, if required, at the middle of joist spans, unless the midpoint is more than 8 feet from the nearest row of blocking. *Note:* To prevent moisture from being trapped between the blocking and the beam, adjust the marks so the blocking will be positioned slightly off the beam instead of directly against it.

Blocking Cut blocking from the same 2-by lumber as the joists. To determine the length of each block, measure the distance between the joists along the chalk line. Theoretically, all these distances are equal, but they usually vary slightly, so measure for every block. The blocking must fit as snugly as possible without bowing the joists.

You can make nailing easier by alternating blocks on either side of the centerline. If you prefer the appearance of straight-line blocking, you will have to toenail one end of each block. Nail each end with three 16d HDG common or spiral-shank nails. As you progress along

a line of blocking, sight along a few joists to see if any are being pushed out of alignment. If so, trim the next block to keep the next joist in line. When you have finished installing the blocking, recheck all the connections. Some of the blocks may have worked their way loose while you were nailing farther along the beam. Tighten them up by tapping a sledgehammer against the whole line of blocking until it is snug.

Bridging The bridging method requires measuring from the top edge of one joist to the bottom edge of its facing joist. The ends of the bridging pieces, usually made from 2×4s, are cut at an angle, which is determined by the distance between the joists and the width of the joist lumber. Cut one bridging piece to length, making sure the ends are cut to the correct angle. If you find that the joist spacing is exactly the same, use this first piece as a pattern to cut all the rest. If the spacing varies, however, you must cut the pieces separately for each joist space. Place each piece against the centerline, alternating pieces on either side of it. Fasten each end with HDG 8d common nails or 2-inch decking screws.

Once you have installed the bridging pieces, recheck and, if necessary, tighten each connection. Some of the pieces may have worked themselves loose as you nailed farther along.

DECKING BOARDS

The decking is a dominant element of any deck, and details make a difference in the overall appearance. Because decking boards are easy and enjoyable to install, you should find it a pleasant challenge to work carefully as you select, place, and fasten each board.

SELECTING A DECKING PATTERN

The decking pattern is what gives a deck character. A simple arrangement is usually the best; complex patterns tend to accentuate rather than hide any defects in the decking. And, as the illustrations show, even the simplest pattern can add interest and dimension to a deck. For an unusual effect, you can arrange 2×4s and 2×6s in repeated sequences. For a clean, finished look, add borders with mitered corners to the perimeter after the decking is installed.

Whatever design you choose, plan its layout carefully, giving particular consideration to the location of joints. This will give the deck a professional, uniform look.

Step 10: Install the Decking

Before you lay the decking, complete any remaining work on the substructure. If you plan to apply a protective finish to the substructure or install plumbing or wiring, do it now while you have easy access. To increase the longevity of the deck, install sealing strips along the top of each joist to prevent moisture from penetrating into the joists along the decking nails.

The most common sizes for decking boards are 2×4 and 2×6. Along with the newer ⁵⁄₄-inch by 6-inch size, these are also the most desirable. Anything smaller or larger tends to sag, warp, twist, or cup. The exact size of decking material you should use is dictated by the joist spans and by the pattern you select for the decking. Most decks are built with 2×6 or ⁵⁄₄-inch by 6-inch lumber.

Laying Out the Boards Before fastening any decking, lay out all but the last few boards on the joists. This allows you to arrange them for the best appearance as well as creates a working platform. (*Warning:* Be extremely cautious where boards butt together at a joist, or overhang the outside edges of the deck!) Leave a space along the house wall about 4 inches wide at the beginning of the layout, so you will have room to maneuver boards as you move them into place for fastening.

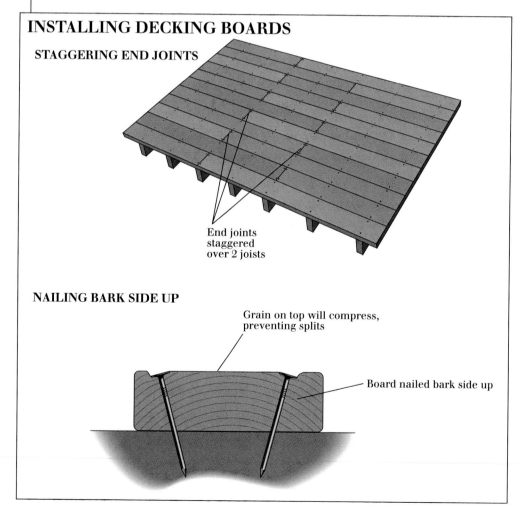

INSTALLING DECKING BOARDS

STAGGERING END JOINTS

End joints staggered over 2 joists

NAILING BARK SIDE UP

Grain on top will compress, preventing splits

Board nailed bark side up

NAILING TIPS

Nailing is the simplest, least expensive way to fasten the decking to the joists. Hand-nailing is better than power nailers; even though nailers will fasten the decking much more quickly, they shoot nails too far into the decking and the nails are more likely to rise up over time. Here are some tips for nailing the decking to the joists.

1. You must use nails long enough to penetrate the joists to a depth equal to the thickness of the decking. If your decking is 1½ inches thick, the nail should penetrate the joist at least 1½ inches.

2. Depending on the width of the decking, use two or three nails to attach the decking at each joist. Keep the nails in straight lines across the decking so the nail heads have a clean appearance. Use a framing square as a nailing guide, aligning it with nails in the previous two boards as you place nails for each joist.

3. Nails driven straight down through the decking can split the decking or soon work their way out. Drive the nails into the decking at about 30° opposing angles.

4. To avoid splitting, especially at the ends of the decking, use this carpenter's trick: Before starting a nail, blunt the tip slightly by tapping it with your hammer or on the head of a nail already driven into a board. Nails with blunted points drill their own holes as they penetrate the wood. If the decking still splits, especially at the ends of boards, drill pilot holes with a power drill. Here is another trick: Nail only into the light part of the grain pattern, not directly on the dark grain lines where the wood is more brittle.

5. When pulling nails, place a wood block under the hammer head for better leverage, to keep from breaking the handle, and to protect the surface of the decking boards. With a curved-claw hammer, pull the handle back toward you. With a ripping claw, rock the handle from side to side.

6. As you drive each nail, be careful not to damage the surface of the decking by missing the nail head, because the hammer head may create indentations where water can collect. This can also happen if you try to drive the nail in too far with a hammer. Always drive the nails in until they rest ¹⁄₁₆ to ⅛ inch above the surface, then use a nail set to drive them below the surface of the board.

7. If you accidentally dent the decking with the hammer, treat the area with a small amount of warm water, which will cause the wood to swell back to its normal size.

8. As the decking weathers, some nails will rise slightly. When the deck is one to two months old, reset the heads just below the surface with a hammer and nail set.

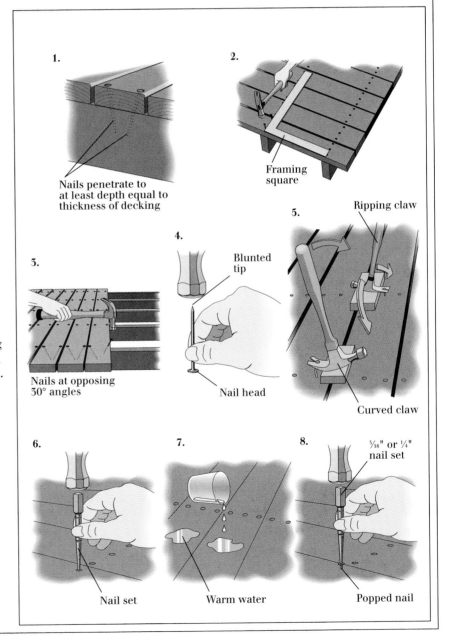

1. Nails penetrate to at least depth equal to thickness of decking

2. Framing square

3. Nails at opposing 30° angles

4. Blunted tip / Nail head

5. Ripping claw / Curved claw

6. Nail set

7. Warm water

8. ³⁄₁₆" or ¼" nail set / Popped nail

ALTERNATIVE FASTENERS

Decking Screws

Although they're more expensive than nails, galvanized decking screws are stronger, and make it easy to remove boards. Buy screws that are long enough to penetrate the joists to a depth at least equal to the thickness of the decking boards. You can fasten them with a power screwdriver. Set the clutch adjustment so the screw heads are countersunk slightly below the surface of the boards. Some power screwdrivers have automatic screw-feeding clips.

Decking Clips

Decking clips are expensive, but if you prefer a deck surface that is smooth and nail-free, the clips are worth the expense. They also last longer than nails or screws. To use decking clips, you start by toenailing the first decking board in place, then use the clips starting with the second board. Mount the clips on the edge of the board that will face the first board, securing one clip about 2 inches from each joist location. Install the decking by sliding the clip's prong under the first decking board, then toenail the opposite edge to the joists. Repeat this process to install the rest of the decking.

Decking Adhesive

The advantages of an adhesive are a nail-free deck surface, faster installation time, and a longer-lasting deck surface. However, adhesive doesn't work well if decking boards are crooked and need to be straightened. Apply the adhesive to the top of the joists with a caulking gun, then set the decking boards in place. Once the adhesive has set up, it will be nearly impossible for you to remove the boards without damaging them and the joists below. This could be a problem if you need to make repairs or access the area underneath in the future.

Continuous-Strip Fasteners

This deck-fastening system, which is relatively new, consists of galvanized metal strips that lie on the top edges of the joists. Each strip has a flange with predrilled holes for nailing it to the side of the joist. The deck boards are laid over the top of the strips, then fastened from below with screws driven up through predrilled holes in the metal strip. No fasteners are visible on top of the decking, and no fasteners penetrate the tops of the joists.

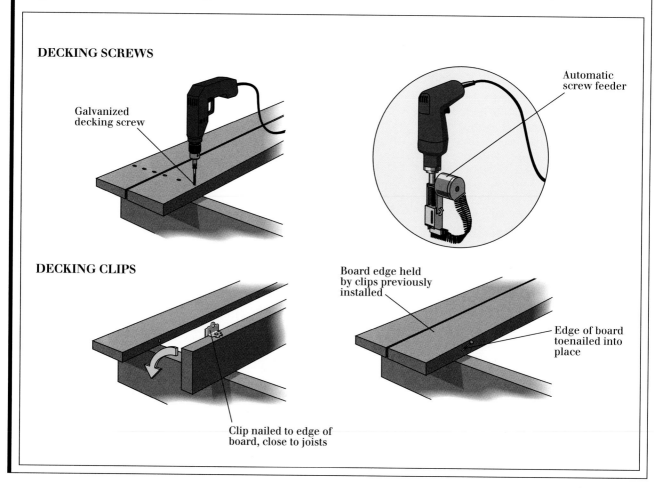

DECKING SCREWS

Galvanized decking screw

Automatic screw feeder

DECKING CLIPS

Board edge held by clips previously installed

Edge of board toenailed into place

Clip nailed to edge of board, close to joists

Ideally, the decking lumber should be just a little longer than the width of the deck, but this may be impossible because of availability, cost, or deck design. If it's necessary to butt decking boards together, plan to position the joints over joists, and stagger them.

When measuring and cutting the decking, let the boards hang over the edges of the outside joists, then trim off the ends after all the decking has been installed. Since the decking is exposed to the elements, you should give it extra protection by coating it with wood preservative after you cut it to size. Be sure to soak the edges and ends with the preservative. When the deck is finished, apply a second coat.

Position the boards so the bark side is up (the half circles of the end-grain pattern resemble a rainbow) to minimize grain separation and splitting on the top of the boards. Also, for a more uniform look, position all the boards so their top grain runs in the same direction. Select knot-free boards to go in front of the doorways, picture windows, stairs, and other entrances to the deck.

Fastening the Decking You can fasten the decking to the joists with nails, screws, decking clips, decking adhesive, or continuous-strip fasteners. Regardless of the method you choose, you may want to use screws in the area above any plumbing or electrical lines so that decking boards can be easily removed for maintenance and repairs.

Start installing the decking with the first board along the house wall. Cut the board to the exact length so you won't need to cut close to the siding when you trim the other boards to length later. Be sure the board is perfectly straight, and leave a ¼-inch gap along the siding so water won't be trapped. If you're working on a stand-alone deck, start at the most prominent side.

As you fasten the decking to each joist, allow a ¹⁄₁₆- to ³⁄₁₆-inch gap between the boards for drainage, ventilation, expansion, and contraction. To keep the gap consistent across the deck, make a guide with a 10d nail driven through a piece of scrap wood. As you install the decking, use the nail to create the crack between the boards, snugging the new board up to it (the wood scrap

Drive decking nails at an angle, with each pair of nails angled toward one another. This gives the nails greater resistance to working loose as the deck boards expand and contract with wet and dry conditions. Drive nails carefully so you don't mar the surface of the wood.

keeps the nail from falling through the cracks).

Straightening Bowed Boards As you fasten the decking, you may come across a few boards that are bowed. This is a problem you can correct with a little know-how. First use one nail at each end of the decking to secure it to the end joists. If the decking bows toward the last board you fastened, carefully force a chisel between the two boards and pry the bowed board outward, then nail it in place. If the bow curves away from the last board, drive the chisel into the joist on the outside of the curve and pull on it to force the board into place, then nail.

Notching for Posts If you need to fit decking around extended posts, cut notches in the decking boards. Lay a piece of decking in position beside the post. On the board, mark the width of the post plus ⅜ inch for drainage. This is the width of the

notch. To determine the depth, push the board tightly against the post, then measure how much the board must slide forward to fit neatly into place. If it's the last board of the layout, this dimension will be the distance from the edge of the board to the outside edge of the header joist, plus ½-inch allowance for an overhang.

Using a combination square, draw the outline of the notch on the board. Then cut the two sides of the notch carefully with a circular saw or handsaw, keeping the blade on the inside of each line. Use a chisel to cut along the third line and remove the waste piece. If the wood grain is not straight and parallel with the cut line, don't try to remove the waste with one bite of the chisel; instead, nibble it away with a series of smaller bites, starting from the edge.

Trimming the Ends After all of the decking is installed, trim off the overhanging ends. Marking and

STRAIGHTENING BOWED BOARDS

Chisel

Chisel

Board bowed inward

Board bowed outward

NOTCHING FOR POST

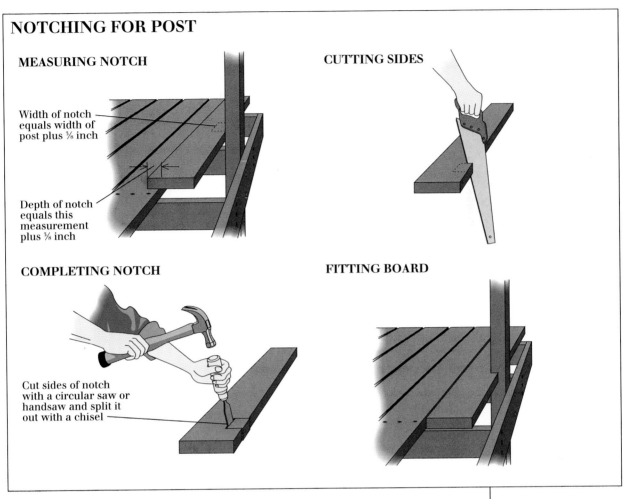

MEASURING NOTCH

Width of notch equals width of post plus ⅜ inch

Depth of notch equals this measurement plus ⅜ inch

CUTTING SIDES

COMPLETING NOTCH

Cut sides of notch with a circular saw or handsaw and split it out with a chisel

FITTING BOARD

TRIMMING ENDS

Chalk line

trimming the decking all at once saves time and makes a uniform, straight edge. Snap a chalk line carefully along the edge of the deck; if necessary, add an allowance for such features as fascia or trim boards to cover the joists, or a ½-inch overhang to create a shadow line. Cut along the line with a circular saw. For a perfectly straight line, tack a board onto the decking to serve as a guide for the saw. Check to see if the joist or header is also perfectly straight, or the saw blade may cut into it as you make the cut. For this reason, take your time trimming the ends, checking your work as you go. Make adjustments gradually, rather than abruptly, to maintain a smooth line. Use a sharp blade to minimize splintering. Smooth the cut edges with a rasping plane or sander.

Adding a Fascia Unless the header joist is an attractive piece of knot-free lumber, or you plan to paint the deck, you may want to install a decorative fascia to give the edge of the deck a trim appearance. To do so, select long, straight, clear pieces of 2-by lumber. Some lumberyards sell a grade of lumber called fascia texture, which is smooth on one side and rough-sawn on the other, depending on the texture you prefer. Attach fascia boards to the deck after you install the stairs (the next task) but before you install the railing. Use miter joints at the corners. If one board is not long enough to span the entire length of the deck, making it necessary to splice two pieces end-to-end, cut the end of each piece at a 45-degree bevel so the ends will overlap at the joint. To prevent nail heads from marring the surface, attach the fascia boards with galvanized decking screws driven through the joists (or header joist) into the fascia from behind.

STAIRS AND RAILINGS

Deck stairs and railings must be designed and built carefully. They affect the accessibility and usability of the deck, they have a strong visual impact, and their design is governed by strict safety considerations.

Step 11: Build the Stairs

Although some low decks may need only a stepping-stone, most decks require at least one flight of stairs. If the deck has more than one stairway, the riser and tread dimensions should be consistent throughout all the flights. Your plans probably specify the stair dimensions, but you should always calculate exact dimensions from the site measurements, not the plans. Support stairs to the ground with a concrete landing, or at least concrete footings for the stringers. To determine the height and location of the landing, consider it another stair tread in the overall calculation of stair dimensions. The landing should extend at least 3 feet in front of the bottom step. You can form and pour a landing at the same time as the deck footings, or wait until the deck is completed to be sure the height and location of the landing are accurate.

Calculating the Dimensions A flight of stairs is made up of risers, treads, and support stringers. Local building codes stipulate the minimum width (as viewed from the side; also called tread depth) of the stair treads and the maximum height of the risers—typically 10 inches for treads and 7½ inches for risers. The tread width plus twice the riser height should equal between 24 and 26 inches. Note that the tread width dimension refers to the dimension on the stringer; the actual tread width is greater, due to the overhang, usually 1 to 1½ inches. Also, the stairs' total rise divided

TYPICAL STAIR DIMENSIONS

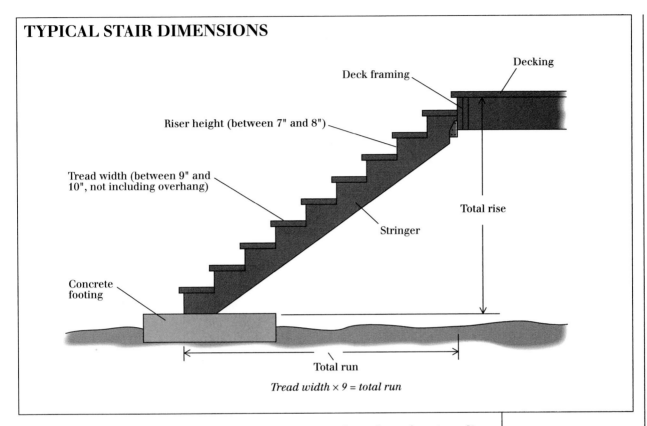

Deck framing

Decking

Riser height (between 7" and 8")

Tread width (between 9" and 10", not including overhang)

Total rise

Stringer

Concrete footing

Total run

Tread width × 9 = total run

by the rise of each step must equal a whole number, since all steps must be equal in rise. The width of the stairs should be no less than 36 inches, wide enough for two people to easily pass each other. *Note:* All of these dimensions are minimum requirements; lower the riser height and widen the treads for safer and more graceful stairways. Just be sure that all of the stairways around a deck have identical riser and tread dimensions.

To determine the number of steps you will need, measure the vertical distance (the total rise) from the surface of the decking to the ground where the stairs will land. Then divide this distance by the desired riser height, according to code. For example, if the deck is 48 inches above grade and you plan on using 6-inch risers, you'll need 8 steps exactly. If, however, the deck height divided by the riser height is

a whole number plus a fraction, divide the next highest number back into the deck height. This will give you the exact riser height you will need for each step. For example, if the deck is 51 inches high and the riser height you want is 7 inches, the number of steps would be 7.285. The next whole number is 8, so divide that into 51 inches, and the new riser height would be 6.375 inches, or 6⅜ inches.

To find the exact width of each tread, subtract twice the riser height from 24 to 26 inches. For a 6-inch riser, the proper width of the tread is between 12 and 14 inches—that is, 24 to 26 minus 12. The riser-to-tread ratio is a 6-inch riser to a 12- to 14-inch tread, or, using the above 6⅜-inch riser, the tread should be between 11¼ and 13¼ inch.

You may want to adjust dimensions so the tread width will be just right for standard lumber dimensions. For example, two 2×6s will make an 11¼-inch-wide tread; or two 2×6s and a 2×4 will make a 14-inch-wide tread. Another way to calculate rise and run ratios is that the product of rise times run should fall between 72 and 76. For example: *6 × 12 = 72; 7½ × 10 = 75; 8 × 9.5 = 76.* Obviously, there is some latitude here, but these ratios make for safe and comfortable stairs.

Finally, you'll need to figure the total run to find out if your measurements will fit the available space. Multiply the tread width by the number of treads. Eight steps with seven 14-inch-wide treads, for example, would have a run of 98 inches. If the steps don't fit in the space, adjust the riser-to-tread ratio, increasing the riser and decreasing the tread. For safety, all steps must have the same riser-to-tread ratio, and all risers must be within ³⁄₁₆ inch of the same height.

Always check local codes. Building codes vary, but most specify minimum allowable treads and maximum rise.

Laying Out the Stringers Stairs are supported by stringers made from 2×12s that are long enough to reach from the top to the bottom level at the proper angle. This size lumber has enough depth for the step notches to be cut out and still carry the load.

Stringers are either cutout or straight styles. Cutout stringers are solid boards with triangular sections removed to accommodate treads and risers. Straight stringers require cleats, brackets, or dadoes to support the treads.

To lay out either type of stringer, you'll first need to determine the length. Measure the total rise (from the top of the footing or cleat to the

LAYING OUT A STRINGER

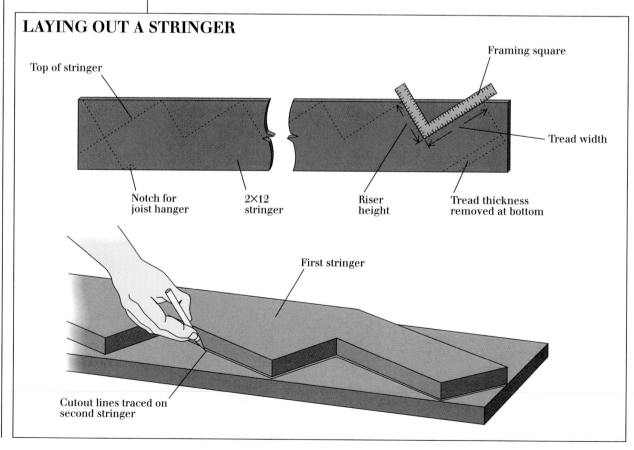

Top of stringer

Notch for joist hanger

2×12 stringer

Framing square

Tread width

Riser height

Tread thickness removed at bottom

First stringer

Cutout lines traced on second stringer

DESIGNS FOR SINGLE STEPS

Many times a deck does not require a full set of stairs, but only one or two steps. Although these are much easier to build than a full set, you must still observe the basic riser and tread ratio (see page 157). The designs illustrated here show some ways of creating a one-step change of level on a deck, or of creating a one-step access to a deck.

Single steps like these can also be made of concrete poured in a form. This is particularly effective if the step matches a concrete path or stepping-stones that approach it.

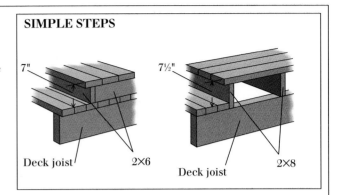

SIMPLE STEPS

7"

Deck joist

2×6

7½"

Deck joist

2×8

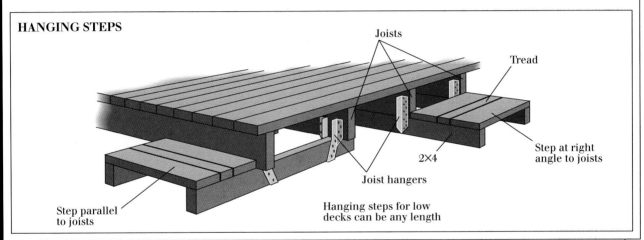

HANGING STEPS

Joists

Tread

Step at right
angle to joists

2×4

Joist hangers

Step parallel
to joists

Hanging steps for low
decks can be any length

top of the decking) and total run of the stairs and mark these distances on a framing square, with the run number on the body of the square and the rise number on its tongue. Measure the distance between these two points to give you the length of the stringers, in feet. Add an extra 2 feet to allow for connecting the stringers to the deck and for cutting off a portion for leveling.

Lay out the lines for the cutouts or the location of the tread support on the 2×12s using the framing square, with the tread dimension on the body and the riser dimension on the tongue. Line up the marks with the top edge of the 2×12; trace the outline of the risers and treads onto it. Use a knife blade or sharp pencil for tracing, to avoid incremental increases in the riser heights.

Cutting the Stringers For a cutout stringer, use a circular saw to begin the cuts and, to avoid overcutting, finish the cuts with a handsaw. Because the tread thickness will increase the height of the first step, measure the thickness of a tread and cut away this amount from the bottom of the stringer. This is called dropping the stringer.

Once one stringer is cut, use it as a pattern to cut the other. Then apply preservative to all cut edges.

If you plan to use a straight, or solid, stringer, measure and mark it in the same manner as the cutout stringer. But instead of cutting away the triangles, use them as guides to attach the cleats or brackets or to cut the dadoes.

Stringer-to-Deck Connection To install the stringers, first set them in place for a test fit. Make sure

CONNECTING STRINGER TO DECK

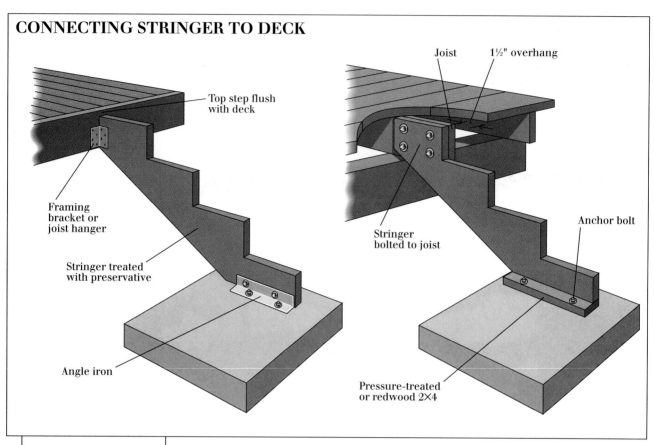

Top step flush with deck

Framing bracket or joist hanger

Stringer treated with preservative

Angle iron

Joist

1½" overhang

Stringer bolted to joist

Anchor bolt

Pressure-treated or redwood 2×4

they are parallel and level with each other by measuring the distance between them and by laying a level on them. Then fasten the top of each stringer to the deck substructure with bolts, lag screws, or metal connectors, depending on how the joists are aligned. Attach the bottom of the stringers to the concrete landing or to individual footings. Attach them directly to the concrete with anchor bolts, angle iron, or metal connectors, or attach cleats to the concrete and toenail the stringers to them with 12d HDG nails, predrilling first. Any wood that touches the concrete must be pressure-treated lumber or the heartwood of a durable species.

Attaching the Treads Generally, the riser space is left open to allow air to circulate. However, it can be closed to hide the substructure of the deck by nailing a 1-by riser board across each riser space before installing the tread. Cut the riser boards slightly narrower than the riser height to allow an air space where the bottom corners join the stringer cutouts. Some jurisdictions require riser closure if the space is greater than 4 inches.

When you cut the tread material to length, the ends of the treads can be flush with the side of the stringer, or they can have a slight overhang. Instead of using one wide board for each step, install two or three narrow boards. The spaces between the boards allow water to drain through, and narrow boards will cup or warp less than a single, wide tread board. But don't overspan the treads; a 3-foot span is too long for a 2×4.

If you are using a cutout stringer, attach the treads directly to the stringer, using 12d HDG common

ATTACHING TREADS

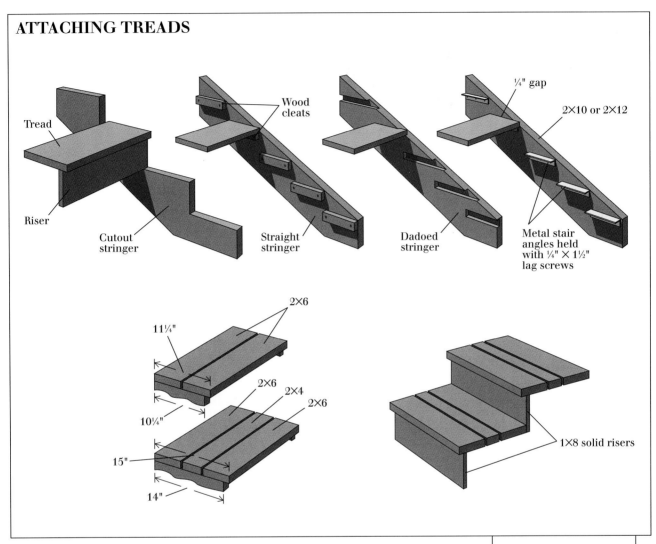

Tread

Riser

Cutout
stringer

Wood
cleats

Straight
stringer

Dadoed
stringer

¼" gap

2×10 or 2×12

Metal stair
angles held
with ¼" × 1½"
lag screws

2×6

11¼"

10¼"

15"

14"

2×6

2×6   2×4

2×6

1×8 solid risers

nails, 16d HDG spiral-shank nails, or 3-inch decking screws.

If you're using a straight stringer, install and support the treads with cleats, metal brackets, or cutaway dadoes. Attach cleats to the stringers with four 3-inch decking screws in each cleat (use washers or clip off the tips of the screws to keep them from penetrating all the way through the stringer). Attach metal brackets, or stair angles, to the stringer with ¼-inch by 1½-inch galvanized lag screws. Then attach the treads to the cleats or stair angles by driving lag screws up through the cleats or stair angles into the treads.

After installing the treads, round the front edges slightly with a rasping plane, smoothing plane, or sander.

Step 12: Build the Railings

Any deck can benefit from railings. The boundaries and visual lines the railings create add a sense of enclosure, safety, and privacy. Railings can be as formal or as rustic as you like, to match the architectural style of your home. There are numerous railing materials available, but the most common are pressure-treated lumber and redwood.

Before you start, consult the local building code. Most codes require

RAILING CONFIGURATIONS

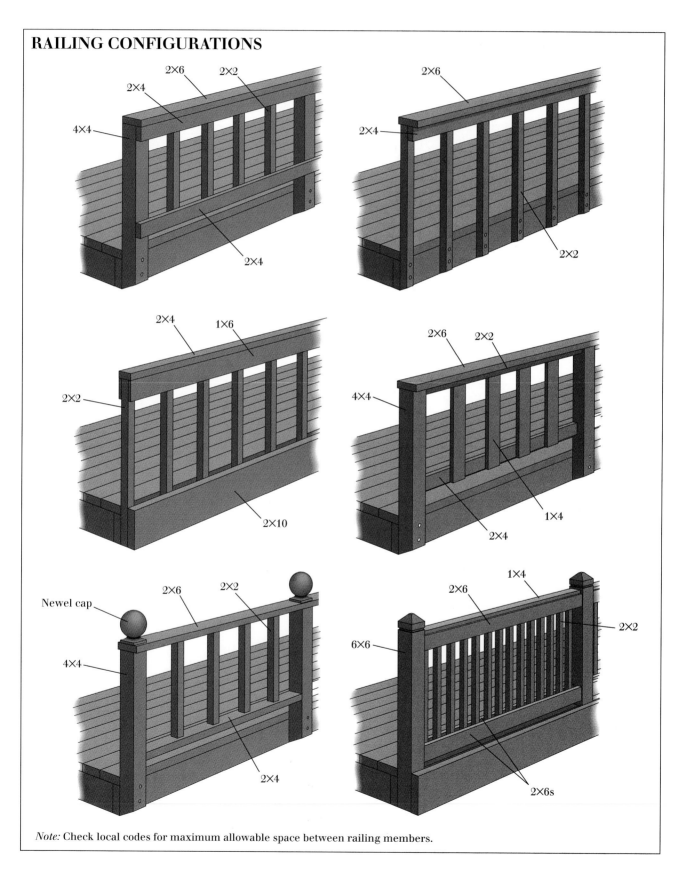

Note: Check local codes for maximum allowable space between railing members.

RAILING CONFIGURATIONS

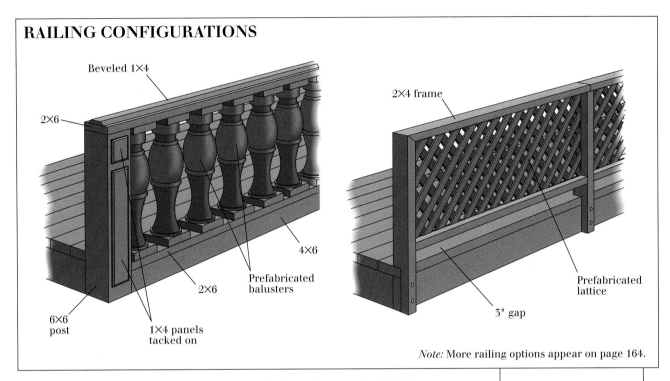

Beveled 1×4

2×6

6×6 post

1×4 panels tacked on

2×6

Prefabricated balusters

4×6

2×4 frame

Prefabricated lattice

3" gap

Note: More railing options appear on page 164.

that decks 30 inches or higher have railings 36 to 42 inches high, and that all stairs with more than four risers have a railing on each open side, 30 to 33 inches above the tread nosings. Spacing between the balusters is closely regulated at 4 to 6 inches maximum. Most codes for residential railings specify that a 4-inch sphere cannot pass through the balusters and that the railings be designed so that they cannot be climbed. This limits design options to a certain extent, but many railing styles meet these requirements.

Railing Options Most styles are variations of two simple designs: top and bottom rails with several intermediate rails in between, or top and bottom rails separated by vertical balusters. The top rail can stand on its own or, if you choose, it can be covered with a cap that is mitered at the corners and beveled on top to shed water.

There are several ways to embellish railings. You can add a cap to the top rail, top off the posts with plain or decorative finials, use rounded spindles instead of flat balusters, or fill the space between the rails with screen, cable, lattice, solid wood, canvas, or hard plastic.

Assembling the Railing Components Assembly techniques vary with the design, but for most railings the process is to cut the posts, rails, balusters, and decorative components to size, then install them as individual pieces, in that order, or fabricate modules that can be installed as a unit.

Posts
The best way to secure railing posts to the deck is to use carriage bolts or metal connectors to fasten their bottom ends to the outside of the joists, header joist, or beams.

With a combination square, mark the location of each post according to the deck plans. Cut each post to length. You may also want to cut embellished tops—a routed, capped, or angled top or a peaked or flat-topped chamfer—with a circular

RAILING CONFIGURATIONS

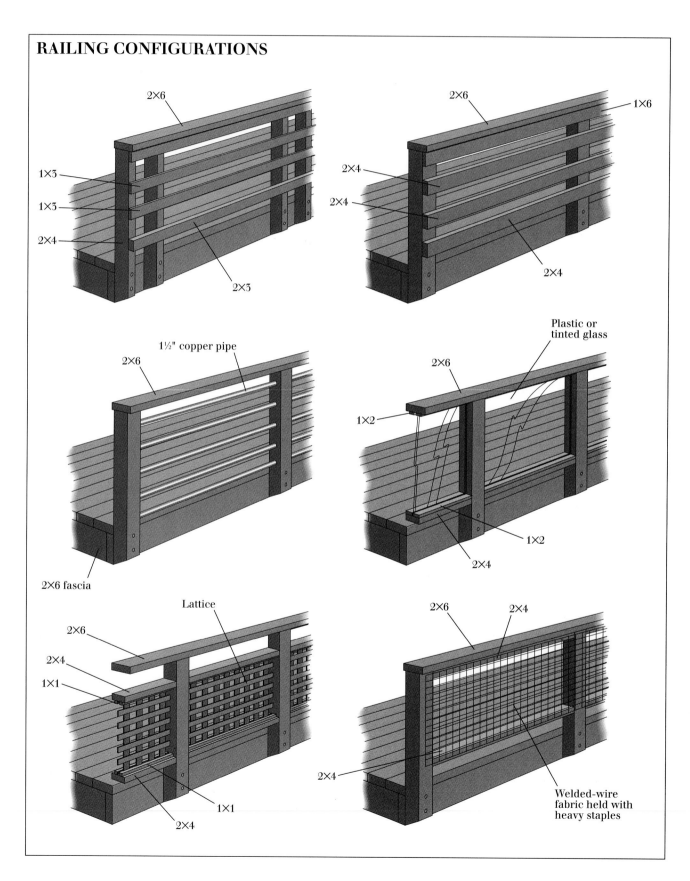

2×6

1×3

1×3

2×4

2×3

2×6

1×6

2×4

2×4

2×4

2×6

1½" copper pipe

2×6 fascia

Plastic or tinted glass

2×6

1×2

1×2

2×4

Lattice

2×6

2×4

1×1

1×1

2×4

2×6

2×4

2×4

Welded-wire fabric held with heavy staples

ATTACHING POSTS

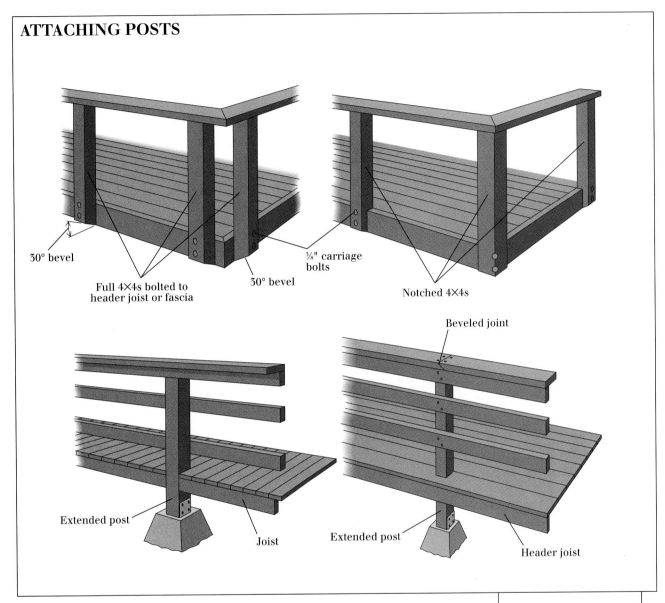

30° bevel

Full 4×4s bolted to
header joist or fascia

30° bevel

⅜" carriage
bolts

Notched 4×4s

Beveled joint

Extended post

Joist

Extended post

Header joist

saw or router. At the bottom end of each post, drill two holes, one above the other. Then slip in the carriage bolts and secure the post to the header joist or beam. If you want the posts set in from the deck edge, cut out a notch at the bottom. The notch should leave at least 2 inches of post thickness and be no longer than the height of the header joist or fascia around the edge of the deck. Attach this post the same way as an unnotched post, but with shorter bolts.

You can also attach the posts with half post bases. These metal connectors attach to the decking boards above the joist. You then secure the post in the base with nails or screws.

If the railing posts are simply extensions of the foundation posts, no additional posts may be necessary, but you should check local codes. Intermediate posts may be required to make the railing strong enough to sustain a prescribed lateral force, typically 15 pounds per square foot.

This unusual and attractive railing is composed of dowels inserted through holes drilled in the bottom rail.

rail end. Choose whichever method will make the nail heads least obtrusive. For either method, predrill holes through the starting member (rail or post). Use 8d HDG common nails for nailing the rail to the post, and 12d HDG common nails for driving through the post into the rail end. With a nail set, countersink each nail head slightly.

For cap rails, use the longest lengths of lumber possible. Locate any necessary joints over a post; cut joints at a bevel so they overlay slightly. For mitered joints at the corners, cut the first piece at a 45-degree angle and nail it in place with two 16d HDG spiral-shank nails facenailed into each post (predrill the cap rail at the ends); lay the second piece in its exact position, with the free end extending over the top of the first piece. Mark a cut line on the bottom of the second piece by scribing along the angled cut of the first piece. Cut it and nail it in place with 16d HDG spiral-shank nails, predrilling for the nails at the joint. In addition to nails driven into the post, lock-nail the two boards together with an 8d HDG common nail (predrill).

Here are three easy ways to install balusters: First, you can attach them to the inside, outside, or both sides of the top and bottom rails and facenail them with HDG box nails. Second, you can toenail the top of the balusters up into the top rail, and facenail the bottom directly against the joists, header joist, or beams. In this case, no bottom rail is needed. Finally, you can place the ends of the balusters in grooves you cut lengthwise in the rails, then toenail them with 6d HDG finishing nails. Regardless of how you install the balusters, be sure to space them evenly by using a spacer block cut from a scrap piece of lumber.

Rails and Balusters

Once the posts are installed, add the top, bottom, and any intermediate rails to the inside or outside of the posts.

To install rails between posts, cut them for a snug fit. There are two ways to toenail them to each post: angling the nails through the rail into the post, or driving the nails through the side of the post into the

CHOOSING AND APPLYING A DECK FINISH

The choice of a deck finish is a matter of aesthetic preference and maintenance requirements. The proper finish, coupled with regular maintenance, will keep the deck looking its best for years.

If you want the deck to have a gray, weathered look, don't do anything—the sun's ultraviolet rays will produce this effect naturally. The best woods for natural weathering are pressure-treated lumber and better grades of cedar, cypress, and redwood.

Generally, it takes two years to complete the weathering process. You can, however, age the wood to the gray you want, perhaps for just a few months, then slow the process by applying a water sealer. This is a good idea even for pressure-treated lumber, as continuous exposure to the elements leads to premature rotting, swelling, and splitting in untreated wood. To accelerate the weathering process, use a wood bleach or a product specifically for weathering decks, following manufacturer's instructions.

The final color depends on the species of lumber. Cedar and cypress weather to a light, silvery gray, redwood turns dark gray, and pressure-treated lumber turns a lighter shade of its original color.

Wood is so vulnerable to weather, ultraviolet light, insects, mold, mildew, and foot traffic that there's no surefire way to permanently protect it from all these factors. You can slow the process considerably, however, with a protective finish.

There are several types to choose from: wood preservatives, semi-transparent stains, solid stains, and paints. Which one is right for your deck depends on the species and grade of lumber, how the deck will be used, the climate, and whether you want to retain the natural color of the wood.

Choosing the proper finishing product shouldn't be a guessing game, yet there are so many different ones on the market, you may be overwhelmed by the options and

HOW WEATHER EXPOSURE AFFECTS WOOD

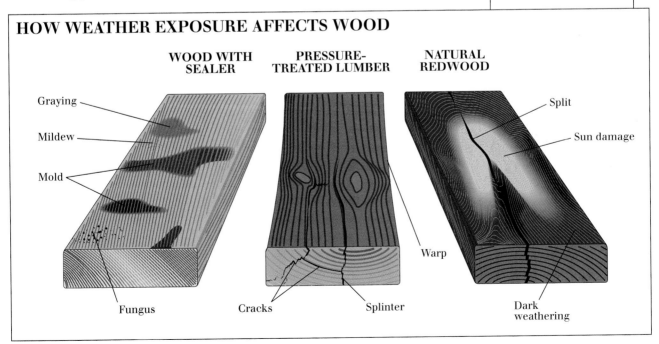

WOOD WITH SEALER   PRESSURE-TREATED LUMBER   NATURAL REDWOOD

Graying — Mildew — Mold — Fungus

Cracks — Splinter — Warp

Split — Sun damage — Dark weathering

APPLICATION TECHNIQUES

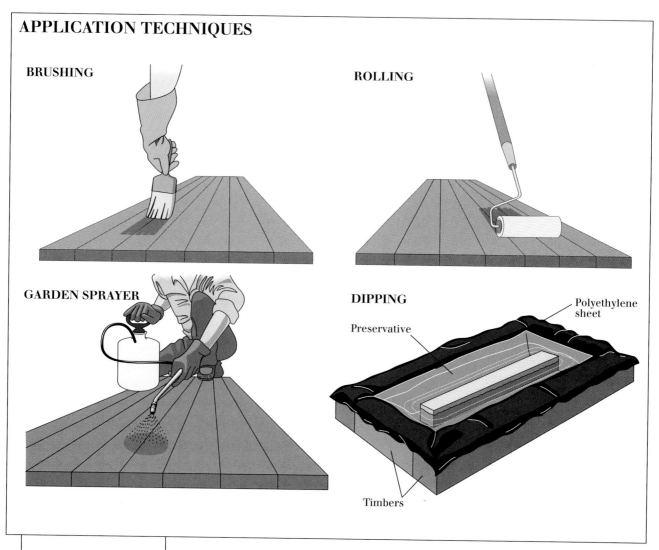

BRUSHING

ROLLING

GARDEN SPRAYER

DIPPING

Polyethylene sheet

Preservative

Timbers

combinations. Some combine wood preservatives with water sealers whereas others couple sealers with stains. Some products even contain fungicides, mildewcides, insecticides, and ultraviolet-light absorbers and inhibitors.

On the upside, the variety gives you plenty of design options. You could choose a finish that lets the wood weather naturally to an appealing gray, or one that preserves the natural color. You could even combine finishes for a unique visual effect, painting the substructure and staining the decking, for example.

Finishes that become slippery when wet are not appropriate

around spas and pools. And wood finished with only a water sealer can't withstand a hot, blanching southern sun. See page 171 for a chart that outlines the advantages and the disadvantages of each type of finish. Once you've pinpointed the one you would like to use, visit your home center. Learn as much as you can about the various products; read the labels and manufacturers' pamphlets. If you use more than one product, make sure they are chemically compatible. Products from the same manufacturer are most likely formulated to work together, but always check the labels for exceptions.

Before any finish can be applied, the wood must be completely dried, or "cured." Use this simple test: Sprinkle water onto a board. If the water is quickly absorbed, the wood is ready for finishing. If the water is not absorbed, give it more time to cure.

Wood Preservatives

Wood preservatives protect the deck from insects, rot, mildew, and mold, but they don't protect against moisture or preserve the natural color of the wood. Pressure-treated lumber already contains preservatives, and its factory treatment outmatches do-it-yourself applications. But if you use cedar or cypress and plan to stain or paint it, you will want to consider using a wood preservative. Some water sealers and stains already contain a wood preservative.

Use products that are safe and effective. Pentachlorophenol, creosote, and arsenic compounds have been banned for health and environmental reasons. One relatively safe, effective, and environmentally acceptable wood preservative is copper naphthenate. It's nontoxic to plants and animals, so it is particularly useful in finishing planters and garden structures. It is available in a clear form, or in a green color that leaves the wood with a green tinge, which will fade as the wood weathers. Renew the treatment every couple of years to maintain the protection.

Apply wood preservative with a brush, or a roller with a 1-inch nap. Always read the manufacturer's instructions and wear rubber gloves and eye protection. If you are constructing a smaller item, such as a planter, you can immerse the boards in a trough of preservative before assembling them.

Sealers

Sealers, or water repellents, are waterlike finishes that serve two purposes. They penetrate the wood to prevent it from absorbing water,

Danish oil, a sealer, is being applied to this deck. Sealers are thin liquids that can be applied with a roller, as shown here, wiped on with a rag, or sprayed on with a garden sprayer. (Clean the sprayer carefully afterward to prevent later clogging.)

This deck has been treated with a semi-transparent stain to match the house.

which would cause swelling, cracking, and warping. They also help retain wood's natural look and color by temporarily delaying the weathering process that inevitably turns it gray.

Sealers can be applied to all wood and pressure-treated lumber. Some products seal and stain in one step. Sealers with ultraviolet-light absorbers provide extra protection against the bleaching effect of the sun. Avoid sealers that form hard surfaces that can become slippery. In addition to their safety problems, the surfaces will eventually crack as the wood expands and contracts, leaving the deck unsightly and vulnerable to water damage.

Stains

Unlike paints, stains penetrate deep into the wood, and rather than conceal the grain pattern, they enhance it. Some stains have preservatives and sealers, protecting the wood from water, mildew, insects, and the effects of ultraviolet light.

There are two kinds of stains: semitransparent (or light-bodied) and solid (full-bodied). Semitransparent stains contain less pigment than solid stains, so the beauty of the wood naturally shows through, and prematurely weathered or worn areas that develop are less noticeable. Use semitransparent stains on the decking boards if they have few or no flaws.

If the decking material is of low-grade lumber with lots of flaws, solid stains make an excellent finish. Because they have some of the characteristics of paint, they hide the wood grain and imperfections and are quite durable. When choosing a stain, select a nonchalking or sealer type made for decks. Stains that contain chalk leave a powdery film on the surface.

CHOOSING A FINISH

Type of Finish	Advantages	Disadvantages
Wood Preservative Principal ingredient is copper naphthenate, an environmentally approved chemical that turns the wood a deep greenish color, which eventually fades.	Soaks into wood. Resists decay and insects. Wood can be stained, painted, sealed, or allowed to weather naturally.	Not water resistant. Wood should also be coated with sealer for moisture protection. Do-it-yourself treatment not as thorough and durable as factory pressure treatment.
Sealer Also called a water repellent. Available in oil-based and water-based types. Oil-based sealers are more durable and suitable for decks. May be applied to all wood species and to pressure-treated lumber. For maximum protection, apply 2 thin coats. May be added to oil-based paints or stains; check compatibility. Do not add to water-based paint or stain.	Penetrates into wood to form protective barrier. Helps minimize formation of water stains. Reduces warping, splitting, shrinking, and swelling of the wood. Delays natural weathering process that turns wood gray. Some sealers are specifically formulated to retain natural color and texture of a particular species. Surface coating is durable, not easily abraded. Dries clear, unless pigment added. Some contain fungicides and mildewcides. Some contain ultraviolet light inhibitors, absorbers, or blockers. Both oil-based and water-based stains and paints may be applied over sealers.	Not effective on previously stained or painted surfaces because it is unable to penetrate the wood properly. Toxic to fish and wildlife. You must take care not to contaminate water when cleaning equipment, and dispose of container and rags properly.
Stain Semitransparent and solid stains protect and add color. There are oil-based and water-based types. Some are specially formulated for use on decks. Choose a nonchalking type and possibly one with a sealer or preservative added.	Penetrates into wood to protect it from damaging moisture and the bleaching effects of ultraviolet light. Adds color. Comes in many assorted colors or may be custom mixed to match or complement your home. Easy to apply.	The color is sometimes unpredictable because it's influenced by the species, grade, color, and condition of the wood. Always test the color in an inconspicuous place or on a piece of leftover lumber. Must be renewed, usually once a year.
Semitransparent Stain Also called light-bodied stain. Contains a small amount of pigment. Resulting color is blend of 2 colors—the stain and the wood.	Lets the wood grain and texture show through for a more natural look. Best choice for the surface of the decking and stairs. Weathered and worn areas will be less noticeable as the deck ages. Suitable for new or previously stained wood in the same semitransparent color range.	Can't be applied to wood that is painted or stained with a solid stain. Overlap marks will occur if you fail to work from a wet to a dry area. Ideally, stain the full length of each board at a time. Requires periodic reapplication to keep the benefits of the stain effective.
Solid Stain Also called full-bodied stain. Contains heavy pigment that acts and looks like paint. Reapply as needed to keep deck looking attractive.	Contains more pigment than semitransparent stains. Hides flaws, knots, grain patterns, and the wood's condition. Ideal for low grades of lumber. Lets the texture of the wood show through. Quite durable. Suitable for new, old, stained, or weathered wood.	Shows premature wear in high-traffic areas such as stairs and deck surface.
Paint Available in oil-based and water-based types. Choose a nonchalking type and one that is specially formulated for decks so it withstands the abuse of foot traffic. Reapply when worn, faded, peeling, or chipped.	Ideal for refinishing older decks or low grades of lumber. Hides flaws, knots, grain, and the condition of the wood. Integrates deck constructed from several different woods. Durable, stain resistant, and moisture resistant. Marine grades are most durable and expensive. Unlimited colors. Coordinates deck with house.	Generally more time consuming to apply. More expensive than other types of finishes. Once painted, components can only be repainted. Slippery when wet—mix in silica sand for traction. Tends to crack as wood contracts and expands repeatedly.

tive or sealer to weather for a minimum of 90 days prior to application of the stain.

Two thin coats are more durable than one thick one. For smooth, consistent color, apply the stain evenly without overlaps and wipe off any excess.

Paints

Paint hides knots and other imperfections better than any other type of finish, making it ideal for use on low-grade lumber. Paint takes longer to apply, however, and is more expensive and harder to maintain. If you plan to use low-grade lumber for the decking and to cover its flaws with paint, the money you save on lumber will probably be spent on the finish. Once you've painted the deck, you are committed to a paint finish in the future, because after the wood's pores have been filled with paint pigments, it is impossible to return to a natural wood finish.

Paradoxically, its good coverage also makes paint a poor choice of finish for the decking. It inevitably wears away under foot traffic, creating noticeable patterns across the deck, and its smooth surface tends to crack when the wood expands and contracts. It may be wisest to reserve paint for the deck's structural underpinnings.

If you do choose to paint the deck surface, find a product formulated for the wear and tear a deck endures, such as a self-priming alkyd-based deck paint. Regular exterior acrylic paints cannot hold up and they easily peel and chip.

A painted deck surface is quite slippery when wet. You can remedy this by mixing silica sand into the paint before applying the final coat to high-traffic areas, such as the stairs and entrances. Read the label on the bag of sand for mixing directions and coverage.

Semitransparent stains seal the wood and also change its color. They can be applied by any method used for sealers, but should be wiped off afterward to avoid uneven color.

To ensure consistent color, check that the batch numbers on all of the cans are alike; if custom-mixing, have all the cans mixed at the same time. If you are staining pressure-treated wood, select a stain formulated especially for this purpose.

How the stain will color the deck cannot be predicted by a store's sample or color chip. The wood species, grade, condition, and natural color will affect the outcome, so before you do the entire deck, test the color in an inconspicuous area and allow pressure-treated lumber and woods that have already been treated with a preserva-

DECKS YOU CAN BUILD

This section features plans for decks you can build easily. Each plan is complete, ready to build, and includes a full materials list. The structural details conform to most model building codes, but you should consult the local building department and get proper permits before starting any construction.

The plans progress from low ground-huggers to more-complex structures. Each deck is designed for a specific site, but can be adapted to any number of locations as required. The plans are intended to reflect design principles that make each deck more than just an outdoor activity space.

Together, these deck plans also offer an encyclopedia of construction details. They will help you see how footings, structural components, decking, railings, stairs, benches, and trim details interconnect with one another to make a complete deck. Although each plan is self-contained, you may find it helpful to go through all the plans; the techniques and details presented for the simpler designs will make the more-complex designs easier to understand. You may also find ways to combine components from various decks.

THE 3 BY 3 DECK MODULES

This simple deck system is made up of modular sections that can be laid directly on the ground or on a level surface such as a patio, pool area, or even a rooftop. It is more akin to a patio than a raised deck, with a low profile that maintains privacy and creates a sense of intimacy with the surrounding garden. Another advantage is its flexibility—you can change its shape and size to meet various needs by

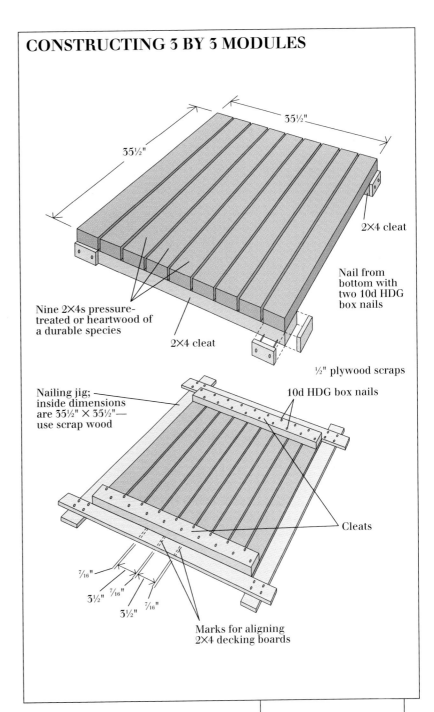

CONSTRUCTING 3 BY 3 MODULES

35½"

35½"

2×4 cleat

Nail from bottom with two 10d HDG box nails

Nine 2×4s pressure-treated or heartwood of a durable species

2×4 cleat

½" plywood scraps

Nailing jig; inside dimensions are 35½" × 35½"— use scrap wood

10d HDG box nails

Cleats

⁷⁄₁₆"

3½" ⁷⁄₁₆"

⁷⁄₁₆"

3½"

Marks for aligning 2×4 decking boards

recombining sections into different configurations.

This kind of deck system has a wide range of applications. It can be the main deck in a small yard or it can serve as a landscaping accent in a large yard. Modules are often used to transform an unused rooftop into

MATERIALS LIST

For 12 modular sections, set on sleepers

Base	108 sq ft 4-mil polyethylene sheeting (for weed control)		
	1 cu yd sand or well-graded gravel		
Sleepers	2×4s	2	12' lengths
	2×6s	2	12' lengths
12 Modules	2×4s	33	12' lengths (cut into 35½" pieces)
Nails	10# 10d HDG common		

a pleasant garden retreat. Because the modules are portable and can be stacked for easy storage during winter, they are ideal for temporary, seasonal decks.

Because a deck composed of modules has no structural system of its own, it requires a stable, level surface. And because modular sections have no footings, they may move and shift over time. This problem is easily solved by making periodic adjustments, by fastening the sections together, or by installing the deck over long sleepers. Soils that are highly expansive may not be appropriate for this type of deck, however.

The following pages provide ideas and techniques for installing a modular deck, whether you build your own or use prefabricated sections. There are instructions for installing deck modules on the ground, on concrete or masonry patios, and on rooftops.

The deck shown on these pages is only one of an endless number of possible configurations, all of which are based on a single 3-foot-square module that you can build yourself. These small modules are easy to carry and do not have to be constructed on-site—you can assemble them in your garage or basement. You can build the modules in almost any size or shape (see page 176 for one option). If you want to build larger modules, just add more cleats. If you build

smaller modules, there will be considerably more nailing and cutting and more joints between sections.

Besides varying the size of the module, you can vary the size of lumber. If you need to reduce the overall weight or thickness of the deck, you can use 1×4s for the decking. If you do, add a third cleat halfway between the other two. You may prefer 2×3 or even 2×2 decking for a finely textured pattern. These sizes also require three cleats.

Materials
Use pressure-treated lumber for the cleats, which make contact with the ground or other surfaces. For the 2×4 decking, use either pressure-treated lumber or a naturally durable wood such as redwood, cedar, or cypress. Because they span almost 30 inches, for maximum strength the boards should be construction-grade lumber with few, relatively small knots. If needed, add a pressure-treated 1×4 as a central cleat.

Cutting
Because all pieces are the same length, you may find it easiest to have the supplier cut them for you. Most lumberyards will do so for a modest fee. Otherwise, note that the 35½-inch length requires two cuts for each 6-foot board, rather than simply cutting them in half. Remember, when cutting pressure-treated lumber, wear long-sleeves, eye protection, gloves, and a dust mask.

Assembly
To construct each module, build a nailing jig as shown on page 173. Place nine of the 2×4s inside the jig, with their best-looking faces down. Lay the two cleats over them as shown on page 173. Before nailing, be sure each 2×4 decking board is aligned for proper spacing. To avoid splitting the decking, especially

SLEEPER SYSTEM FOR INSTALLING MODULES ON THE GROUND

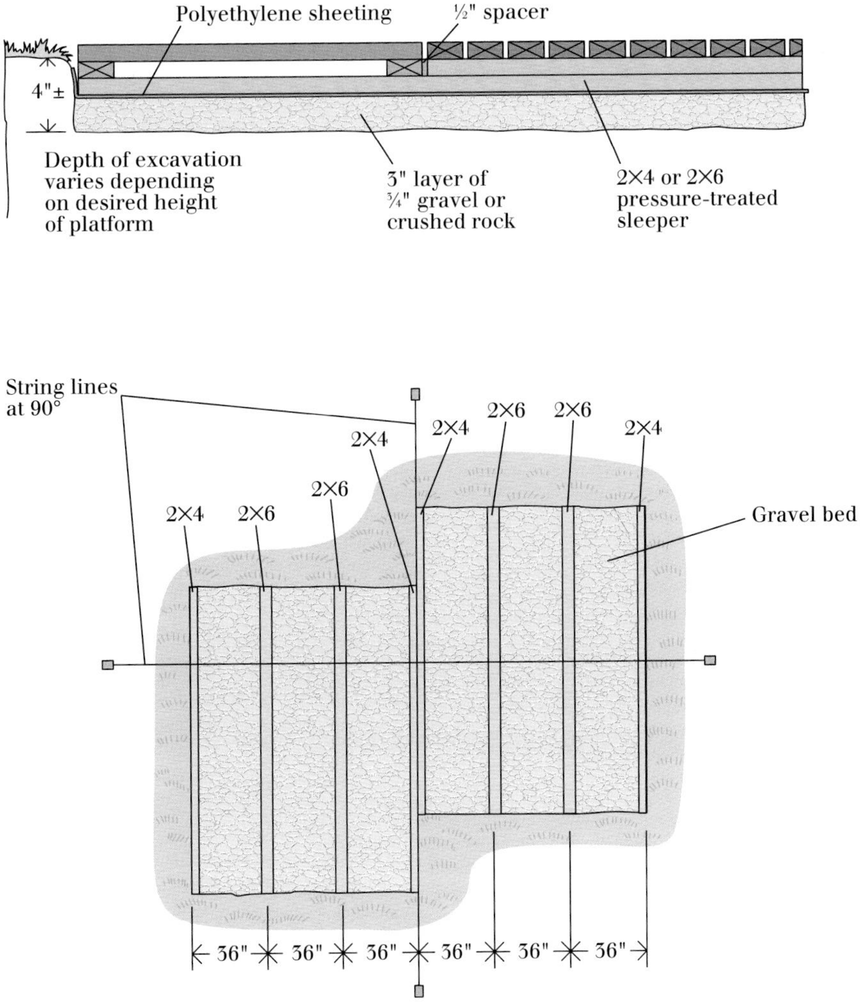

Polyethylene sheeting   ½" spacer

4"±

Depth of excavation
varies depending
on desired height
of platform

3" layer of
¾" gravel or
crushed rock

2×4 or 2×6
pressure-treated
sleeper

String lines
at 90°

2×4   2×6   2×6   2×4

2×4   2×6   2×6

Gravel bed

←36"→←36"→←36"→←36"→←36"→←36"→

when nailing close to the ends, drill pilot holes or blunt the point of each nail. An easy way to blunt a nail is to place it upside down on a nail that has already been driven into the deck and strike the point with a hammer.

After assembling the modules, nail ½-inch plywood scraps on two sides of the module to provide uniform spacing between modules. Some modules will not need spacers, so you may wait to attach the scraps until you decide on a final configuration. See pages 167 to 172 for details about finishing decks.

DECK MODULES ON A ROOF

Rooftops offer an exciting option for outdoor living. A modular system can be built at a convenient location and transported to the rooftop, can be moved for roof maintenance, and can be easily expanded. If you are an apartment or condominium dweller, this is an ideal project to approach as a cooperative venture, pooling resources and efforts with neighbors to develop a pleasant outdoor space that you can enjoy together.

Before considering a rooftop deck, check that the roof can support the weight of one. Most residential roofs are designed to support only their own weight. A roof intended as living space will be designed to support an additional 30 or 40 pounds per square foot live load. Roofs on large buildings or where snow loads are expected may already have a framing system that can handle the extra load. Hire a professional to evaluate the roof and, if necessary, recommend structural changes.

The roof should be sound and have a slope of at least ¼ inch per foot so that puddles won't form.

A 3' × 6' DECK MODULE

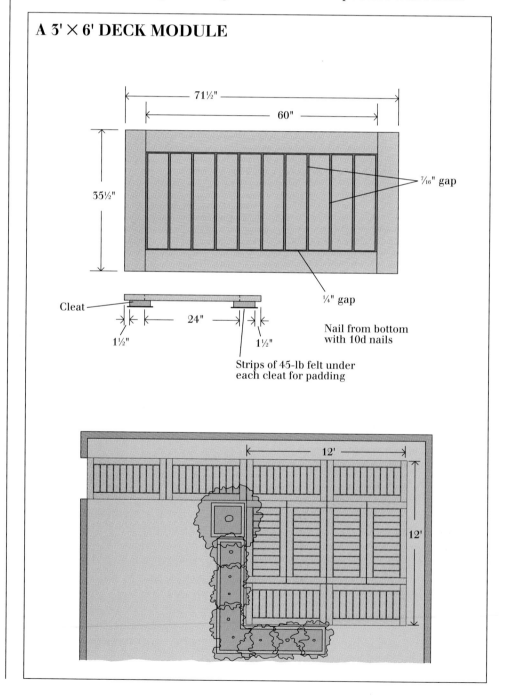

Flashing should be in good condition, especially at parapets or other walls. A fundamental consideration is access. To avoid damaging roof membranes, access should lead directly to the deck. It may be more bother to construct a stairway or roof hatch than to build a deck elsewhere. You also need to consider safety requirements, such as railings or parapets, and protection from nearby power lines. And, if you intend to do any gardening, you'll need a water faucet handy.

Construction Techniques

The modules featured in this plan are different from those in the previous section, but you could use either design. These larger modules distribute the loads better and are less likely to shift. They use 2×6s instead of 2×4s but are constructed the same way. The only difference is that the cleats are set in from the edge of the module rather than flush with it (see page 173).

You can use 1×6 decking boards to reduce overall weight or 2×4s for a finer texture; 1×6s will require a third cleat.

Installation

The modules can be set directly on most roof surfaces, although gravel should be swept away and strips of 45-pound felt or rubber pads (made by a number of roofing manufacturers) placed under the cleats. The modules will slope the same as the roof. If you want to level them, use long sleepers with shims underneath.

Choose an area of the roof that drains well. It should also have a protective parapet, railing, or other safety barrier and be close to an access door. Simply lay each section in place, and presto! . . . instant deck. Planters should be placed off the deck to maximize usable space.

AN ELEGANT DECK FLUSH WITH THE GROUND

This plan (see page 178) features another ground-level deck that is easy to build and can be adapted to a variety of settings, including installations directly on the ground, over an existing patio, or on a rooftop. Unlike the modules, this is a unified structure that is less likely to shift or settle. It also uses full-length decking boards, giving it a more restful appearance. This L-shaped deck is ideal for a transition area between house and lawn. Away from the main traffic corridor, it provides a usable space where a table or a pair of lounge chairs invite casual relaxing. Plantings along the side borders help to confine the space. Lowering the structure into a shallow excavation and edging it with a masonry or concrete border makes a graceful transition between lawn and deck.

Construction Techniques

This deck can be built directly on or below grade, so long as you prepare the site carefully and use pressure-treated lumber or other lumber suitable for ground contact. You can alter the size and shape of this deck very easily by changing the length of the decking boards and the length and spacing of the sleepers.

Site Preparation

Choose a site that drains well naturally, or be prepared to install subsurface drainage pipes. Lay out the perimeter of the deck and excavate. The illustrations on page 179 show how the depth of the excavation varies with the height of the deck. Deeper excavations should have a solid border of concrete or brick to retain the edges; install it before you install the deck.

PLAN VIEW

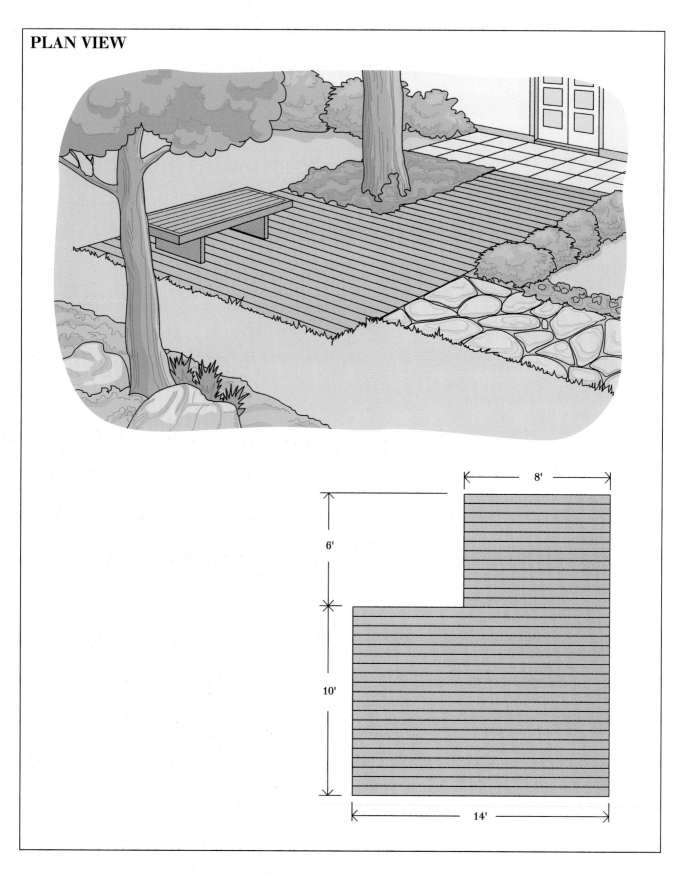

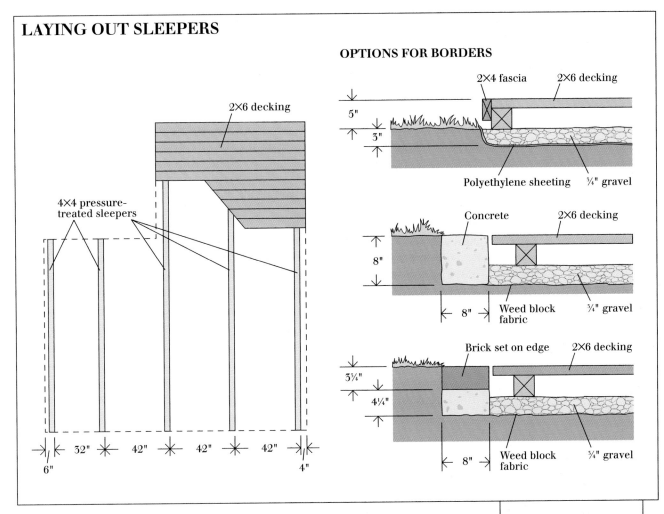

LAYING OUT SLEEPERS

2×6 decking

4×4 pressure-treated sleepers

6"   32"   42"   42"   42"   4"

OPTIONS FOR BORDERS

2×4 fascia   2×6 decking

5"   3"

Polyethylene sheeting   ¼" gravel

Concrete   2×6 decking

8"

8"   Weed block fabric   ¼" gravel

Brick set on edge   2×6 decking

3¼"   4¼"

8"   Weed block fabric   ¼" gravel

After excavating, provide for weed control (see page 121) and install the gravel.

Sleepers and Decking

Cut 4×4s to length for the sleepers and lay them on the gravel bed. You can use 2×4s or 2×6s to reduce the thickness of the deck, but they provide less clearance for air circulation and give less structural rigidity. The sleeper spacing on this deck is 42 inches, which requires the spanning strength of 2×6 decking. If you use 2×4s or smaller decking boards, add more sleepers. Space sleepers for 2×4 decking no more than 24 inches apart; for 1-inch decking, space them no more than 16 inches apart.

MATERIALS LIST

Base	200 sq ft 4-mil polyethylene sheeting		
	1.75 cu yd ¼" gravel		
Sleepers	4×4s	2	10' lengths
		3	16' lengths
Decking	2×6s	12	8' lengths
		20	14' lengths (188 sq ft)
Nails	7# 12d HDG common		
Curb Options			
A) Fascia	2×4s	2	6' lengths
		1	10' length
		1	14' length
		1	16' length
		1	18' length
B) Concrete	1 cu yd concrete		
	120" 1×8 (for forms) (8" × 8" × 60')		
C) Brick	½ cu yd concrete		
	360 common bricks and mortar		

Nail the decking boards with two 12d or 16d HDG nails at each sleeper (use three nails for 6-inch boards), using a string line or straightedge to ensure a straight, even pattern. You can lay the boards diagonally or in a complex pattern (see page 149), but if you do, the actual spans for the decking boards will be greater than the sleeper spacing. To compensate, place the sleepers closer together.

Place any border around the excavation before building the deck. Nail 2×4 fascia boards around the perimeter of above-grade decks. Stain or paint the deck after it has seasoned.

A NEW DECK FOR AN OLD PATIO

A sleeper deck system is a great way to cover an existing patio. Although a patio is certainly a useful and pleasing design element for any landscape, some patios may be too small, may absorb too much heat from the sun, or may be cracked and damaged. Covering a patio with a deck might be easier than replacing it, and you may prefer the color, texture, and line patterns of natural wood over the appearance of concrete or masonry. The deck featured in this plan is for a condominium with a small yard

A NEW DECK FOR AN OLD PATIO

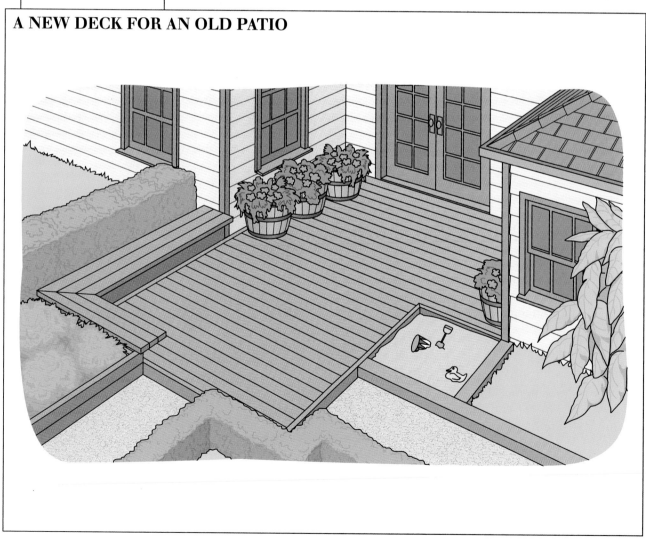

FRAMING PLAN AND SECTION

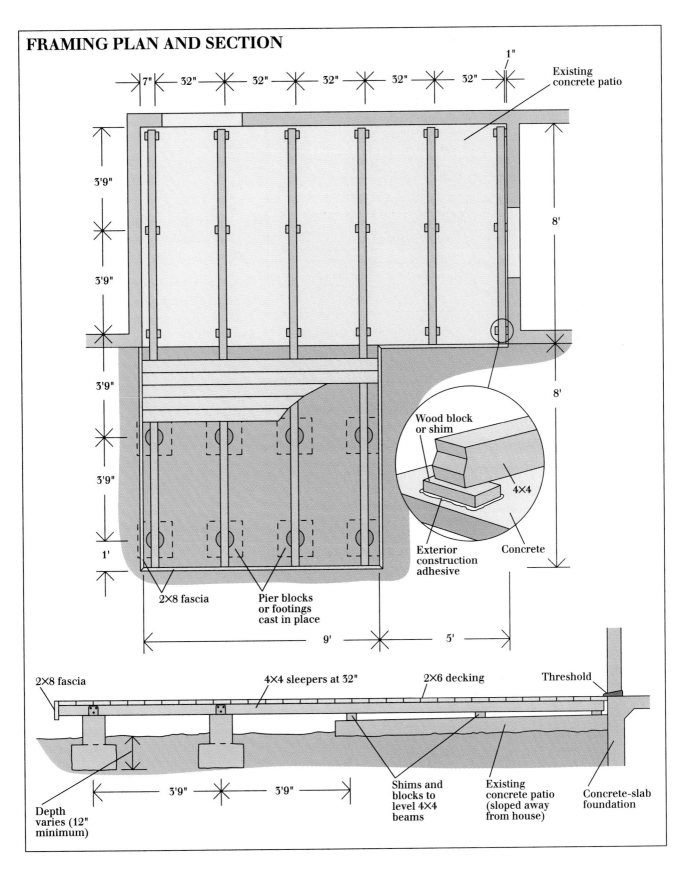

7" 32" 32" 32" 32" 32" 1"

Existing concrete patio

3'9"

3'9"

8'

3'9"

3'9"

8'

3'9"

1'

Wood block or shim

4×4

Exterior construction adhesive

Concrete

2×8 fascia

Pier blocks or footings cast in place

9' 5'

2×8 fascia

4×4 sleepers at 32"

2×6 decking

Threshold

3'9" 3'9"

Shims and blocks to level 4×4 beams

Existing concrete patio (sloped away from house)

Concrete-slab foundation

Depth varies (12" minimum)

MATERIALS LIST

Footings	(Materials for 8; number can vary)		
	10.5 cu ft concrete		
	{for 8 piers (8" × 8" × 8") and footings (12" × 12" × 12")}		
	8 metal post anchors		
	16 ⅜" × 4½" carriage bolts with nuts and washers		
Sleepers	4×4s	2	8' lengths
		4	16' lengths
	Shims and scrap blocks		
	1 tube exterior construction adhesive		
Decking	2×6s	16	14' lengths
		8	18' lengths (184 sq ft)
Fascia	2×8s	2	8' lengths
		1	14' length
Nails	8# 12d HDG common		

and a correspondingly small patio. The deck solves these problems by extending usable activity space beyond the patio. It provides a strong focal point for the yard and creates an inviting access to a shade garden or lawn. It has ample room for two separate activity areas, perhaps one for outdoor dining and the other for a children's play area.

Site Preparation and Footings

A concrete or masonry patio is an excellent base for a deck and requires no particular preparation. It should slope away from the house. If you want to extend the deck beyond the patio, as this plan shows, you must provide bearing for the sleepers. If the patio is level and the area around it well drained, you may be able to prepare a gravel bed beyond the patio and lay sleepers directly on it (see page 179). More likely, the patio is sloped and the ground beyond it cannot easily be raised to its level. In this case, you'll need to provide concrete piers and footings for the sleepers. This plan shows typical dimensions for footings, although depths and sizes will vary according to local

conditions (see pages 129 to 137). Because the sleepers will lie directly on the piers, with no posts, the piers must be level with each other. The easiest way to ensure this is to form and build the piers and footings together rather than use precast piers.

Installing Sleepers

When laying sleepers on a patio, you can minimize warping by attaching them to the concrete with exterior construction adhesive, concrete nails, or expansion bolts designed for concrete. If the patio slopes, level each sleeper with shims. Nail the shims to the bottom of the sleeper first, and then turn it over and nail or glue the sleeper to the patio. This plan uses 4×4 sleepers because they also act as beams. The spacing between footings (and therefore the number of footings) can be adjusted by using sleepers having a greater depth. Using sleeper material of a different size can also vary the height of the deck. In all cases, the lumber must be pressure-treated or of a durable species, and long boards set directly on the patio should run parallel to the slope to avoid becoming dams that trap water.

The spacing between sleepers depends on the span limits of the decking. This plan uses 2×6s, which allow a wider distance between sleepers than 2×4s or 1-by lumber.

Installing Decking

Nail or glue the decking to the sleepers, as described on page 179. It is best to lay out all the boards first so you can adjust for any variations in appearance. Nail 2×8 fascia boards around the exposed edges of the deck. Designs that use sleepers and decking thicker than those in this plan will require fascia material sized accordingly.

A SIMPLE GARDEN PLATFORM

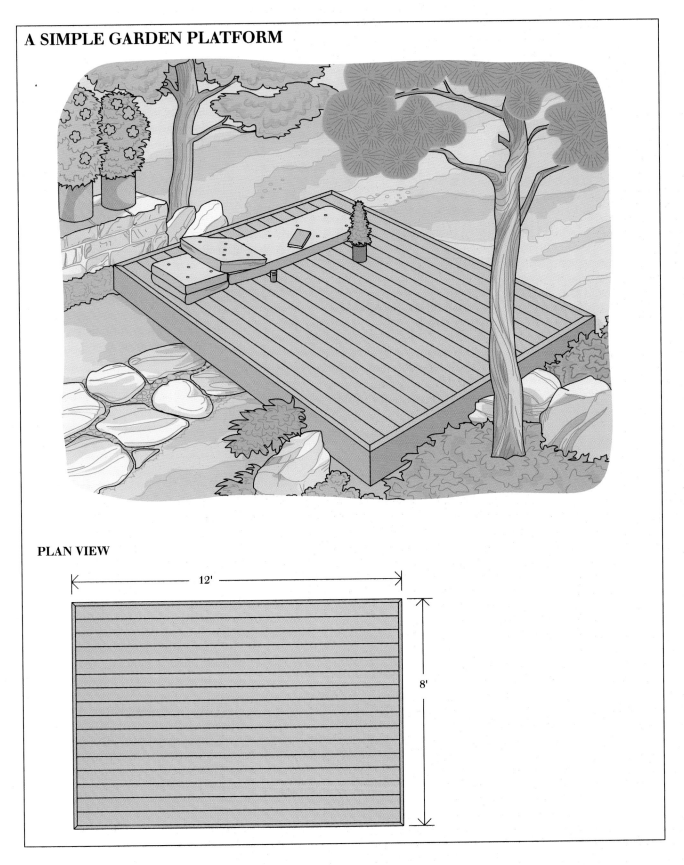

PLAN VIEW

MATERIALS LIST

Footings	15.5 cu ft concrete		
	{for 6 piers (8" × 8" × 8") and footings (18" × 18" × 12")}		
	2×6s	6 blocks for piers	
Framing			
Beams	4×6s	2	12' lengths
Joists	2×6s	10	8' lengths
Joist hangers	2×6s	20	
Decking	2×6s	16	12' lengths (96 sq ft)
Fascia	2×10s	2	8' lengths
		2	12' lengths
Nails	2# joist hanger nails		
	7# 12d HDG common		
	5# 12d HDG common		

A SIMPLE GARDEN PLATFORM

This freestanding deck (see page 183) is a permanent, raised platform that can go anywhere in a level yard. It is an ideal solution for a problem area, such as a drab corner that never seems to get used or an area unsuited for plants. Use it as a retreat, a dining area, a fantasy platform for children's play, or a planter display area. Because it is wood, it blends well with the garden and will not overheat in direct sun. It is raised high enough to provide some detachment from other areas of the yard but is low enough to maintain intimacy with the surroundings and to retain the privacy provided by existing fences or shrubbery.

Because it is a simple rectangle, the deck can reflect other landscaping or architectural forms, such as fences, lawns, planting beds, and the house itself. Locate it carefully, however, so that its straight edges are oriented along an existing visual axis; otherwise, its size and strong form can make it look out of place or create a disturbing tension. Even if placed strategically, there may be some danger of too many hard edges and straight lines

if the landscape already has an abundance of geometric forms. The easiest solution is to soften the deck with plantings around its perimeter. You could also add a meandering pathway of curved pavers leading to the deck, or alter the corners of the lawn or planting beds so they are curved rather than square. The overall effect and visual impact of this deck are limited only by imagination. It can look stark and striking surrounded by an expanse of level lawn, or subtle and rich nestled into a grotto of trees in a remote corner of the yard.

Construction Techniques
This small platform is intended to be as low to the ground as possible and still maintain required clearances between earth and wood. Because it's not attached to the house, you may be able to reduce the clearance normally required for an attached structure. Check local codes.

Layout and Footings
The piers for this deck are on the perimeter. Locate string lines so the outside edges of the piers will be flush with the outside face of the beams and so the fascia can cover them. All piers must be level because the girders rest directly on them. To connect the piers and beams, use pressure-treated woodblocks rather than metal post anchors, because woodblocks can be set flush with the outside edge of the pier and beam. Embed the blocks in the piers while the concrete is wet.

Beams and Joists
For the structural members of a deck this close to the ground, use pressure-treated lumber suitable for ground contact or heartwood of redwood or cedar. Use HDG nails, including the joist-hanger nails, and leave a ¼-inch gap between the ends of the joists and the beams.

The end joists are 7 inches longer than the others and are attached to the beam ends with facenailing rather than joist hangers. It may be necessary to excavate under some of the joists to provide adequate clearance.

Decking

This plan shows 2×6 decking, but because the joists are spaced 16 inches apart, you can use decking of smaller dimensions.

FRAMING PLAN AND SECTION

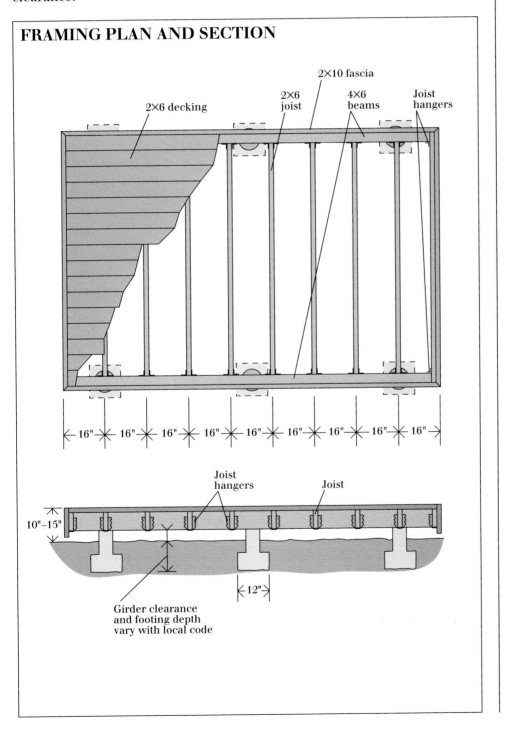

2×10 fascia

2×6 joist

4×6 beams

Joist hangers

2×6 decking

16" 16" 16" 16" 16" 16" 16" 16" 16"

Joist hangers

Joist

10"–15"

12"

Girder clearance and footing depth vary with local code

Fascia and Finish

The 2×10 fascia provides a skirt for the deck that hides the piers, keeps out leaves and debris, helps the deck hug the ground, and creates a finished border for the decking boards. If the deck is set into a shallow excavation and is therefore closer to the ground, you can use other sizes or thicknesses of lumber for the fascia, such as 1×12 or 2×8. If the deck is more than 10 inches above grade, you should provide a low step (see page 159 for techniques). Finish the deck as desired with stain or paint, or allow natural weathering.

FRAMING PLAN AND SECTION

2×6 decking   2×10 fascia

4×8 beams

9"

3'3"

3'3"

9"

8'

16"   9'4"   16"

12'

Step

15"

6"

Depth varies with local codes

A SIMPLE VARIATION

This plan (at left) is a variation of the low garden platform, with the decking running the short distance rather than long. Its shorter decking boards "widen" the short dimension and make the deck feel less like a corridor. This is an important feature where serenity and repose is important, as well as with elongated decks.

Construction Techniques

The structural system for this deck consists of only three beams. The beams are 4×8 instead of 4×6, so only two footings are needed for each one. You can change the size of the deck by lengthening the beams or by adding new beams to widen it. With this system it is possible to make large platforms set low to the ground, although they require more footings than a joist-over-beam system.

Layout and Footings

Because the footings are set in from the perimeter, you can center the piers under the beams instead of setting them flush with the edges. Keep the piers level with one another, because the beams rest directly on them.

Beams and Decking

Use pressure-treated or other decay-resistant lumber for the beams. Run the decking over their tops and nail. Use full 8-foot pieces and then trim them to 7 feet 9 inches, preferably along both sides to produce clean, straight edges. The 7-foot 9-inch length allows an 8-foot fascia board, but if you use longer fascia material, you needn't trim the decking.

Fascia and Finish

On this deck the fascia is more than decorative. It also stabilizes the overhanging ends of the decking boards, which might warp and twist. The fascia boards along the sides need to be connected to the decking as well as to each end of the short fascia boards. If you nail the fascia onto the ends of the decking boards, the large number of nails required will look like upholstery tacks. A solution to this problem is to nail a 2×4 cleat inside the fascia board before installing it and then nail the decking boards down onto the cleat. To temporarily stiffen the fascia against the downward pressure of this nailing, place a car jack or blocking under the section being nailed. Because this deck uses deeper beams, it is 15 inches high and requires a low step. Running such a step along one entire side makes a nice bench for sitting, relaxing, or displaying plants. For construction details see page 192.

AN L-SHAPED COMBINATION

This plan shows one way to combine the two structural systems featured for low platforms. The result is an L-shaped deck that is large enough for both a transition walkway and a separate activity area. Plantings help define the direction of flow, create a sense of closure, and define the grassy open space embraced by the deck. This deck is really a combination of the simple garden platform and the simple variation (pages 184 to 186). One section is supported by two 18-foot

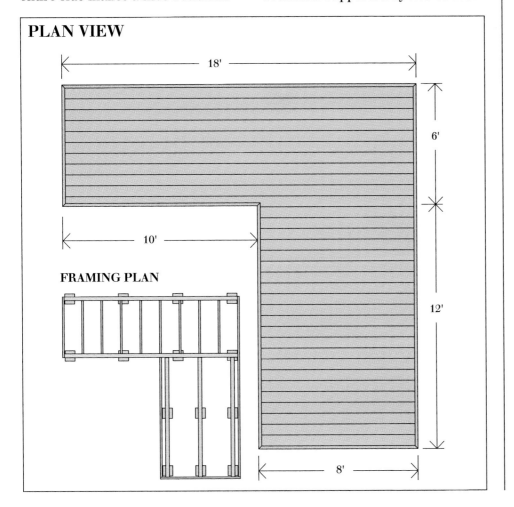

PLAN VIEW

FRAMING PLAN

A FLOATING DECK FOR GENTLE SLOPES

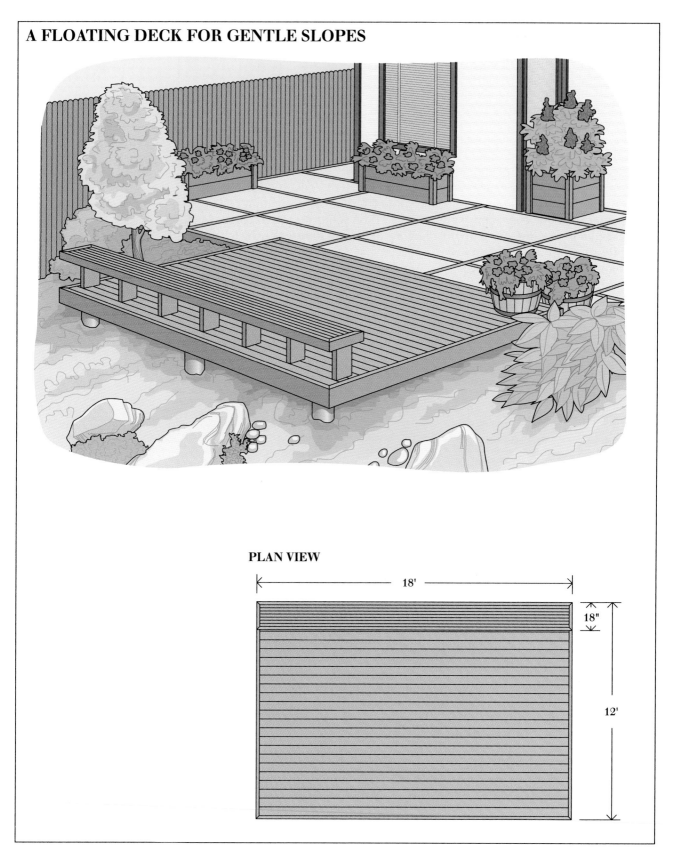

PLAN VIEW

18'

18"

12'

beams placed 6 feet apart, with 2×6 joists hung between them on 24-inch centers. The footings are 5 feet 6 inches on center.

Framing Plan

The other section is identical to the deck on page 186, except that the girders are 4×6 instead of 4×8 and each one has three supports. Beam hangers attach the 12-foot beams to the 18-foot beam. Note that the center footings for the 12-foot beams are closer to the intersection (4 feet 6 inches) than to the end of the 8-foot-wide arm (7 feet 6 inches). A long, low step along the edge of the grass completes this deck, providing easy access to the grass as well as additional seating or display space. Use 2×6 fascia on the deck edge so the step can tuck under it, making the deck appear to float out over the step.

A FLOATING DECK FOR GENTLE SLOPES

This deck (opposite) is the perfect solution for a neglected sloping corner of the yard or for small yards that have no level space. It could even be lengthened to extend across an entire backyard that slopes away from the house. It is featured on a gentle slope here, but the same structure could easily be adapted for steeper slopes by lengthening the posts and increasing the footing depths. A railing would be required along any side of the deck that is more than 30 inches above the ground (or whatever local codes require). For gentle slopes, a bench is sufficient protection, if needed.

Access to the deck is easiest from the uphill side, so it is most appropriate for yards that slope away from the house or main part of the garden. To make the approach

cleaner and the deck even more accessible, you could build a simple retaining wall of masonry or pressure-treated timbers along the uphill edge of the deck (see page 242). One or more steps would be required for approaches from the downhill side.

The joist-and-beam structure of this deck allows the footings to be set back from all the edges 1 to 2 feet, or even more with larger-sized lumber. This conceals the piers and posts, making the deck appear to float.

This effect creates interesting possibilities for breaking up flat space, accenting horizontal planes, or extending level areas. Although this plan is designed to accommodate sloping ground, it can be built on level ground as well. Page 190 shows a possible setting for this deck in a level yard.

MATERIALS LIST

Footings	23 cu ft concrete {for 9 piers (8" × 8" × 8") and footing (18" × 18" × 12")}		
	9 metal post anchors		
	18 ⅜" × 4½" carriage bolts with nuts and washers		
Framing			
Posts	4×4s	1	8' length (for 6 short posts; length will vary)
Beams	4×6s	3	18' lengths
Joists	2×6s	10	12' lengths
Blocking	2×6s	1	18' length (cut into 9 22½" ± pieces)
Decking	2×6s	24	18' lengths (216 sq ft)
Fascia	2×8s	2	12' lengths
	2×8s	2	18' lengths
Bench			
Uprights	2×8s	2	10' lengths (cut into 10 23½" pieces)
Cleats	2×4s	1	14' length (cut into 10 15" pieces)
Seat	2×2s	9	18' lengths
Trim	2×4s	2	20' lengths
Bolts	20 ⁵⁄₁₆" × 3½" carriage bolts with nuts and washers		
	20 ⅜" × 3½" carriage bolts with nuts and washers		
Nails	5# 8d HDG box or finish (for bench)		
	10# 12d HDG common		
	7# 16d HDG common		

A FLOATING DECK FOR LEVEL GROUND

A FLOATING DECK FOR LEVEL GROUND

Here is the same deck as the previous plan, used as a freestanding platform in a level yard. Its structural system makes it higher than the floating deck for gentle slopes; but for a very large deck, it has the advantage of fewer footings. Its overhangs also create a hovering effect that gives clear definition from the surrounding garden. Because it is not high enough to require a railing, it provides both contact and detachment at the same time. Access is provided by a step and transition platform. Other possibilities might be a bridge from the house or from part of the yard, or you might want to attach the deck to the house (see page 121 for specific techniques).

Construction Techniques

The structural system of joists resting on beams is a common and versatile approach to deck framing. You can move the footings in from the edges of the deck, redesign the structure for varying conditions without changing the size of the deck, or adapt it to any change in overall size or shape. For instance, this deck has three beams in order to use low-profile, 2×6 joists. If you wish to reduce the number of footings or increase the deck's thickness, however, you could use 2×8 joists, 16 inches on center, and only two beams.

FOOTING AND FRAMING PLAN

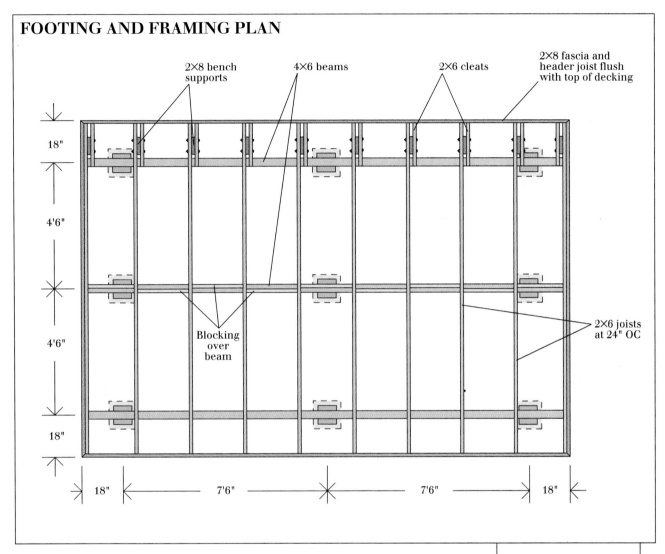

2×8 bench supports

4×6 beams

2×6 cleats

2×8 fascia and header joist flush with top of decking

18"

4'6"

4'6"

18"

Blocking over beam

2×6 joists at 24" OC

18" 7'6" 7'6" 18"

Layout and Footings

To mark the footing locations, stretch three string lines to represent one edge of each of the beams, and another to represent one end of the deck. You will need these lines later to install posts. Use layout techniques for slopes, which means measuring all distances along a level plane rather than along sloping ground.

When excavating for footings on a slope, dig the holes slightly deeper than the code requirements for level ground (2 or 3 inches for gentle slopes). Always measure the depth of the hole from the downhill edge.

In spite of being on a slope, the footings and piers for this deck are easy to build because only those at the top of the slope have to be level with each other. Make sure the pier blocks or metal anchors for each beam are in perfect alignment.

Posts, Beams, and Joists

Install the top beam first, attaching it directly to its three piers. Use shims to level it, if necessary. Then install posts for the other two beams. Cut the posts slightly long before installing them, rather than to exact length. If the posts are not made of pressure-treated lumber,

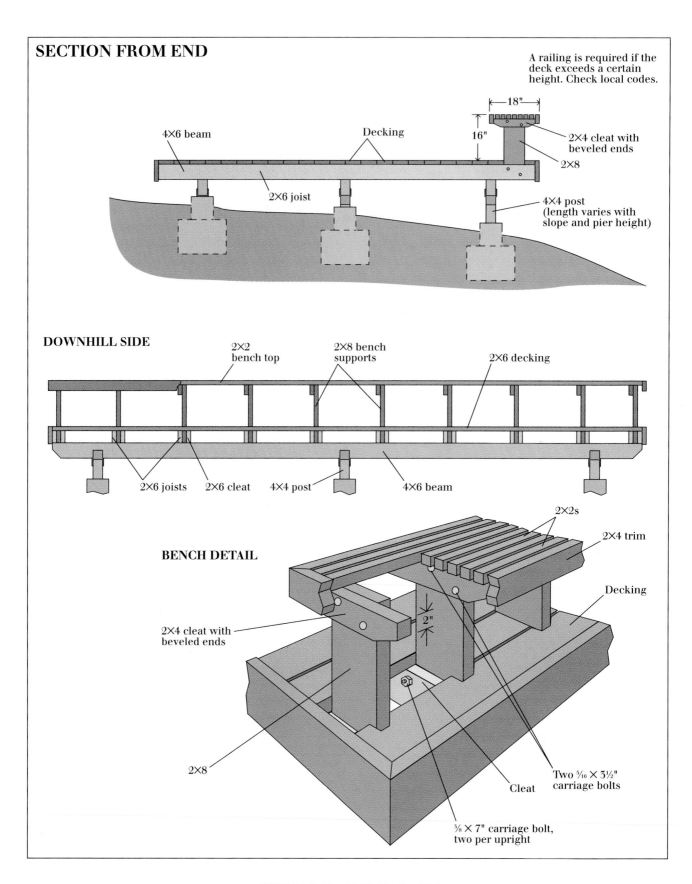

SECTION FROM END

A railing is required if the deck exceeds a certain height. Check local codes.

18"

16"

4×6 beam

Decking

2×4 cleat with beveled ends

2×8

2×6 joist

4×4 post (length varies with slope and pier height)

DOWNHILL SIDE

2×2 bench top

2×8 bench supports

2×6 decking

2×6 joists

2×6 cleat

4×4 post

4×6 beam

BENCH DETAIL

2×2s

2×4 trim

Decking

2×4 cleat with beveled ends

2"

2×8

Cleat

Two ⁵⁄₁₆ × 3½" carriage bolts

⅜ × 7" carriage bolt, two per upright

soak the ends in wood preservative. When the posts are in place, plumb them and nail temporary diagonal braces. Then level each post to the bottom of the top beam and mark the post for cutting. Align the ends of all the beams with the string line, and attach girders to the posts with metal connectors. Then toe-nail the 2×6 joists to the beams. Install blocking over the center beam and header joists along both sides. Trim the joist ends for a straight, clean edge. Install the header joists the same day as the field joists; otherwise, their ends may warp.

Decking and Fascia

Nail or glue the decking boards. When you get to the 2×8 bench uprights, provide support for the decking by nailing a wood cleat onto the side of each upright opposite the joist it is bolted to. Then either notch a long decking board or cut short lengths of decking to fit between the uprights. Finish out the deck with a full-length board. The top edge of the fascia is flush with the deck surface. This plan uses 2×8s to maintain a sleek look, but if you want to conceal more of

the understructure, or if you are using deeper joists than 2×6s, you can use wider fascia boards. You can use a 2×12 fascia to hide the beam ends, or you can bevel them.

Bench

Any bench design can be used for this deck, but the one shown is very sturdy and has a simple, clean look. (On a larger deck, widen the top to 24 inches and change the uprights to 2×12s.) When you install the 2×8 uprights, be sure they are all level. The easiest way is to mark each one exactly 18 inches from the top and align this mark along the top edge of the joist when bolting it. Then cut the 2×4 cleats, beveling each end so it doesn't protrude below the 2×4 trim piece. Bolt them in place so they are centered on the 2×8 upright and level. Nail 2×2s into the cleats, toenailing from the sides so the nails don't show. Predrill before nailing into any ends to avoid splits. When all the 2×2s are in place, trim the ends; then install the 2×4 trim boards by nailing them into the cleats. Miter the corners for a more finished look.

HOW TO ADAPT A PLAN
If you need to adapt a plan to fit your particular situation, follow these guidelines:
■ To expand a deck outward from the house, lengthen the joists. You can safely extend them beyond the beam—this extension is called a cantilever—as long as the length of the cantilever section is less than half the joist span between beam and ledger. To extend the deck even farther, add a second beam or move the first beam out and make all the joists larger.
■ To extend the width of a deck, lengthen the ledger and beam and add more joists. The longer beam will require an additional footing or two, or you can enlarge the beam and increase the spacings between posts.
■ To shorten a deck along its length, reduce the number of joists and use shorter decking boards.

The beam and ledger must also be shortened accordingly.
■ To make a deck narrower, move the beam closer to the house and use shorter joists. You will also need fewer decking boards.
■ The easiest changes to a deck's shape involve variations on a basic rectangle. For instance, wrapping a deck around a corner of the house or adding an extension will change the deck from a rectangle to an L. Structurally, this change involves the same principles as enlarging a deck, except that you are lengthening only some of the joists, adding a short beam under the new addition instead of the entire deck, and so on. You can also vary the basic rectangle by treating the extensions as separate decks joined to the original platform to create an L, T, or other shape.

PATIO CONSTRUCTION

A patio can be simpler to install than a deck—basically, it's no more than a paved area. This patio is a quiet haven in a densely populated urban neighborhood.

Patio design and construction differ from deck design and construction in significant ways. Decks float above the ground plane; patios are bedded onto or into the earth. In fact, most patios comprise earth materials such as rock or clay, transformed into paving materials—concrete aggregate, brick, and tile. The task is to combine these smaller units into a smooth surface designed to facilitate outdoor living. Technically, the task is pretty straightforward—no span tables to worry about here. The challenge is the hard work that patio installations require. Most of the difficulty lies in excavating the site and moving relatively heavy materials. But the results are rewarding—a smooth surface tailor-made for outdoor living, melding beautifully with the landscape.

DRAWING WORKING PLANS

Working drawings clearly illustrate overall dimensions, footings, and material patterns. They are essential for planning construction steps and ordering materials. They are used to demonstrate to the building department that the design is in keeping with municipal codes. You'll need the following views, by themselves or combined into one drawing.

❑ The *base plan* (see pages 21 to 29) shows the patio's position relative to the overall landscape. You likely will have completed this earlier, but will need have it in hand when applying for necessary permits. If the site is sloped, the base plan will be invaluable for working out the various patio levels, the rise and run of any stairs, and rough dimensions for preparatory grading.

❑ A *final site plan* provides an overhead view of the lot that details all the known facts—the patio shape, dimensions, and pattern, including the concrete finish or brick layout, and where permanent features and plantings will be located in relation to the patio.

❑ *Elevation drawings* are sections that show the details of footings and the depths of the various layers of materials that make up the patio. Draw these as if you are directly in front of, and level with, the area being viewed. All patios require a gravel bed for stability, whether the final surface is laid on sand, mortar, or concrete—or even if the final surface is concrete itself.

COMMON PATIO SITING OPTIONS

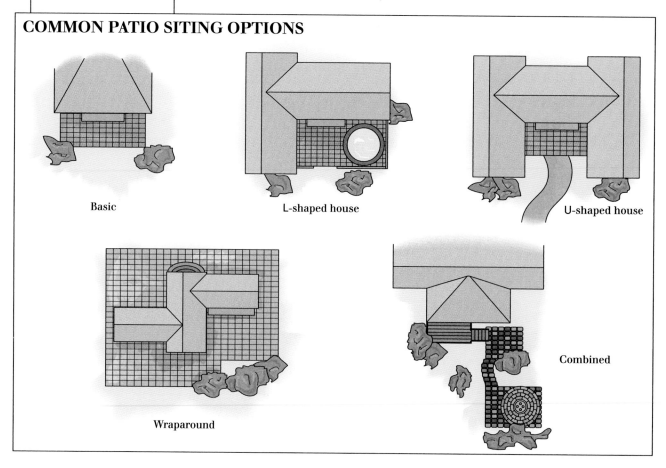

Basic

L-shaped house

U-shaped house

Wraparound

Combined

SITE PREPARATION AND LAYOUT

Preparation and layout tasks vary widely, depending on the complexity of the site and patio. If the site is level and you plan a simple surface such as brick on sand, you may need to just mark the patio perimeter. If the installation involves multiple levels and footings, however, careful layout and grading are required.

Rough-Grading the Site

In most cases grading is simply a matter of flattening high spots, filling in low spots, and making sure the site slopes in the right direction. You may have to rough-grade an area larger than the patio to make a smooth transition to the surrounding landscape. As you remove plants, make sure that you don't leave any roots thicker than 1 inch. Once roots decompose, they leave cavities in the ground that can cause a patio to buckle.

Laying Out a Square or Rectangular Patio

Begin by driving temporary stakes to mark the patio boundaries. Next, to square up the patio and establish guidelines for grading, construct batter boards. Made of a 2×4 crosspiece attached to two sharpened 2×4s pounded into the ground, batter boards let you attach mason's lines and adjust them as needed. Drive the 2×4 stakes 3 feet outside of the patio perimeter. (If space doesn't permit this, attach the 2×4 crosspiece to a nearby fence, shed, wall, or other structure.)

Using a hydro level, a long straightedge with a carpenter's level, or a line level, mark on each stake (or fence or wall) a point exactly 6 inches above the final patio surface. With 16 penny (16d) duplex nails, nail a 3- to 4-foot 2×4 crosspiece to the stakes so the top

FOUNDATIONS

FOUNDATION FOR SAND INSTALLATION

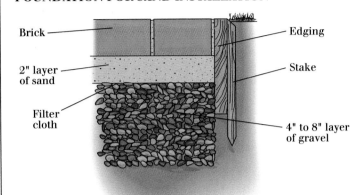

Brick — Edging
2" layer of sand — Stake
Filter cloth
4" to 8" layer of gravel

FOUNDATION FOR POURED CONCRETE

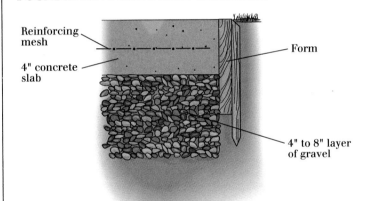

Reinforcing mesh — Form
4" concrete slab
4" to 8" layer of gravel

FOUNDATION FOR MORTARED INSTALLATION

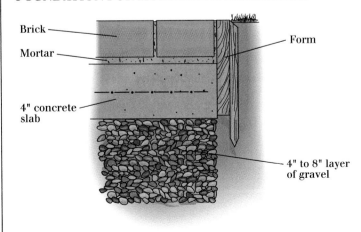

Brick — Form
Mortar
4" concrete slab
4" to 8" layer of gravel

ROUGH-GRADING THE SITE

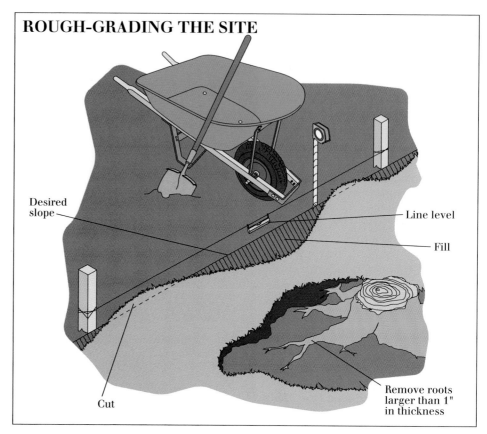

Desired slope

Line level

Fill

Cut

Remove roots larger than 1" in thickness

LAYING OUT A CURVED PATIO

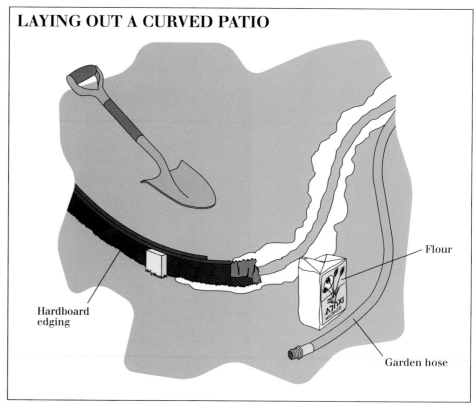

Flour

Hardboard edging

Garden hose

is even with the marks, attaching it to the sides of the stakes facing away from the patio. Brace the stakes diagonally with a 1-by piece of scrap lumber. Stretch out each string line again and drive a 6d nail into the top of each crosspiece where the line crosses over it. Tie the strings to the nails.

Next build batter boards for a third string line that will cross the first two at right angles on a line marking the outside edge of the patio. Use a line level to check that this line is level with the other two. Square the lines using the 3-4-5 tri-angle method: Mark a point along the house 3 feet from the outside edge of the patio. Attach a piece of tape to the string 4 feet from the house. Measure the distance be-tween the two marks. The corner is square when the distance is ex-actly 5 feet. (For greater accuracy, use multiples of 3–4–5: 6–8–10 or 9–12–15.) As a final test, measure between opposite corners. The diagonals will be exactly the same if the patio is square. Once all is square, drive a nail into each batter board where the string crosses it and tie the string to the nail.

Laying Out Curves and Radii

To mark for a curved edge, lay a garden hose in the exact shape of the future patio and pour flour on top of it. (A hose charged with water holds its shape best.) When you remove the hose, you will have a clearly defined line. If you plan a circular patio, lay it out using a compass made of mason's twine at-tached to a stake. Hold a can of spray paint at the desired radius and mark the ground as you walk along the arc. To mark for initial excavation, make the radius 6 inch-es longer than needed.

BUILDING BATTER BOARDS

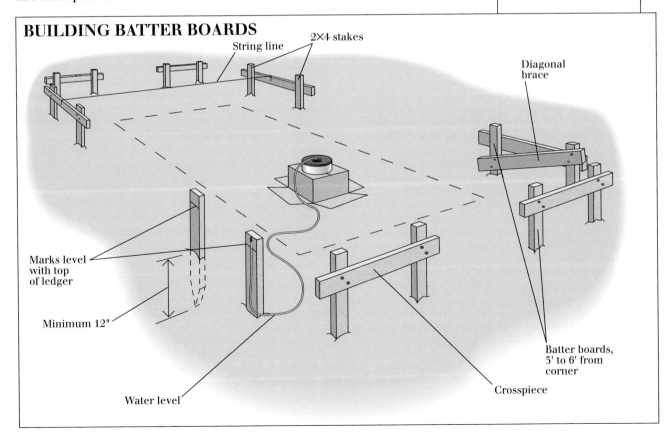

2×4 stakes
String line
Diagonal brace
Marks level with top of ledger
Minimum 12"
Water level
Batter boards, 3' to 6' from corner
Crosspiece

A GRID FOR CHECKING EXCAVATION DEPTH

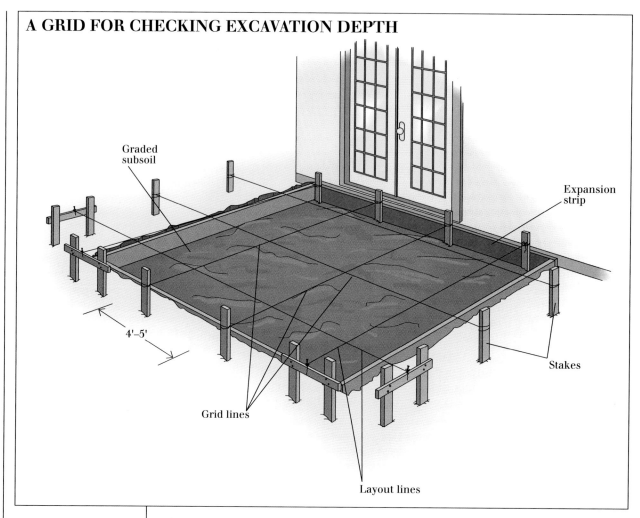

Graded subsoil

Expansion strip

4'–5'

Stakes

Grid lines

Layout lines

Completing the Final Grading

Use 2-foot 2×4s to make one stake for every 4 feet of perimeter, shaping a point on one end. Drive the stakes about 2 feet outside the patio edge, starting with the sides that slope. Mark a reference point on the house 6 inches above the projected finished surface. Using a hydro level or line level, mark a batter-board stake level with that reference point. (If you're using a hydro level, check that both ends show the correct level before you make the mark. With a line level, position it roughly in the center of the line run rather than near either end; check for accuracy by reversing the level—it should read exactly the same when facing either direction.)

Now set the slope by measuring down 1 inch for every 8 feet of length. Mark that point, screw on the crosspiece, and tie the string in place. Use this grid to smooth the surface by digging and filling as necessary. Measure down 6 inches from the grid to occasionally check the grading.

Providing for Drainage

Patios can accumulate tremendous amounts of water. A certain amount will percolate through sand-based patios, but in most cases a means of drainage must be built into the site. For patios that need to accommodate only the water that accumulates

DRAINING A PATIO SURFACE

SUBSURFACE DRAINAGE PIPES

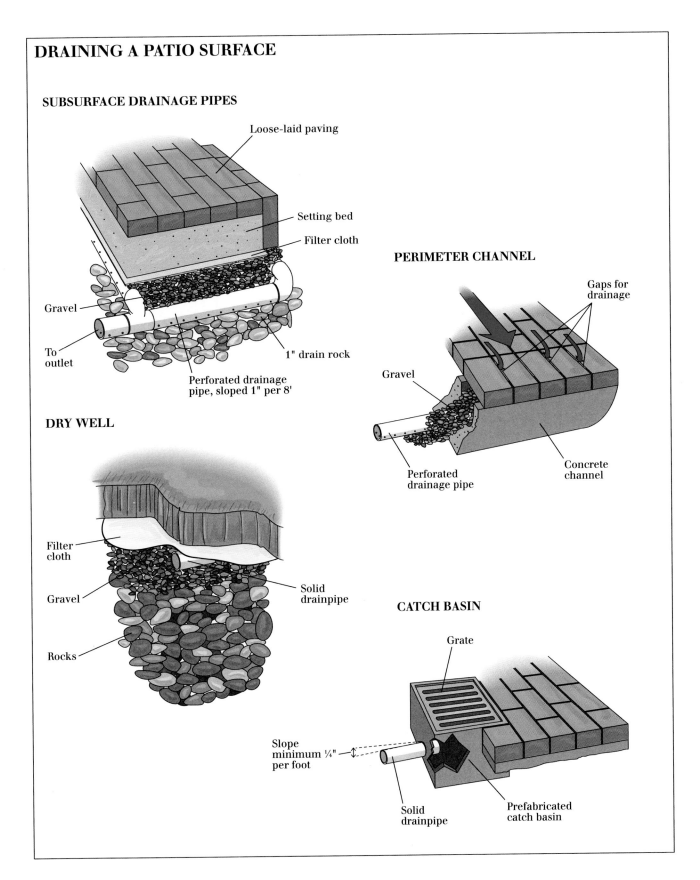

Loose-laid paving

Setting bed

Filter cloth

Gravel

To outlet

1" drain rock

Perforated drainage pipe, sloped 1" per 8'

PERIMETER CHANNEL

Gaps for drainage

Gravel

Perforated drainage pipe

Concrete channel

DRY WELL

Filter cloth

Gravel

Rocks

Solid drainpipe

CATCH BASIN

Grate

Slope minimum ¼" per foot

Solid drainpipe

Prefabricated catch basin

Brick-in-sand paving doesn't need extra drainage provisions. Water percolates down through the sand and will drain away as fast as in bare soil. Mortared brick, however, is almost impervious to water, and perimeter drainage must be considered.

directly on the patio surface, a border of gravel along the low edge of the patio will suffice. But in regions with heavy rainfall where patios are large or must handle runoff from adjacent hillsides, higher-capacity drainage systems must be installed.

Subsurface Drainage Pipes To help permeable patios cope with excess drainage, install subsurface perforated drainage pipe. Set it in a gravel bed and slope the pipe 1 inch for every 8 feet of run. Place

filter cloth over the gravel-filled trench to keep the pipe from clogging with sediment.

Perimeter Channel For a mortared brick patio, a perimeter channel made of concrete provides adequate support while carrying away water through voids left in the mortar at the low end of the patio.

Catch Basin For patios with impermeable surfaces, a catch basin acts as an enlarged drain that bears the water away to a dry well. The

patio should be inclined 1 inch for every 8 feet of run on all sides of the catch basin.

Dry Well The problem of what to do with runoff is solved by a dry well. Essentially a hole in the ground filled with rock, a dry well fills with water at times of high runoff, letting it slowly percolate into the surrounding soil. Completely buried in the ground, it is topped by a layer of filter cloth to slow sediment buildup.

These solutions require heavy excavation and careful planning to be effective. And though compensating for drainage is one of the least glamorous aspects of constructing a patio, it can make the difference between a sanctuary and a swamp. If the site is steeply sloped or at a low spot where runoff accumulates, consult a landscape designer for help.

INSTALLING A BRICK-IN-SAND PATIO

Ideal for the do-it-yourselfer, a sand- or crushed stone–based patio is easy to install, attractive, and durable. It is also relatively inexpensive. Along with attractiveness and ease of installation, a brick-in-sand patio offers another tremendous advantage: You can lay as much or as little material at a given time as you wish, because you don't have to worry about mortar setting up. And you can use the patio as soon as it is finished, because you don't have to wait for mortar to dry or concrete to cure.

CROSS SECTION OF BRICK-IN-SAND PATIO

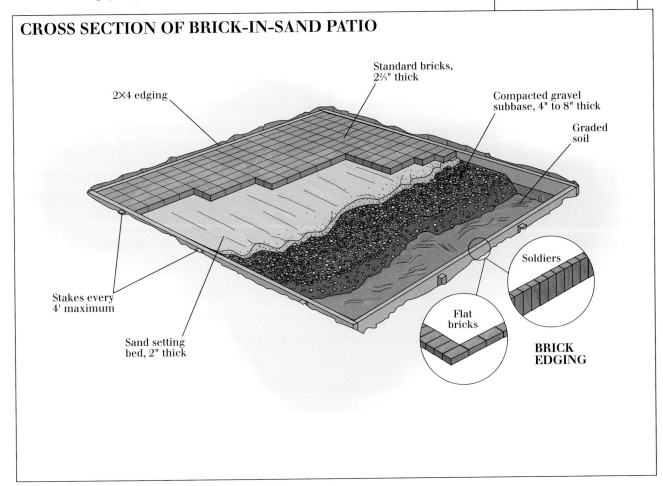

2×4 edging

Standard bricks, 2⅔" thick

Compacted gravel subbase, 4" to 8" thick

Graded soil

Stakes every 4' maximum

Sand setting bed, 2" thick

Soldiers

Flat bricks

BRICK EDGING

TOOLS FOR LAYING BRICKS IN SAND

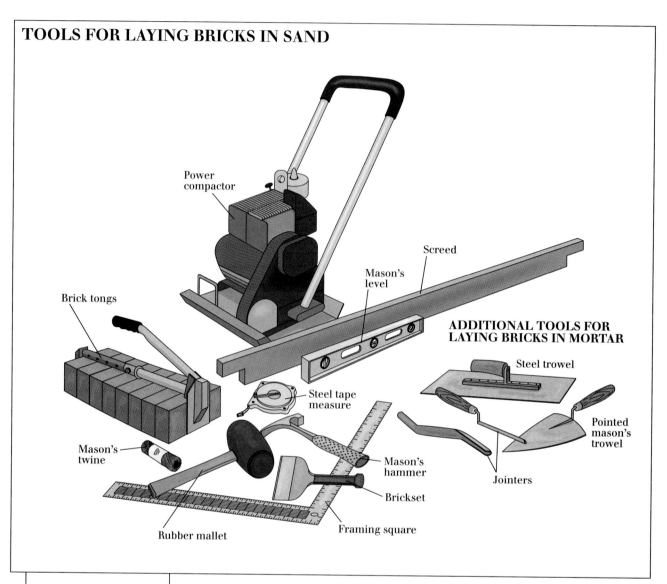

Power compactor

Screed

Mason's level

Brick tongs

ADDITIONAL TOOLS FOR LAYING BRICKS IN MORTAR

Steel trowel

Steel tape measure

Pointed mason's trowel

Mason's twine

Mason's hammer

Jointers

Brickset

Rubber mallet

Framing square

The Necessary Tools

There are very few specialized tools and even fewer technical skills required to install this type of patio. Besides measuring, counting, leveling, and shoveling, you will have to be able to cut bricks, which can be quickly learned if you have the right tools. Tools for laying bricks, concrete pavers, or stone on a sand base include a steel tape measure, a framing square, a 2-foot-long carpenter's level, a hammer, a mallet, mason's twine, a line level, a wheelbarrow, and safety goggles. In addition, to make the job easier you need the following specialized tools, which you can borrow, rent, or buy:

❏ A mason's level, at least 4 feet long, for checking level over large areas.
❏ A brickset or broad-bladed cold chisel for cutting and trimming bricks.
❏ A mason's hammer for trimming the rough edges of cut bricks.
❏ Brick tongs for carrying several bricks at a time.
❏ A screed for leveling the sand.
❏ A power compactor, to pack the gravel, sand, and brick paving.

Installing the Edging

The first step after the site is prepared is to install the edging to hold the sand and bricks firmly in place. Install edging after the subbase is laid and compacted but before laying the setting bed and paving. Dimensional lumber, a concealed concrete footing, poured concrete, and bricks set into the soil all provide the stable edging this kind of patio needs. See page 92 for a discussion of the different types of edging materials, and pages 238 to 241 for installation techniques.

Making the Setting Bed

A brick-in-sand setting bed consists of a 2-inch-deep layer of sand on top of the gravel subbase. Use the formula for estimating how much concrete to order (page 75) to determine how many cubic yards of sand you need.

Wet down the gravel subbase and cover it with sand. Using a shovel, spread the sand as evenly as possible over the gravel. Then screed or level it into a uniform, 2-inch-deep layer over the entire surface. This is the most important step in constructing this type of patio—a level base at this point directly translates into a smooth and level finished surface.

Make a screed by cutting 1½-inch-deep notches at each end of a straight 2×4. Make the screed long enough to ride on the patio edging and/or temporary guides. Working 3-foot-wide sections at a time, pull the screed in a sawing motion as you level the sand. Tamp the sand with a power compactor until the surface is firm. Add more sand if needed, and screed and tamp until you have a firm, 2-inch-deep layer.

LEVELING SAND SETTING BED

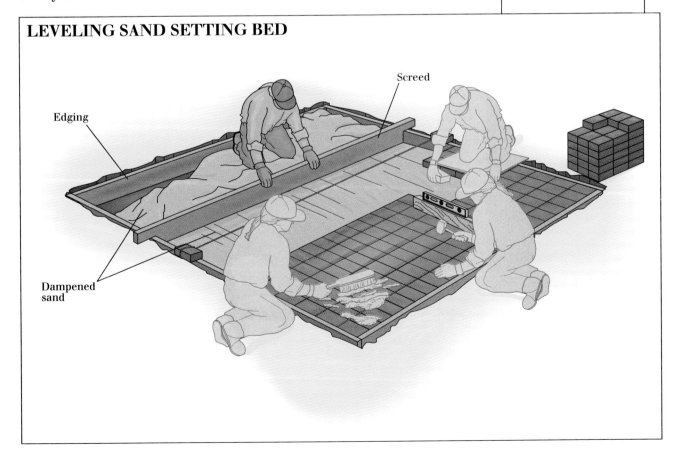

Edging

Screed

Dampened sand

SETTING BRICKS

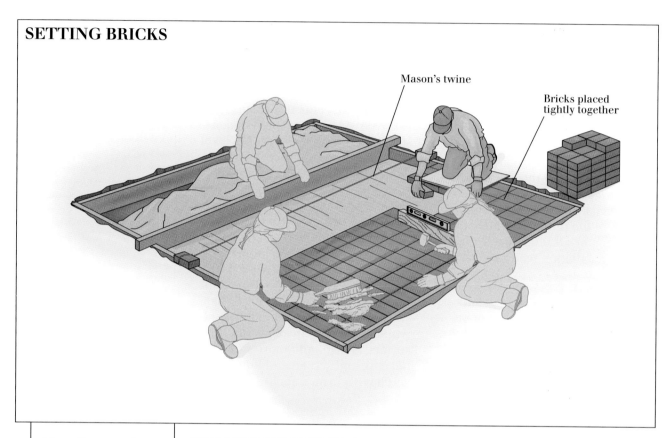

Mason's twine

Bricks placed tightly together

More than most other pavements, a sand-laid brick patio requires a firm edging to hold the bricks in place.

Laying the Bricks

Once you establish your rhythm, brick goes down with ease, and it is satisfying to watch the surface develop beneath your hands. Begin by dampening the sand. Then start laying the bricks in one corner, butting them tightly together in your chosen pattern. Do not slide the bricks into place—this shifts the sand. Instead, place each brick straight down into the sand and press it firmly into place with a hammer handle or rubber mallet. Lay one course at a time, using mason's twine to keep them straight. Frequently as you work, use a carpenter's level on a straight 2×4 to check for level. If you want the patio surface to be sloped for drainage, cut the 2×4 to a tapered shape to represent the degree of slope (⅛ inch per foot of length) so the level will read accurately. If a brick is too low, lift it and tamp a little damp sand under its low side to level it. If it is too high, lift it and gently scrape out some of the sand and tamp to level it.

Cutting the Bricks

Inevitably, you must cut some bricks to make the pattern fit within the patio space. Always wear safety goggles to protect your eyes from the flying chips and grit that

CUTTING BRICKS

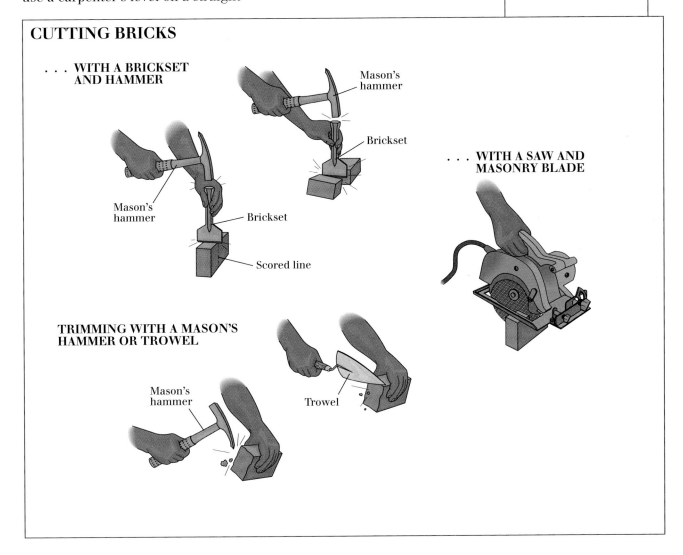

. . . WITH A BRICKSET AND HAMMER

Mason's hammer

Brickset

Mason's hammer

Brickset

Scored line

. . . WITH A SAW AND MASONRY BLADE

TRIMMING WITH A MASON'S HAMMER OR TROWEL

Mason's hammer

Trowel

are created when you cut brick. If you have just a few cuts to make, use a brickset or broad-bladed cold chisel to do the job. Use the tool, its beveled edge facing the waste piece, to score a cut line on all four sides. Do this by tapping the handle gently with a hammer. Then lay the brick flat on the sand, face side up, and place the tool on the scored line, its beveled edge again facing the waste piece. Strike the handle with a sharp blow of the hammer. The brick will break into two pieces along the scored line. Trim the rough edges with the brickset or a mason's hammer.

If the job involves many cuts, wait until the end and make them all at one time to ensure speed and accuracy. In this case, consider renting a hydraulic brick cutter. This large, stationary tool uses pressure to score and cleanly cut bricks, although you still have to trim them somewhat. If you need to make a lot of angle cuts or need very smooth cuts, rent a diamond-bladed tile saw.

Adding the Sand Fill

When all of the bricks are laid, cover the entire surface with a thin layer of fine sand. Work it around with a broom until the joints are filled. Spray the surface with a fine stream of water to compact the sand, being careful not to flood the joints. Repeat the sanding and spraying procedure until all the joints are packed full of sand. You can create an even more stable installation by using the power compactor to pack the bricks after filling the joints with sand. Place pieces of plywood over the bricks and run the compactor over them a few times, just as you did to tamp the gravel base and setting bed. After vibrating the brick, add a little more sand in the joints, clean up, and then have a party on your new patio.

SEATING BRICKS AND SPREADING SAND FILL

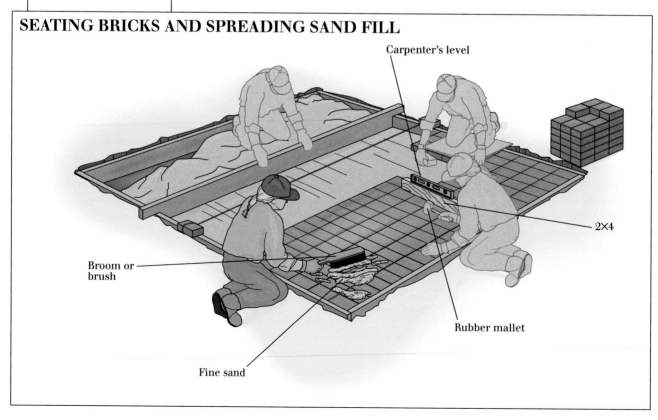

Carpenter's level

2×4

Rubber mallet

Fine sand

Broom or brush

INSTALLING INTERLOCKING CONCRETE PAVERS

Interlocking concrete pavers are a recent product, a hybrid made out of concrete and used like brick. The installation techniques are essentially the same as for bricks. Lay them on a bed of compacted sand, with a firm edging material installed along the side where you will begin (install the rest of the edgings as you complete the final row of pavers). Pavers can be cut using a brickset or a diamond-bladed tile saw. If the pattern requires perfectly straight lines, every few courses use a 2×6 and a mini sledgehammer to tap the side of the row. Use a taut mason's line to check for trueness. Concrete pavers usually have cleats built onto the sides to maintain a small space for sand fill between them.

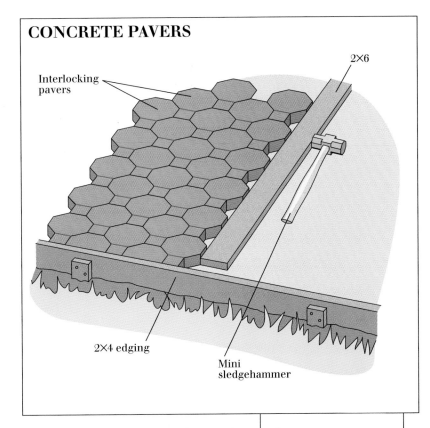

CONCRETE PAVERS

Interlocking pavers

2×6

2×4 edging

Mini sledgehammer

Concrete pavers come in a variety of patterns, creating effects from formal to casual.

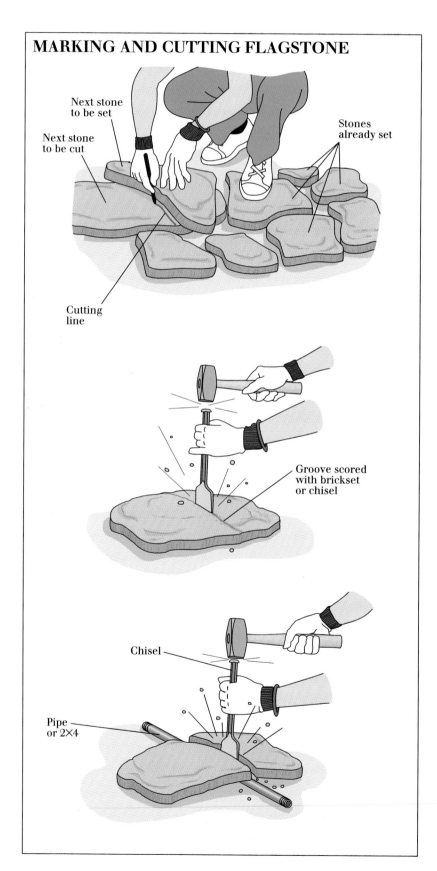

MARKING AND CUTTING FLAGSTONE

Next stone
to be set

Next stone
to be cut

Stones
already set

Cutting
line

Groove scored
with brickset
or chisel

Chisel

Pipe
or 2×4

INSTALLING A FLAGSTONE PATIO

Flagstone is a natural material for patios and ideally suited for a sand- or crushed-stone base. Although the surface of a flagstone is smooth, the thickness can vary. Flagstones are typically quarried from stratified stone and are split in thicknesses ranging from 1 to 3 inches. The adjustable base provided by sand or crushed stone makes it easy to accommodate the variations. Flagstones are usually slate, sandstone, and limestone.

Setting the Pattern

If you spend enough time arranging the stones, cutting will be reduced to a minimum. Be careful about the scale of the stone. Don't put all the big stones at the beginning and the smaller ones at the end; try for a even mix throughout. When you have determined where each stone fits into the pattern, number the stone with chalk so you can repeat the pattern exactly as you set the stones in place.

Cutting Flagstone

You will generally flip and turn the flagstones until you find a natural fit, but sometimes you have to cut them. Fortunately, this isn't difficult. To cut flagstone, first mark and score a line on one side with a pitching chisel. Then place the stone over a piece of pipe or a 2×4. Strike it sharply on the scored line with a hammer and chisel. To cut a curve to match another stone, use the other stone as a template and mark the cut line with a crayon or piece of chalk. Be sure that the scoring is fairly deep and as even as possible. Don't be discouraged if some stones break incorrectly.

Finishing Flagstone With Dry Mortar

The variation in flagstone makes it difficult to maintain even gaps between the stones. Often these gaps are too wide to be filled only with sand. Dry mortar is a straightforward alternative that produces a more stable installation in which the stones are less inclined to shift. Once the stones are laid, simply fill the joints with a mixture of sand and cement mortar, and gently wet the surface.

Laying an Edge

If the permanent edging will be a material other than wood, place temporary wood strips along all edges to hold the stones in place while you are working. Coat each edge form with oil so the mortar will not stick to it. The wood form can be installed as a permanent edging if heart redwood or pressure-treated wood is used. Stake the edging tightly in place so it will not shift while you work or while the mortar is hardening. Temporary edging can usually be removed after about 12 hours, although if conditions are wet and cool, you may have to wait as much as three days before removing it.

Mixing and Applying Dry Mortar

Combine 3½ parts plaster sand, 1 part portland cement, and ½ part masonry lime, or use a prepared bagged mix. Once the stones are laid out and the temporary or permanent edging is in place, fill the joints with the premixed dry mortar and tamp it down. If you are using temporary edging, pay particular attention to the joints next to the outer edge so that there will be no spaces or voids when the edging is removed. Before wetting the mortar, use a soft brush to remove any that has spilled onto the stones. Wet the mortar with a fine spray, being careful not to dislodge any of it; do not apply enough water to cause puddling. After five minutes wet the area again. It is important that the water penetrate through to the base. It may take a number of applications to properly soak all the material.

Filling the spaces between flagstones with dry mortar makes a rigid surface, suitable for heavier use than sand-filled cracks can support.

FLAGSTONE INSTALLED WITH DRY MORTAR

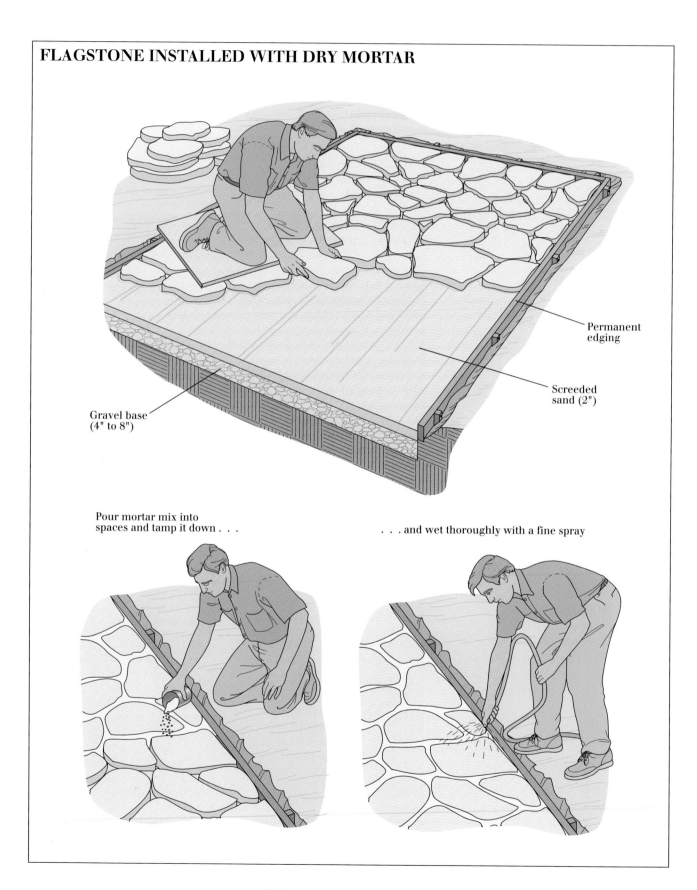

Permanent
edging

Screeded
sand (2")

Gravel base
(4" to 8")

Pour mortar mix into
spaces and tamp it down . . .

. . . and wet thoroughly with a fine spray

Some of the mortar joints may settle, depending on how well you tamped them. Fill any gaps. Let set for 12 hours, then use a heavy-duty sponge or a coarse material such as burlap or toweling soaked in water to wipe away the mortar stains. If water alone is insufficient, clean the stains with a solution of TSP (trisodium phosphate), available in any hardware store. Mix ½ cup TSP with a gallon of water. Always wear goggles and rubber gloves when working with cleaning compounds.

INSTALLING A POURED CONCRETE PATIO

Although more involved than setting bricks in sand, building a concrete patio is relatively inexpensive and is within the abilities of most do-it-yourselfers. There are dozens of interesting ways to create an attractive finished surface, or you can use the basic concrete slab as a foundation for other paving materials.

Concrete provides a stable patio surface that lasts a lifetime if it is

Poured concrete can be colored, shaped, and stamped to mimic almost any other paving material. This concrete pool deck looks like flagstone, but it was installed at a much lower cost and is more durable.

correctly installed. However, fresh concrete is a cumbersome material. It is heavy and requires that you work fast. Once the pour starts, you can't stop until the section is complete—struck-off, floated, edged, grooved, and troweled. That means you need two or more helpers for a patio measuring 12 by 15 feet, more if the patio is larger or if you have to transport concrete to the work site in wheelbarrows. It also means that you must be prepared: The forms have to be in place, you need the right tools on hand, and the concrete order must be accurate.

There is no advantage to mixing concrete yourself for a project as large as a patio. As dramatic as the concrete pour itself is, it is relatively unimportant to the final outcome of the project when compared with what must go on before and after. In effect, all concrete work is divided into two phases—

before the pour and after the pour—so you shouldn't focus on the pour itself any more than you have to. Handling bulk materials and mixing concrete is misplaced effort. For a discussion of figuring cubic footage and ordering concrete, see page 75.

The Necessary Tools

Besides a wheelbarrow, square-sided shovel, line level, and steel tape measure, you probably don't have the specialized tools necessary to give concrete a professional finish. You need these finishing tools to do a credible job:

❑ A pointed mason's trowel to smooth, cut, scrape, and chip concrete.
❑ A screed or strike-off board to level the wet concrete.
❑ A bull float or a darby to smooth out the wet concrete. A bull float is a long-handled float used on large surfaces. A darby is a

CONCRETE TOOLS

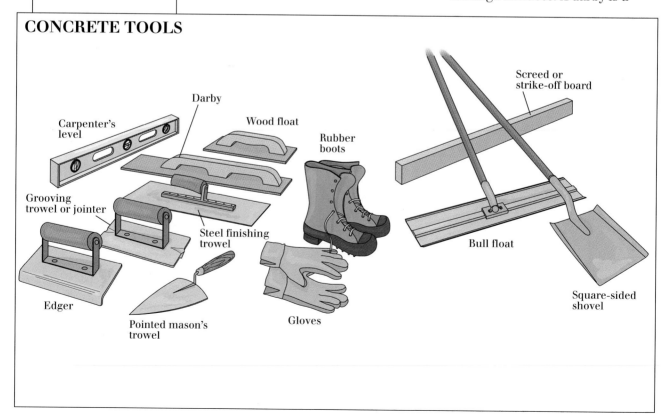

Carpenter's level

Darby

Wood float

Rubber boots

Screed or strike-off board

Grooving trowel or jointer

Steel finishing trowel

Bull float

Edger

Pointed mason's trowel

Gloves

Square-sided shovel

handheld wood tool used to float small surfaces.

❏ A wood float to give concrete a slightly coarse finish.

❏ A steel trowel to give concrete a smooth, glassy finish.

❏ An edger to form smooth edges.

❏ A metal grooving trowel or jointer to cut expansion or control joints.

You also need protective clothing. This includes thick work gloves to protect your skin from the caustic concrete, and heavy rubber work boots. Don't wear any clothes you can't afford to throw away when the job is done; standard cleanup should take care of most stains, but you don't want to take any chances.

Building the Formwork

Concrete is heavy and must be contained in well-braced forms. Make the forms and stakes with 2×4 lumber. Remember, 2×4 lumber is actually 3½ inches wide, whereas the concrete slab is actually a true 4 inches thick. To make up for this difference in depth, place ½ inch of backfill under the lumber so its top edge is flush with the ground and so concrete cannot seep under it during the pour.

There are two types of forms: temporary, which are removed after the concrete has cured, and permanent, which are incorporated into the patio surface.

CONCRETE PAVING FORMS

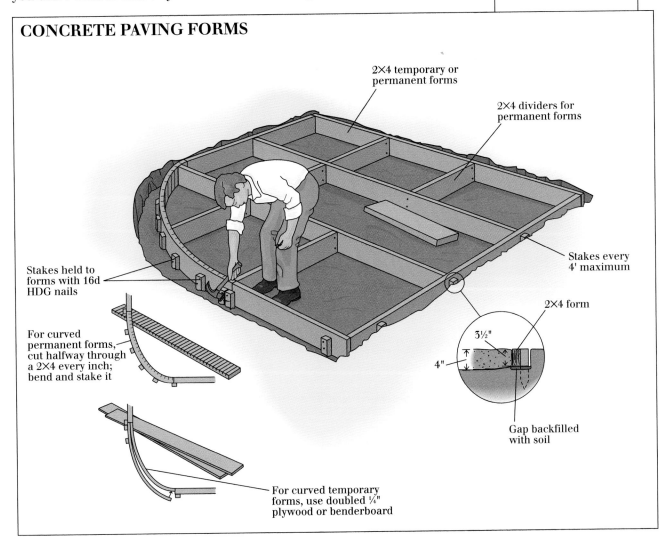

2×4 temporary or permanent forms

2×4 dividers for permanent forms

Stakes every 4' maximum

Stakes held to forms with 16d HDG nails

For curved permanent forms, cut halfway through a 2×4 every inch; bend and stake it

2×4 form

3½"

4"

Gap backfilled with soil

For curved temporary forms, use doubled ¼" plywood or benderboard

Temporary Forms Place the form boards around the patio perimeter, butting them end-to-end. The inner side of the boards form the slab's finished edge. Drive the stakes into the ground at 4-foot intervals and at every joint along the backside of the 2×4s. Drive them slightly below the top edges of the boards. Secure them by driving 16d hot-dipped galvanized (HDG) duplex nails through the stakes into the forms. Just before the pour, dampen the forms with an oil or release agent to make them easier to remove.

Permanent Forms Permanent forms become part of the patio's decorative treatment. Make them with heart redwood, cedar, or cypress that has been given a coat of clear wood sealer, or with pressure-treated lumber, which requires no preparation except coating any cut ends with preservative.

Join the boards at the corners with butt or miter joints. Drive the stakes 1 inch below the ground. Secure them by driving 16d HDG nails through the stakes into the boards. Also drive 16d HDG nails horizontally through the boards from the outside edge at midheight every 16 inches around the perimeter. These nails will help anchor the boards to the concrete. Cover the top edges of the forms with masking tape to prevent staining and other damage during the pour.

As you build both types of forms, check them frequently with a level to make sure the proper grade and slope are maintained. And with both types of forms, install a band of flexible concrete joint foam where the patio abuts the house.

CROSS SECTION OF A CONCRETE PATIO

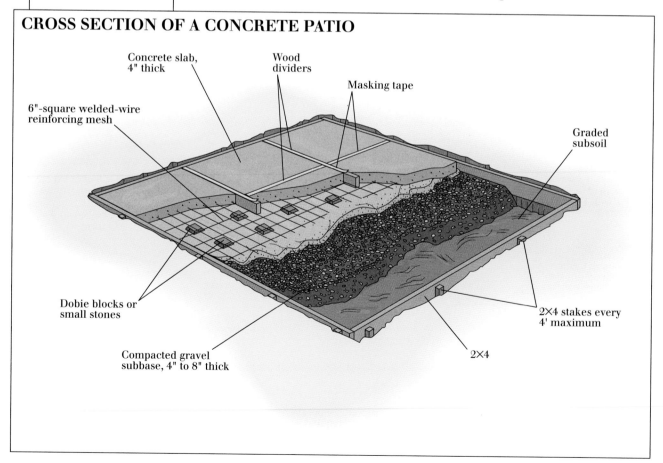

Concrete slab, 4" thick

Wood dividers

Masking tape

6"-square welded-wire reinforcing mesh

Graded subsoil

Dobie blocks or small stones

2×4 stakes every 4' maximum

Compacted gravel subbase, 4" to 8" thick

2×4

Making the Setting Bed

Once the formwork is built, dampen the compacted gravel subbase. Lay 6-inch-square welded-wire reinforcing mesh (called 6-6-10-10 reinforcing mesh) over the gravel. At frequent and regular intervals, lift the mesh and slip small stones or pieces of brick under it so it is held 1 to 2 inches above the gravel. If you install the wire in sections, overlap the sections by one square. Be careful when working with the mesh; it must be cut with a hacksaw or bolt cutters, and should be straightened as you unroll it, or it might spring back into a coil shape without warning.

Adding Divider Strips

If the patio is large, install divider strips at this time. They replace control or expansion joints as well as give the patio a decorative finish. They also give you the advantage of breaking the patio surface into sections that can be poured and finished one or two at a time.

Place these divider strips at a maximum of 10-foot intervals in both directions. Because they will remain in the concrete, make them of 2×4 heart redwood, cedar, or cypress or pressure-treated lumber. Give redwood, cedar, or cypress dividers a coat of clear wood sealer before installing them; pressure-treated dividers need no chemical treatment except at the cut ends.

No matter what wood you select, join the intersecting strips with butt joints and secure by toenailing. Reinforce the divider joints with stakes driven into the ground outside the forms at 4-foot intervals. Drive 16d HDG nails through

INSTALLING DIVIDERS

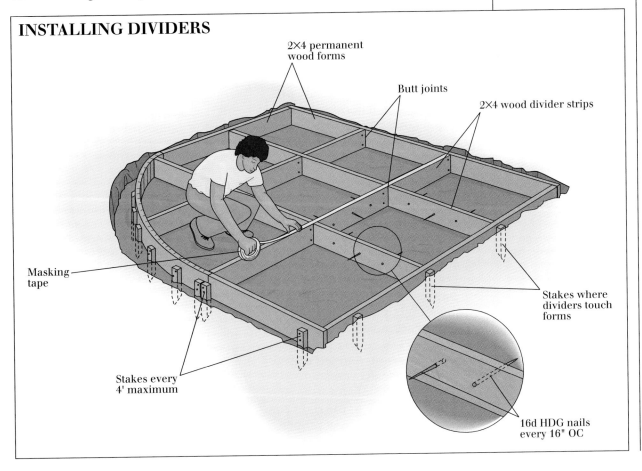

2×4 permanent wood forms

Butt joints

2×4 wood divider strips

Masking tape

Stakes every 4' maximum

Stakes where dividers touch forms

16d HDG nails every 16" OC

MIXING CONCRETE

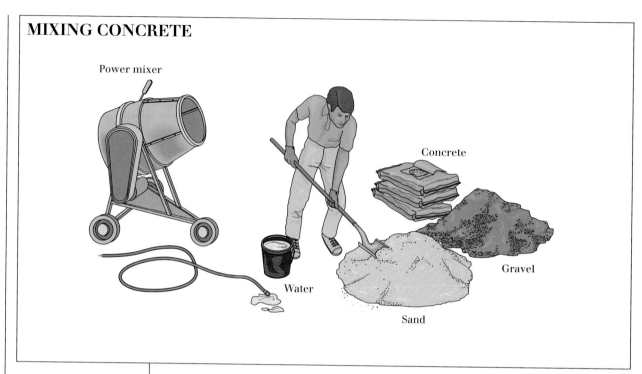

Power mixer

Concrete

Gravel

Water

Sand

these interior dividers to help anchor the concrete after it is poured (the same as with the permanent forms—except drive them alternately from opposite sides of the boards). Cover the top edges of the dividers with masking tape to prevent them from being stained or damaged during the pour.

Mixing Concrete Yourself

Mixing your own concrete with bulk dry materials can save you money on a large project. It may be more convenient to buy the ingredients in ready-to-use bags of dry concrete mix, but this is expensive for all but the smallest jobs. Mixing your own is worthwhile only if you are paving a small area, or if you can pour and finish the concrete in workable sections that are no more than 3 feet square. With either method, do-it-yourself concrete mixing means you and you alone are responsible for its quality. You must get a mix of the right consistency using the correct proportion of ingredients.

If you decide on dry ready-mix, see page 77 for estimating how much to order. Follow the manufacturer's mixing instructions to the letter. Dry ready-mix is usually used to hand-mix small batches of concrete for patching, setting posts, and pouring footings for edgings. It is too expensive to use for paving large areas such as a patio.

If you decided to mix your own concrete using bulk ingredients, see page 219 for estimating how much cement, sand, and aggregate to order. Remember, a good concrete comes from the proper combination of cement, sand, aggregate, and water. A standard mixture for patios and walkways is 1 part cement, 2¼ parts sand, 3 parts coarse aggregate, and ½ part water. You also need to add an air-entraining agent if you live in a region with freezing weather.

Whichever you chose, rent a portable cement mixer; proper mixing is essential, and simply stirring ingredients together will not do. They must be thoroughly mixed

CALCULATING AREA

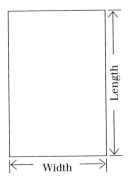

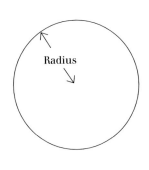

Radius

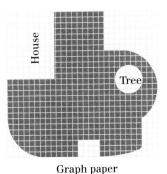

House

Tree

Graph paper

To figure the square feet of rectangular or circular areas, use the formulas you learned in school: for rectangular, length multiplied by width; for circular, 3.14 multiplied by the radius squared.

Complex shapes can be figured by drawing them on graph paper with each square representing 1 square foot—count all the squares within the patio area, including partial squares larger than half a square.

so the cement paste coats every particle of sand and coarse aggregate in the mix. A portable cement mixer makes this possible. It mixes ⅔ cubic yard at a time.

Be advised, however, that sand is always sold wet, and the amount of water you actually use depends on how much water the sand contains. To determine how much water you need, make a test batch in the mixer. Start by estimating the moisture content of the sand: Pick up a handful and squeeze it. If it tends to crumble, it is merely damp, and you need more than ½ part water. If it compacts smoothly without visible water in your hand, it is wet or average and you need ½ part water. If it forms a ball and leaves your hand soaked, it is very wet and you need less than ½ part water.

Based on your estimate of the sand's moisture content, mix a trial batch of concrete. Dump a small amount onto the ground and examine it for stiffness and workability, or slump. *Slump* refers to the number of inches a 12-inch-high pile

PROPORTIONS OF INGREDIENTS FOR MAKING CONCRETE

	Cubic Feet of Concrete				
	4	6	12	18	27*
Cement (90-lb sacks)	1	1½	3	4½	6
Sand (pounds)	200	300	600	900	1,400
Gravel (pounds)	300	450	900	1,350	2,025
Water (gallons)	5	7½	15	22½	33¾
or Water (pounds)	40	60	120	180	270

*1 cubic yard

of concrete slumps when fresh. A 1-inch slump is a very stiff mix, a 10-inch slump very soupy. For residential purposes, a 4-inch slump is average. The ideal mixture is plastic, almost smooth and creamy. With light troweling, all the spaces between the aggregate fill with sand and cement. If the trial batch is not right, adjust the ingredients for another trial batch and combine in the mixer for at least one minute. Check again, and keep adjusting until you get the right mix.

A WELL-COORDINATED CONCRETE POUR

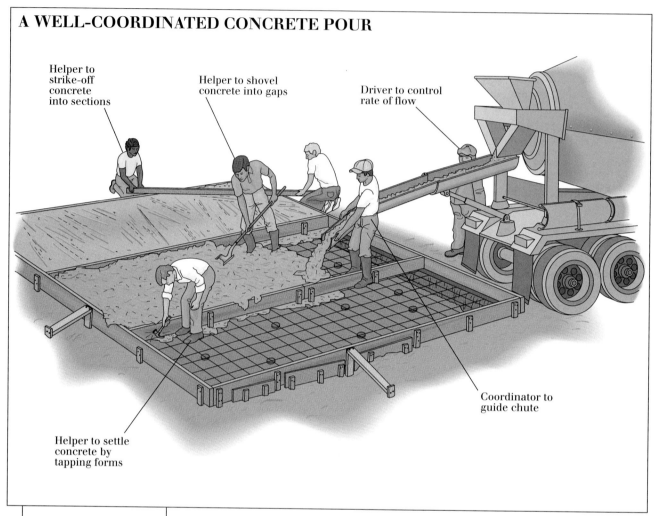

Helper to strike-off concrete into sections

Helper to shovel concrete into gaps

Driver to control rate of flow

Coordinator to guide chute

Helper to settle concrete by tapping forms

Pouring the Concrete

Before you pour the concrete, give the forms a final check for trueness to grade and proper slope. Then wet down the forms and the gravel so they do not wick water away from the concrete.

Begin the pour in a corner at one end of the patio and work across and forward in the space. Place each batch uniformly to the full depth of the form and as close as possible to its final position. Each batch also goes up against previously placed concrete. As each batch is placed, immediately begin spreading it with the square-sided shovel. Work it up against the forms and tamp it into the corners and down into the reinforcing mesh. Spread it only enough to compact it firmly and eliminate voids. Do not overwork it—this brings excess water and inert silt to the surface.

Leveling and Smoothing Concrete

As soon as the concrete has been spread and compacted, strike-off and float the slab. Both steps must be done before water oozes out and collects on the surface.

The strike-off involves using a screed to level the concrete with the forms. The screed can be a wood straightedge or a straight 2×4 that is 12 to 18 inches longer than the width of the slab. It takes two people to strike-off a large slab. Work the screed with a person at each end, sliding it slowly along the tops of the forms in a sawing motion. Do a 36-inch-long section in one pass and then go back over the section a second time to remove any remaining bumps or low spots. You can strike-off batch by batch. One person can strike off one section at a time if the slab has dividers.

Floating immediately follows the strike-off. It levels ridges and fills voids left by the screed and helps compact the concrete. It also embeds the coarse aggregate slightly below the surface. Use either a darby (for small surfaces) or a bull float (for larger surfaces) for this job.

❑ For smaller surfaces, hold the darby flat against the concrete and work it back and forth in a sawing motion. When the surface is level, tilt the darby slightly and go over the surface again, working in the same direction. Although a wood darby works fine, rent or borrow a magnesium float if you can; it slides more evenly over the concrete without the slight drag of a wood float or darby.

❑ For larger surfaces, push the bull float away from you, the front end of its blade raised slightly so it doesn't gouge the concrete. Then pull it back with the blade flat on the surface.

Immediately after floating, use a mason's trowel to cut the concrete away from the forms to a depth of 1 inch. Then let the concrete begin to set up before continuing with the finishing steps. This waiting period can be as long as several hours, depending on the weather.

Finishing Concrete

Concrete is ready for finishing when its water sheen is gone and foot pressure leaves no more than a ¼-

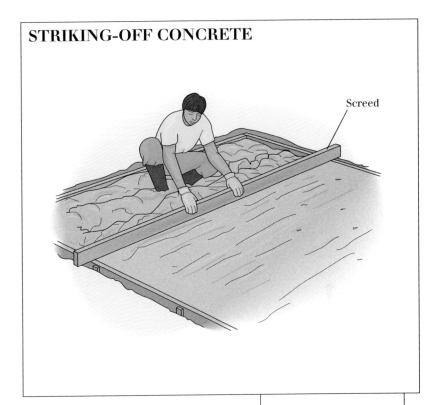

STRIKING-OFF CONCRETE

Screed

inch-deep indentation. Waiting for the concrete to reach this stage is the only way to get a durable surface. When the slab reaches the desirable point, continue with the finishing steps in this order: edging, jointing, hand-floating, and troweling.

Edging This first finishing step produces a neat, rounded edge that resists chipping. It also compacts and hardens the concrete surface next to the forms. Hold the edger flat on the surface next to the forms and run it back and forth to make a shallow, smooth edge. Raise its front edge slightly when moving it forward, and its back edge when moving backward, so you don't gouge the concrete.

Jointing Immediately after edging, cut or groove control joints in the slab. This is the most important finishing step because it provides a place for the concrete to crack as it expands and contracts with the

EDGING AND CUTTING JOINTS

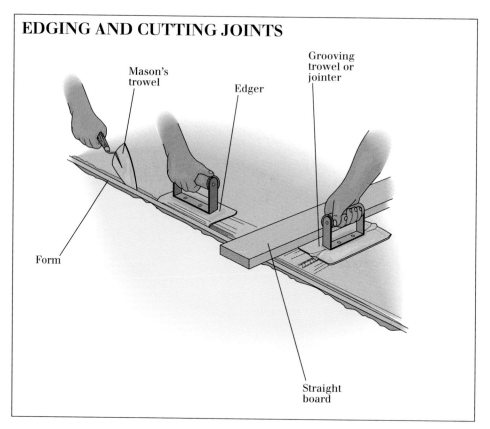

Mason's trowel

Edger

Grooving trowel or jointer

Form

Straight board

FLOATING CONCRETE

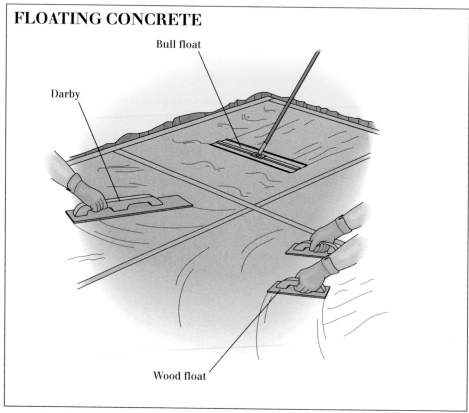

Bull float

Darby

Wood float

FINISHING CONCRETE

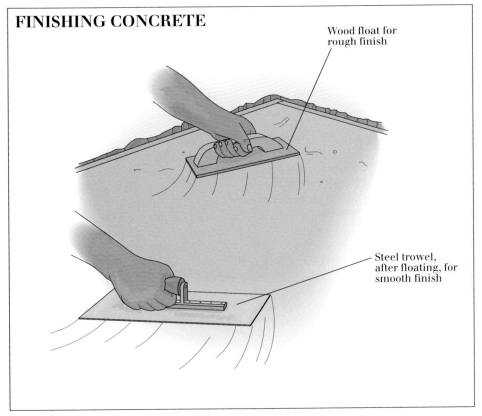

Wood float for rough finish

Steel trowel, after floating, for smooth finish

weather. If the slab has wood dividers, you have already provided these joints and you can skip this step. If you don't have dividers, mark the joint locations on the concrete surface with a chalk line. With a 1×6 as a straightedge, and a scrap of wood to kneel on, cut the joints with a handheld metal grooving trowel or jointer or a circular saw fit with an abrasive blade; guide the tool along the straightedge for a straight line.

❏ When cutting with a grooving trowel, use one with a sharp bit deep enough to cut a 1-inch joint in the slab. Push it down into the concrete and slide it forward. Apply pressure at the back of the groover to keep it from gouging the concrete. When the cut is complete, turn the groover around and go back over the joint to create a smooth finish.

❏ When cutting with a circular saw, make saw joints when the surface is hard enough not to be torn or damaged by the blade. Normally, this is 4 to 12 hours after the concrete hardens. Cut the joints 1 inch deep and finish them by running the edger over them.

Hand-Floating Hand-floating removes imperfections, compacts the concrete surface, and prepares it to receive a finish. Use a handheld wood float to produce the skid-resistant finish recommended for a patio. Hold it flat against the surface and move it in a sweeping arc with a slight sawing motion. If you want a slightly rougher texture for the patio, float the surface a second time and skip troweling. Floating usually removes the marks left by the edger and groover. If you want these marks for decorative purposes, rerun the edger and groover over the edges and joints after this step.

COLORING CONCRETE

Concrete is naturally gray and dull, but it doesn't have to be that way. You can color it in any of five ways—one-course, two-course, dry shake, chemical stains, and paint. The first four methods give the most satisfactory results because the colors become integral to the concrete and are subtle and attractive. They soften and subdue the gray rather than mask it.

One-Course Method

In this method pigment is mixed with the concrete to produce a uniform coloration throughout the body. The pigment is pure mineral oxide or a synthetic iron-oxide colorant prepared for use in concrete. Both types of pigment yield satisfactory results. Buy them from building-supply outlets. Make sure the pigment you choose is insoluble in water, free of soluble salts and acids, and sunfast. For subtle, pastel colors, use 1½ pounds of pigment to every bag of cement. For stronger color, add 7 pounds of pigment to every bag of cement. The colors range from white, cream, and buff to green, pink, rose, and brown.

Two-Course Method

Similar to the one-course method, this technique uses a base course of standard concrete and a topcoat of colored mortar (cement, sand, water, and color pigment). The pigments are the same as for the one-course method. The surface of the base course is left rough enough to provide a good bond for the topcoat. After it stiffens slightly and the surface water disappears, mix the pigment into the mortar and apply in a ½-inch- to 1-inch-thick layer. Apply a commercial bonding agent or a cement grout before floating and troweling the mortar in place.

Dry Shake Method

Shake a dry colored powder over the concrete as soon as it has been hand-floated. The first coat consists of about two thirds of the color. Sprinkle it evenly over the slab. As soon as the powder absorbs some of the moisture, thoroughly hand-float it into the surface. Immediately shake the remaining powder evenly over the surface, allow it to become absorbed, and hand-float into the slab. The powdered color consists of pigment, white portland cement, and a silica sand or fine aggregate. It acts as a concrete hardener.

Chemical Stains

These stains enhance dull, gray concrete surfaces with striking colors in mottled and drifted color patterns. They are made by blending together metallic salts, water, and acid solutions. The eight standard colors can be mixed and diluted to produce an infinite variety. A licensed applications contractor spreads the solution on a clean, dry concrete slab and allows it to stand for a specified period of time as it color-etches the surface. It can be used in combination with the previous coloring methods described here to make interesting patterns.

Paint

Paint is the least desirable way to color any masonry surface. It simply does not stand up well to heavy traffic and weathering and it requires constant upkeep. Use it only if absolutely necessary. Before painting, the surface must be cured for 28 days to 6 months and completely cleaned. Use a primer and paint specifically formulated for use on concrete surfaces.

COLORING CONCRETE

1" thick layer of colored concrete

Dry shake method

Paint or chemical stain

CURING CONCRETE

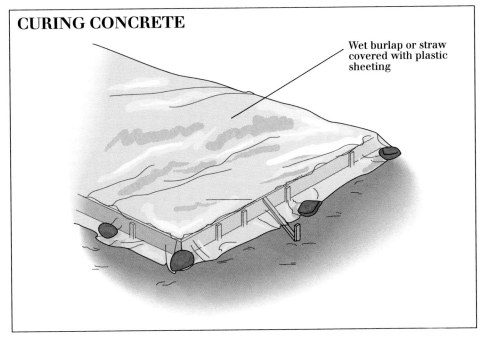

Wet burlap or straw covered with plastic sheeting

If you are planning to color the concrete, there several easy and convenient methods for applying color compounds at this stage (see opposite page).

Troweling Troweling produces a smooth, hard surface considered undesirable for patios. However, it makes a good surface on which to apply textured finishes. Using a steel trowel, place the blade flat on the surface and move it in a sweeping arc, each pass overlapping the previous pass by half its width. If this step doesn't produce as smooth a texture as desired, do a second and even a third troweling. Leave the forms in place for 24 hours after this last step, but begin curing immediately.

Curing Concrete

Curing keeps the concrete moist and warm so it hardens properly. When done correctly, this step gives the concrete slab maximum strength and durability. There are three ways to keep it moist.

❑ Use an oscillating lawn sprinkler or soaking hoses. Apply the water continuously and uniformly so the slab does not partially dry out; wet/dry cycles cause cracks.

❑ Cover the slab with burlap or straw and keep the material uniformly wet. Covering the burlap or straw with plastic sheeting helps.

❑ Cover the slab with plastic sheeting, wet burlap, waterproof paper, or curing compounds that prevent moisture loss. These materials must be laid flat, thoroughly sealed at the joints, and anchored carefully along the edges.

Continue the curing process for five days in warm weather (70° F or higher), for seven days in cool weather (50° to 70° F). Add three days to the curing time for every day the temperature falls below 50° F. Do not allow the temperature of the concrete to fall below 50° F during this curing period.

When moist curing is complete, remove the coverings or stop sprinkling and let the slab dry out naturally. This is a long, slow process that takes up to several months. Do not walk on the concrete during the first 24 hours after curing.

Decorative Finishes

Applying a decorative surface treatment gives concrete a pleasing texture and improves its traction. There are nine finishes from which to choose.

Exposed Aggregate This is the most popular concrete finish. It is slightly rugged, naturally colorful, and attractive in most settings. This finish is achieved by exposing the aggregate mixed into the concrete

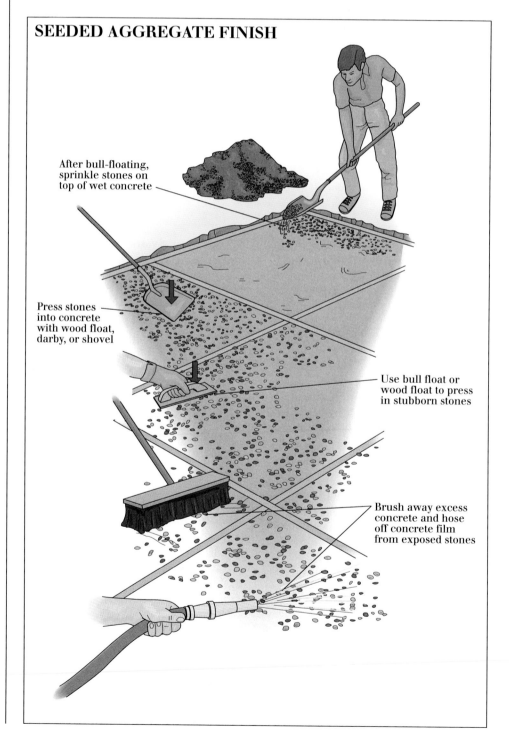

SEEDED AGGREGATE FINISH

After bull-floating, sprinkle stones on top of wet concrete

Press stones into concrete with wood float, darby, or shovel

Use bull float or wood float to press in stubborn stones

Brush away excess concrete and hose off concrete film from exposed stones or by seeding additional aggregate into the surface.

❏ Exposing the internal aggregate. Construct the slab through the first floating stage. Be careful not to overfloat, pushing the coarse aggregate too deep into the slab. When the water sheen disappears and the slab bears your weight on knee pads without indentation, brush away the top layer of concrete with a stiff nylon brush or broom until you have just exposed the aggregate. Clear away the concrete debris. Spray the surface with a hardener, cover it with plastic sheeting, and let it cure for 24 hours. Then repeat the brooming process, accompanied by a fine spray of water, until about half the surface of the large stones is exposed.

❏ Seeding aggregate. If you plan to seed aggregate into the slab, build the forms ½ inch lower than the desired final surface. Construct the slab through the first floating stage. Spread the aggregate over

Decorative finishes for concrete include a rock salt finish (top left), stamped and stained concrete (top right), broom finish (bottom left), and exposed aggregate (bottom right).

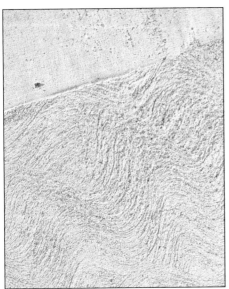

the surface in an even layer. Using a wood float, a darby, or a straightedge, tap the aggregate into the concrete. Then use a bull float or wood float to embed the aggregate in the concrete until the mortar just surrounds all the pebbles. This surface aggregate should not intermix with the base aggregate. Make sure the surface remains flat, then expose the seeded aggregate in the same way you expose internal aggregate.

Troweled Finish This is a swirled pattern made with a steel finishing trowel. It gives a patio an interesting texture and good traction. Build the slab through the first hand-floated stage. Texture the surface by holding the trowel flat, pressing on it, and moving it in a swirling motion. Make different patterns with a series of uniform arcs or twists.

Broomed Finish This technique produces an attractive, nonslip texture created by pulling a damp broom across freshly floated or troweled concrete. Apply the texture in straight, curved, or wavy lines. Use a street broom or a broom specifically made for texturing concrete.

Travertine Finish This attractive surface resembles travertine marble. It requires a two-step procedure. After the slab has been edged, it is broomed to permit a bond with a finish or mortar coat, which is made by mixing white portland cement with sand, color pigment, and water. The mortar is thrown onto the slab with a dash brush. When the concrete can support you on a knee board, use a steel trowel to flatten the ridges and spread the mortar, leaving voids in the low areas. This finish is not recommended for regions with freezing weather.

Rock Salt Finish This is a slightly pitted, roughened surface created by rolling rock salt (ordinary water-softener salt) into the concrete. It creates an interesting texture and provides excellent traction. Scatter the salt over the surface after it has been hand-floated, troweled, or broomed. Use a wood float to press the grains into the concrete until only their tops remain exposed.

TEXTURING WITH BROOM

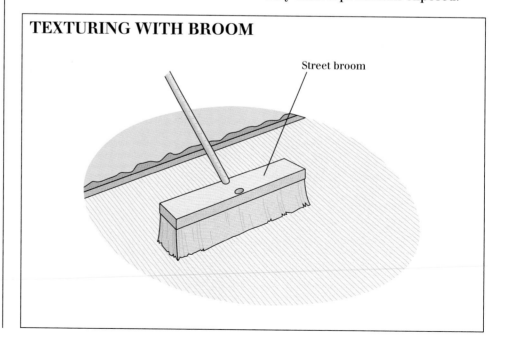

Street broom

TEXTURING CONCRETE

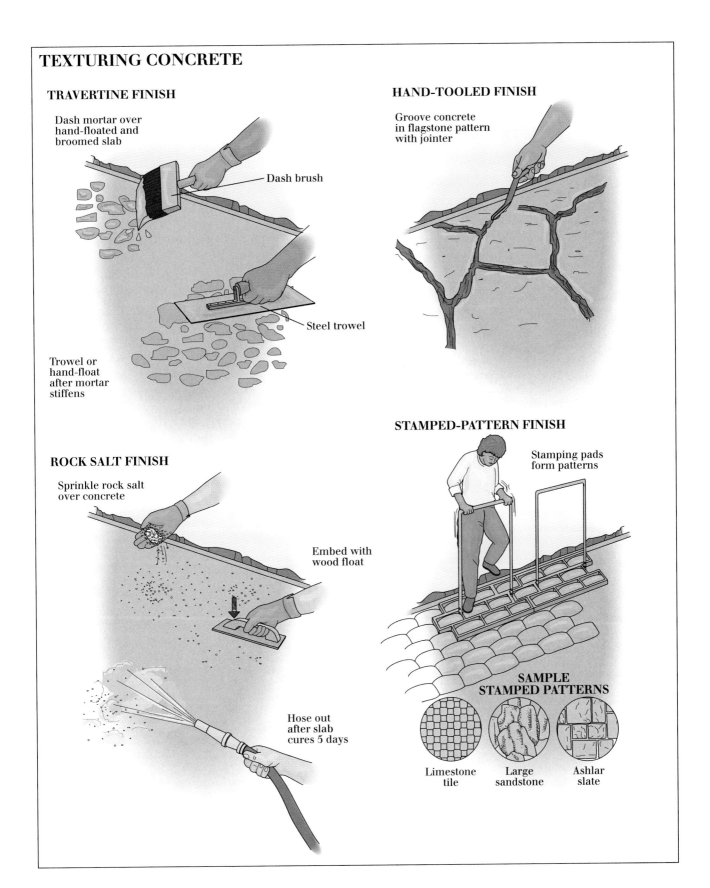

TRAVERTINE FINISH

Dash mortar over hand-floated and broomed slab

Dash brush

Steel trowel

Trowel or hand-float after mortar stiffens

HAND-TOOLED FINISH

Groove concrete in flagstone pattern with jointer

ROCK SALT FINISH

Sprinkle rock salt over concrete

Embed with wood float

Hose out after slab cures 5 days

STAMPED-PATTERN FINISH

Stamping pads form patterns

SAMPLE STAMPED PATTERNS

Limestone tile

Large sandstone

Ashlar slate

Obviously, a water cure won't work with this finish; instead, cure it for five days under plastic sheeting or waterproof paper. Then wash and brush the surface to dissolve the salt. Continue curing as needed. This finish is not recommended for areas with freezing weather.

Semismooth Finish This is a slightly coarse texture produced by hand-floating the concrete with a wood float and stopping there. The wood float drags, creating the texture. This is a good texture for a patio needing a nonskid surface.

Smooth Finish Create this surface by troweling the concrete two or three times with a steel finishing trowel. This tool compacts the concrete, producing a hard, smooth surface. This is not an ideal surface for a patio, but it does make a good base for texturing techniques such as brooming and salting.

Stamped-Pattern Finish Concrete often is made to resemble other paving materials by incising it with stamping pads, which come in patterns that resemble brick, cobblestone, flagstone, cut (ashlar) stone, slate, pavers, and exotic paving materials such as seashells and wood boardwalk. After floating the slab, push the pads into the concrete and align them with one another. Then step from one pad to the next, cutting the pattern into the concrete. After stamping, use a jointer to clean up the joints.

Hand-Tooled Finish Cut random patterns into concrete with a concave jointer or a piece of bent ½-inch to ¾-inch copper pipe. After the slab is bull-floated, score the pattern into the surface. Score a second time after the slab has been hand-floated.

See page 92 for edging options.

TEXTURING WITH TROWEL

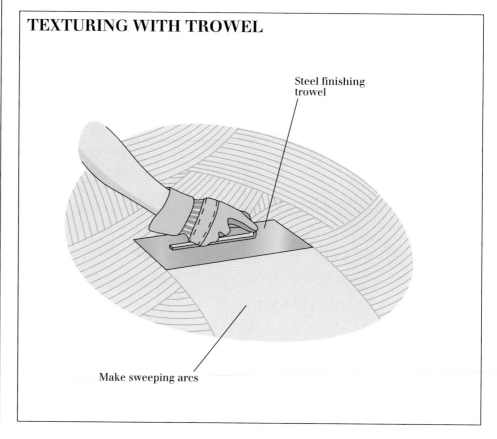

Steel finishing trowel

Make sweeping arcs

INSTALLING TILE ON A CONCRETE BASE

Though not suited for colder climates, tile is a durable, decorative surface ideal for patios. Applied with mortar to a concrete base, tile offers a wide variety of colors, textures, and patterns.

Laying Out Tile

For square or rectangular slabs, begin at the most visible corner farthest from the house. Lay out a row of tiles, allowing for the grout joint if the tile does not have tabs or spacers. Check to be sure you won't end up with a thin sliver of tile at the end of a row. Instead, position the tiles so no tile will be cut to less than half its original size. No slab, even one you have painstakingly formed up yourself, will be exactly square. As a result, use guidelines rather than rely on the edge of the patio.

Establish two guidelines at right angles to each other. Use a chalk line for rough layout purposes. Once you've settled on the location of the guides, stretch mason's twine just high enough to clear the finished tile surface by ½ inch. If the slab has an expansion joint, you will have to line up a grout joint along it. (Overlaying an expansion joint will eventually cause the tile to crack.) Use the expansion joint as one of the guidelines and run another guideline at a right angle to it. For free-form patios, set guidelines spanning the two widest areas of the patio.

Installing the Tile

Mix mortar as described on page 245, substituting latex tile setting liquid for water. Dampen a roughly 6-square-foot area. Apply mortar to a smaller area—about 3 square feet—using a serrated trowel with

LAYING OUT TILE

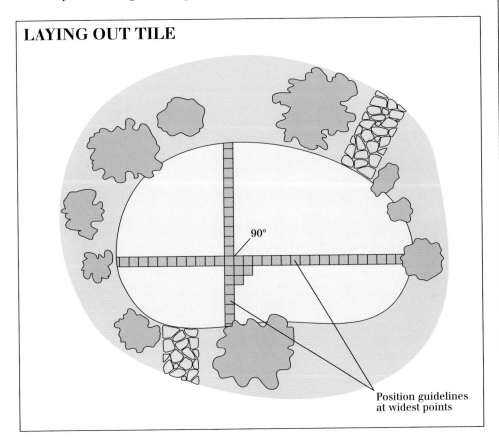

90°

Position guidelines
at widest points

SETTING TILE IN MORTAR

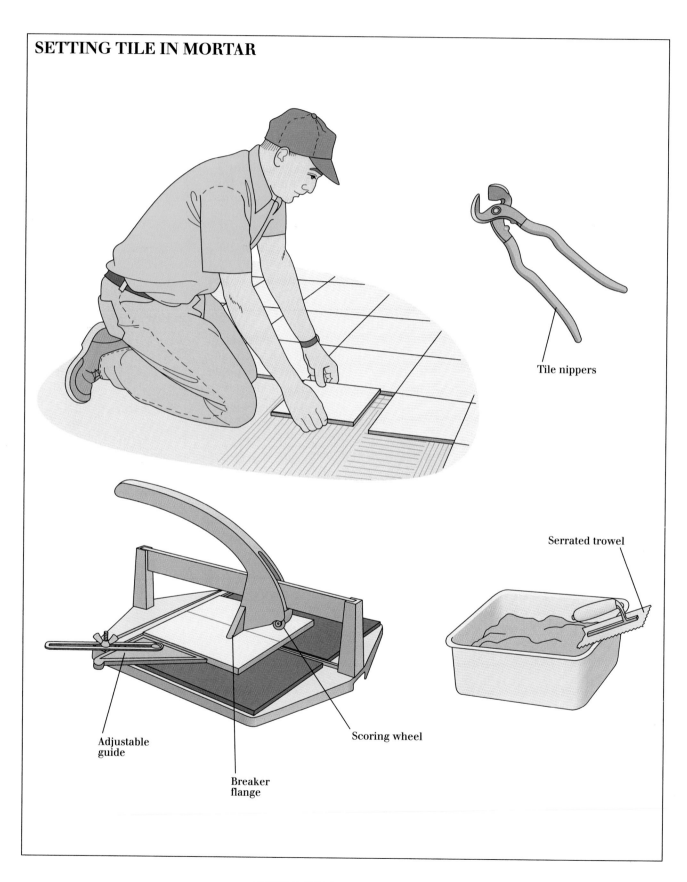

Tile nippers

Serrated trowel

Adjustable guide

Breaker flange

Scoring wheel

¼-inch notches. Smooth it as evenly as possible. Holding a tile with your fingertips, lower it directly on top of the mortar. Push the tile firmly in place, but don't use undo force. Every three or four tiles, check that the surface is even. Use a rubber mallet to tap down any raised tiles. Repeat the process, working away from the intersection of the guide-lines until the patio is complete.

Grouting the Joints

Give the mortar 24 hours to set up. For narrow joints, float grout over a 3- to 4-square-foot area using a moistened grout float to push the grout into the joints. Kneel on a piece of plywood to distribute your weight over the still-curing mortar base. After joints have dried for 15 minutes, remove any excess grout with a damp sponge. Rinse the sponge but ring it out well to avoid oversaturating the grout. Follow the manufacturer's specific direc-tions for curing the grout, a process usually involving the occasional dampening of the surface the first couple of days after grouting.

For wider joints, use a grout bag. Mix Type M mortar to a consistency that will allow you to extrude the mortar out of the ½-inch nozzle. Fill the bag, and roll the end until the mortar coils out to fill the joint. Pack and smooth the mortar with a ½-inch jointer. Wait one hour before removing any excess mortar. After three hours, brush joints smooth and wash the patio.

Tile makes a pleas-ing contrast to brick. A brick patio here might have been just too much brick.

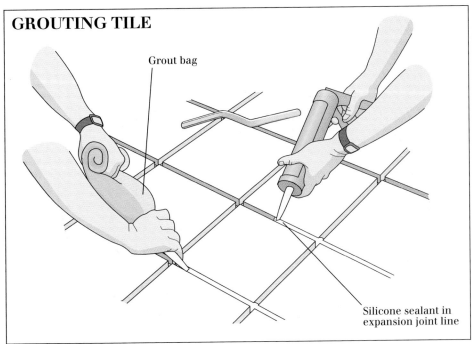

GROUTING TILE

Grout bag

Silicone sealant in expansion joint line

INSTALLING BRICK ON A CONCRETE BASE

There is a long tradition for this type of patio. It is permanent and attractive and combines the benefits of a concrete slab with the warmth and elegance of brick. The grouted joints create a strong pattern, setting this type of patio apart from brick-in-sand installations.

To check the exact size needed for the concrete base, use a flat surface, such as a lawn area, driveway, or garage floor, to experiment with brick patterns. Lay out an area large enough so that you can visualize the pattern over the entire patio surface. Space the brick with correct mortar joint widths so the pattern is accurate. When satisfied with the look, measure a typical section that includes an entire pattern. Use these measurements to accurately calculate the edges of the base slab. If the pattern requires a border, be sure to allow for it when pouring the base slab.

Providing a Foundation

Laying bricks in wet mortar creates a handsome and stable surface that is especially desirable in rainy climates. You need a concrete slab as a base. It can be a new slab or an existing one that is in good condition. Be sure the slab is thoroughly clean and roughen the surface to promote a solid bond between the old and new surfaces. If building a new slab, float it with a wood float to give it a roughened surface; then cure. Wait two weeks after the initial curing before laying the bricks.

For heavy-duty use, brick laid on a concrete base is almost as strong as the concrete it covers.

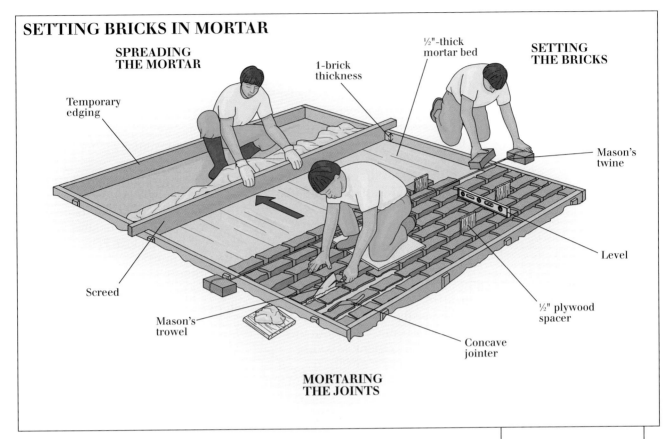

SETTING BRICKS IN MORTAR

SPREADING THE MORTAR

SETTING THE BRICKS

Temporary edging

1-brick thickness

½"-thick mortar bed

Mason's twine

Screed

Level

Mason's trowel

½" plywood spacer

Concave jointer

MORTARING THE JOINTS

Setting the Bricks

First, following the instructions on page 240, install the brick edging around the slab perimeter. The top should extend above the slab a distance equal to one brick thickness plus ½ inch. This type of installation lends itself to half-bricks, which are face bricks only half as thick as conventional ones. (If you will be using some other type of edging, install temporary wood edging before laying the bricks.)

Wet the bricks and the existing concrete slab thoroughly so they will not wick water out of the mortar. Use a dry ready-mix or make your own mortar by mixing 1 part cement with 4 parts wet sand. Mix only the amount you can use in one hour. Plan to work a 3-foot-square section at a time.

Spread the mortar in the working section and strike-off to a ½-inch depth. Using mason's twine to align the bricks, lay them in the desired pattern, leaving ½-inch open joints between them. As you set each brick in place, tap it gently with a rubber mallet to seat it in the mortar. Check frequently for level as you work. Wait at least 24 hours before finishing the joints.

Mortaring the Joints

Add ½ part hydrated lime to the mortar mix to improve workability. Pack the mortar into the joints between the bricks with a pointed mason's trowel, keeping it off the bricks as much as possible. Immediately clean up any spills with a moist rag and let the joints harden for about 30 minutes. Then finish the joints by lightly tooling them with a jointer. Keep the mortar wet for 24 hours by covering with plastic sheeting. Stay off the brick surface for at least three more days.

INSTALLING FLAGSTONE ON A CONCRETE BASE

The best way to build a flagstone patio is to bed the stones in mortar over a structural concrete slab. If frost is a problem in your area, the slab should be poured over an 8- to 12-inch-thick gravel base. You might also consider reinforcing the slab with ½-inch-diameter rebars at 16 inches on center in both directions. The concrete slab should be at least 4 inches thick.

Setting the Flagstones

Position and cut stones before beginning to set them in mortar (see page 210). Mix the mortar thoroughly. For the base mortar, use a mix of 3 parts masonry sand to 1 part portland cement. Mix this fairly stiff (leaning toward dry) so that it will support the weight of the stones. Make certain that the stones have been brushed or washed clean. If you are working with very porous flagstone and the weather is dry, the stones should be kept moist (not wet) to prevent them from absorbing moisture from the mortar and inhibiting the bond.

Plan the layout of a flagstone patio carefully, fitting the pieces together like a puzzle and cutting stone where necessary. Then set the stones in mortar a few at a time.

Spread a layer of mortar 1 or more inches thick over an area large enough to set two or three flagstones. Place each stone, spacing them about ½ inch from each other and from the edging. Rap each stone with the handle of the mason's trowel to seat the stone; use a rubber mallet for larger pieces.

To align the stones, use a straight 2×4 that spans a number of stones. If a stone is higher than its neighbors, use the mallet to tamp it down. If it is too low, remove it and add some mortar.

In order to keep the concrete base clean, work on top of the stones you have already placed, but do not step on individual stones. Place plywood over the work to distribute your weight evenly. When all the stones have been placed, let the base mortar set for 24 hours or more. Then fill the joints, being careful not to spill wet mortar on the stones. Trowel the joints to a smooth finish. Keep a bucket of water with you and sponge off any mortar that drips on the surface.

If the base mortar has dried, use the sponge to dampen the surface a little before adding the joint mortar.

Curing the Mortar

For mortar to cure properly, it must not be allowed to dry too rapidly; slow curing greatly increases its strength. The best curing method is to cover the entire patio with 2 mil polyethylene sheeting. Weight the plastic at the edges and at all joints to keep the moisture in. An adequate although less-effective alternative is to keep the patio hosed down for a few days, but if the weather is hot and dry this could mean spraying every hour or so. Do not walk on the patio surface for four or five days.

LAYING FLAGSTONE OVER A CONCRETE BASE

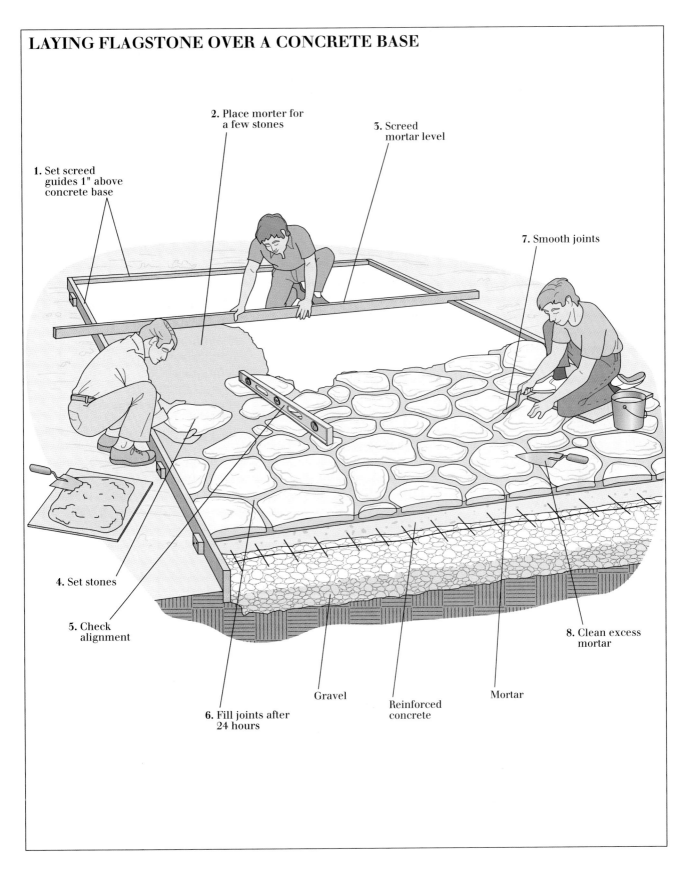

2. Place morter for a few stones

3. Screed mortar level

1. Set screed guides 1" above concrete base

7. Smooth joints

4. Set stones

5. Check alignment

6. Fill joints after 24 hours

Gravel

Reinforced concrete

Mortar

8. Clean excess mortar

ADDING EDGING

Patios require an edging to keep loose-laid materials in place. Edgings define traffic areas and keep plantings and loose surface materials where they belong. Edgings also serve a decorative function by providing distinct borders and, where contrasting materials are used, adding interesting design effects.

Edgings can be constructed from a variety of materials, from brick, stone, and concrete to wood beams, benderboard, and plastic strips. They can be flush with the surface, below grade, or above ground. Decorative bricks, set on edge, are an easy way to make a curved edging. Use a wood beam or railroad tie to edge a concrete patio. A 2×4 on edge can be set flush between a patio and adjacent lawn, or set

a 2×4 above grade to bridge the different levels between a patio and a lawn. The combination of wood and concrete makes a well-defined and permanent edging. A raised concrete edging will give a curb around a patio. A flush concrete edging helps blend the patio into the surrounding landscape while still providing a definite edge.

When selecting an edging, consider such aspects as contrast (to emphasize lines and shapes or to relieve large expanses of paving material), maintenance (some lawn trimmers require a straight edge), safety (smooth versus jagged edges), durability, and ease of installation. To help you evaluate the options, the following section summarizes the various installation techniques.

Even when they aren't necessary to strengthen a patio, edgings add a decorative touch. The contrasting edging around this patio emphasizes its spare geometric shape.

COMMON EDGING INSTALLATIONS

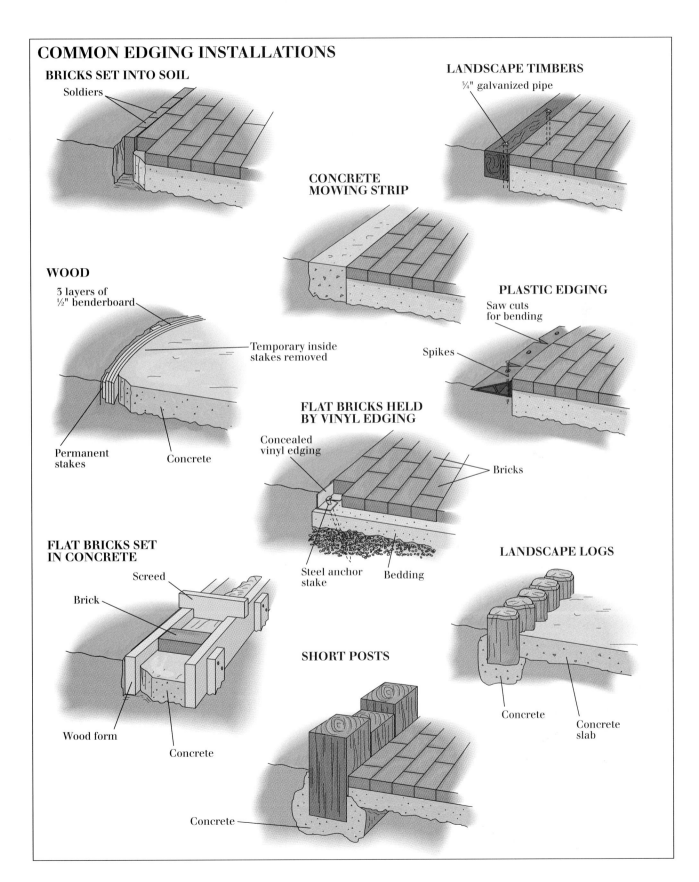

BRICKS SET INTO SOIL
Soldiers

LANDSCAPE TIMBERS
¼" galvanized pipe

CONCRETE MOWING STRIP

WOOD
3 layers of ½" benderboard

Temporary inside stakes removed

Permanent stakes

Concrete

PLASTIC EDGING
Saw cuts for bending

Spikes

FLAT BRICKS HELD BY VINYL EDGING
Concealed vinyl edging

Bricks

Steel anchor stake

Bedding

FLAT BRICKS SET IN CONCRETE
Screed

Brick

Wood form

Concrete

LANDSCAPE LOGS
Concrete

Concrete slab

SHORT POSTS
Concrete

Brick

The brick-in-soil edging is the easiest to build. It's a natural border for a brick patio; it also adds a decorative as well as functional edge to a patio of concrete or wood. Place the bricks on end, called soldiers, or flat and at right angles to the patio. Flat bricks should be set in concrete; soldiers may not need concrete footings if they extend below grade far enough to butt against the patio's base material.

To set bricks in concrete, first build a form around the patio, using stakes and long lengths of 2-by lumber. The form should be deep enough for at least 4 inches

BRICK POSITIONING TERMS

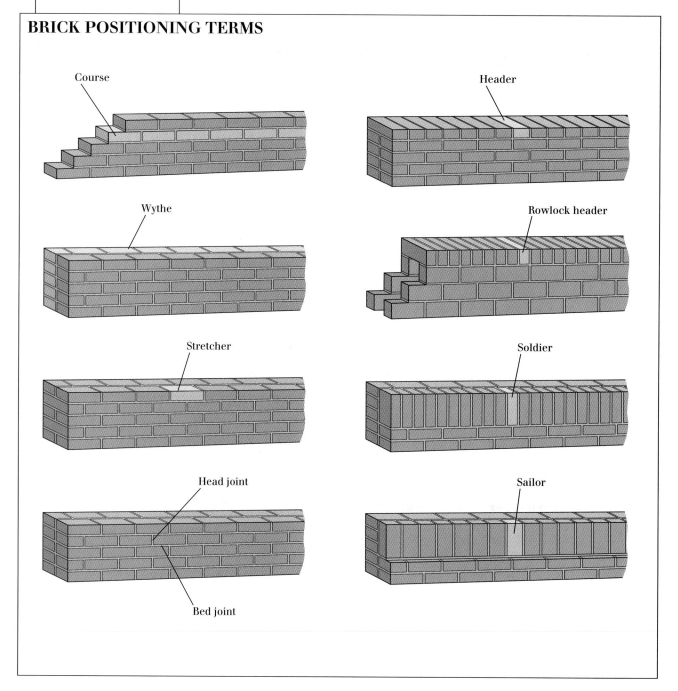

Course

Header

Wythe

Rowlock header

Stretcher

Soldier

Head joint

Sailor

Bed joint

of concrete and one brick laid flat, and wide enough to accommodate the length of one brick (or width, if you lay them lengthwise). The top of the form should be level with the patio surface. Fill the form with enough concrete so that when a brick is laid on top of it, the brick will be flush with the top of the form; then place bricks into the wet concrete. Butt them together and set them with a rubber mallet so the tops are level with the form. Allow the concrete to cure for five days before removing the forms and packing soil around the border.

For a variation on this installation, angle the bricks, laying them against one another, so they extend above the patio to make a serrated or scalloped edging.

Wood

Build wood edgings with highly rot- and insect-resistant species, such as heart redwood, cedar, and cypress, or pressure-treated lumber. The typical wood edging is made with 4×4 or 6×6 beams or with 2×4s or 2×6s on edge. The mason's twine with which you have outlined the patio perimeter marks the inner edges of the edging. Dig a narrow trench deep enough and wide enough to hold the wood, its top edge aligning with the patio surface. Place the beams in the trench, end to end, aligning their inner faces with the twine. Secure them to the ground with ½-inch galvanized-steel pipe. Or, make a staked wood edging by lining the trench with 12-inch-long 1×3 or 2×3 stakes placed 4 feet apart. Set the studs against the stakes, with their inner faces aligning with the mason's twine. Use wallboard screws to secure the studs to the stakes and to each other at the corners. Pack soil around the outside.

You also can use 12-inch-long round posts ranging from 4 to 6 inches in diameter, or 4×4 or 6×6 beams cut into 12-inch-long post lengths, to make standing wood trim that rises 4 to 6 inches above the patio surface. Secure these posts to the ground by setting them in concrete footings.

Stone

Flagstones, boulders, or cobblestones make a rugged and natural-looking patio edge. As with flat bricks, stone edgings should be installed on a concrete bed—the stones can be placed directly onto the wet concrete or set in mortar over hardened concrete. Do a test layout of the stones before you do the permanent installation in concrete or mortar.

Concrete

A concrete edging flush with the ground, called a mowing strip, is fairly easy to build and provides a smooth, clean patio edge. The width can vary, but most mowing strips are 4 to 6 inches wide. Using stakes and long lengths of 2×4 lumber, build a form along the patio perimeter; the top of the form should be level with the patio surface. To make curves, use benderboard or similar thin boards and double them up. Screed the concrete level with the top of the form. Run an edger along the outside form board to give the concrete a rounded edge. Finish the surface as you would for concrete paving (see page 221).

Plastic Strips

Plastic edging strips give do-it-yourselfers an easy and convenient way to edge a patio. These are concealed edgings, so they do not add a decorative element to the patio, but they are practical and economical to use. Follow the manufacturer's installation instructions.

BUILDING RETAINING WALLS

Garden walls serve many functions. They can create privacy, screen out wind and noise, define an activity area, provide seating around a patio, or retain sloping ground. Walls impart a feeling of permanence and quality. Most walls—especially those under 3 feet high—are within the homeowner's ability to build. Your main considerations in planning a wall are function, height, material, and structural design.

In makeup, retaining walls differ from standard walls only in the way they are reinforced or keyed into the earth they hold back, and the way in which allowance is made for draining water buildup behind the wall (see page 243). Hydrostatic pressure (the buildup of water be-

hind a wall) is the primary reason why retaining walls fail. Because of this, retaining-wall design is legislated in most areas. Typically, if the wall is more than 3 feet high, it must be designed by an engineer or other qualified professional.

Types of retaining walls range from stone walls built to lean into the earth they retain, to concrete or concrete-block walls reinforced with additional rebar and cast support sections. "Green walls," walls made from stacked precast concrete sections in which plants can be established, are designed to be set at an angle that leans into the hillside. Retaining walls made from landscaping timbers use T-shaped "deadmen" to lock the wall into the hill.

Concrete retaining walls can be faced with other materials, such as

Besides their practical uses, the terraces formed by retaining walls add a vertical element to the garden and create little "stages" where small plants can star.

stone, brick, stucco, or even wood. A retaining wall that depends on its mass weight for its strength should be built with a batter—a sloped face—so that gravity can assist with the retaining (see page 260). If you need a large retaining wall, consult a local masonry supplier or landscape contractor about the materials available in your area.

As many jurisdictions require that retaining walls taller than 3 feet be designed by an engineer, use the details illustrated here for preliminary design and estimating purposes only. Hire a professional for the final structural design.

Building Wall Footings

Except for those made of loose-laid stone or wood, all garden walls should be supported by a continuous concrete footing. The width and thickness of the footing depend on the size of the wall, and the depth depends on local soil conditions. Most footings are twice the width of the wall, but the footing of a retaining wall is usually two thirds the height of the wall. The footing should be at least 8 inches thick for low walls; construct 12-inch footings for walls over 2 feet tall. Depth also depends on the local frost line. The minimum depth for a footing and its gravel bed is 14 inches below grade.

A footing should have a 6-inch layer of gravel beneath it. This controls the heaving that occurs in locations where there is unstable soil or deep frost. Be sure to dig the trench deep enough; in areas that get a lot of frost, the top of the gravel should be below the frost line.

The footing should contain at least one horizontal rebar—two or three would be better. Also place vertical rebar every 24 inches in the footing to protrude up into a brick or concrete-block wall. Stone is usually too irregular to accom-

modate it, although you may be able to lay stone around a few bars. For specifics on footings for mortared stone walls, see page 257.

Providing for Drainage

Any wall built next to a bank or along sloping ground may be subject to considerable additional pressure during wet months. If the soil behind the wall becomes saturated, the wall may crack or lean, be pushed out of line, or actually topple. To prevent this, adequate

Concrete is being pumped from the curb into this footing. If the footing is of substantial size, a concrete pump saves much labor. Vertical rebars are placed in the wet concrete.

DRAINAGE CONSIDERATIONS

Drainage to carry water around wall

Drainage through wall

drainage is essential. There are two basic drainage systems, depending on the amount of water you expect behind the wall. One system carries the water away from behind the wall and the other lets the water drain through the wall.

The first type of system is excellent on sloped ground and is made by placing rigid, perforated drainage pipe, such as the type used for septic field leach lines, in a bed of gravel behind the wall. The pipe has two rows of holes; when you set the pipe, keep these holes toward the bottom, not facing up as you might think. This allows the water

to percolate up into the pipe and then run down the narrow channel between the holes. This approach reduces the silting that would occur if the water entered from above.

If the ground is not sloped and you cannot channel the water away, drains must be run through the base of the wall. Weep holes at the bottom of a wall can provide the necessary drainage. When building a brick wall, for example, cut 1 inch off the end of a brick every 4 feet so a length of ¾-inch plastic can be inserted through the wall. Extend the pipe about 6 inches beyond the back of the wall and surround it with gravel. Drill holes along the sides of the pipe to allow more water to enter. To prevent staining, extend the pipe slightly past the face of the wall.

For small structures such as brick planter boxes, effective drainage can be achieved simply by putting short lengths of cotton clothesline between the head joints of the base bricks. These work like wicks to drain excess water.

BUILDING BRICK WALLS

The ease and speed with which a professional bricklayer deftly "butters" each brick and taps it in place comes only with years of experience. Still, bricklaying is an enjoyable and satisfying skill by which you can add otherwise expensive features to your patio. This ancient art has a terminology all its own. Here are some terms worth getting acquainted with:

❏ *Bed joint.* The layer of mortar under a brick.
❏ *Wythe.* The thickness of the wall. A wall one brick thick is a single-wythe wall. A wall two bricks thick is a double-wythe wall.
❏ *Head joint.* The mortar between the ends of adjacent bricks.

❏ *Course.* One horizontal row of bricks in a wall.

❏ *Header.* A brick laid flat but turned so the end is facing out.

❏ *Rowlock Header.* A brick laid on edge with one end facing out.

❏ *Sailor.* A brick laid on end with the broad face exposed.

❏ *Soldier.* A brick standing on one end with the narrow face exposed.

❏ *Stretcher.* A brick laid flat in a wall with the narrow edge facing out.

Before You Begin

Before you actually start building a brick wall, you will need to choose the pattern and the brick you prefer. There are many sizes, textures, and colors to choose from. Some are better for some patterns than others. Prices vary widely. See pages 77 through 83 for information regarding how to order brick as well as the many options surrounding brick types, sizes, colors, textures, and patterns. Depending on the function of the brick wall, you will probably also have to allow for drainage (see page 243).

It is always a good idea to practice a bit first. Mix some mortar and lay up a sample single-wythe section of wall. Before the mortar dries, knock down the wall and do it over again. Keep laying up bricks until you are comfortable working with mortar.

Patterns for Brick Walls

Select a pattern from the examples on page 246 or combine them to make a unique design of your own.

Know Your Mortar

Mortar is a combination of portland cement, hydrated lime, sand, and

If a wall is to be thicker than two bricks wide, the interior can be of concrete blocks. The resulting wall will be stronger, faster to construct, and less expensive than if it were all brick.

WALL PATTERNS

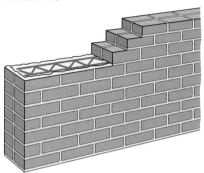

Running bond. This is the most common pattern because it is the easiest. It consists of all the bricks laid as stretchers, with each course offset from the one above and below by half a brick.

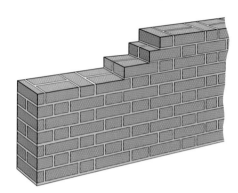

Flemish bond. A variation of the English bond, the Flemish bond consists of alternate rows of stretchers and headers arranged so that the headers and stretchers in every other course are aligned.

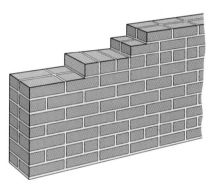

Common bond. Similar to the running bond, the common bond pattern has a course of headers placed every fifth or sixth course.

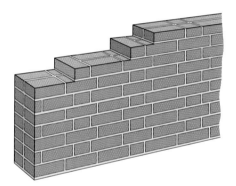

Garden bond. Here, each course has three consecutive stretchers followed by a header.

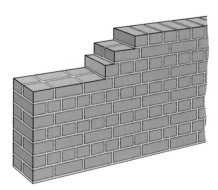

English bond. This pattern is made by alternating rows of stretchers and headers. Note that the vertical joints of all the stretchers are aligned.

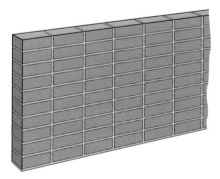

Stack bond. This pattern has each stretcher stacked directly on top of the one below it. Because it is structurally unsound, it can be used only for a brick veneer, not for a retaining wall.

water that binds together the masonry units. Hydrated lime makes the mortar more plastic and easier to work. Sand adds volume and must be free of soil and stones or other impurities that will drastically reduce the strength and bonding qualities of the mortar (beach sand with its salt content will not do). You can buy the raw materials and mix your own mortar, or you can buy premixed dry mortar in bags and just add water. The bagged material is expensive, but it saves time and ensures consistency. Sand purchased in bulk will be damp or even wet, meaning less water will be required in the mix.

There is nothing difficult about mixing mortar; just be careful to combine the correct proportions and use exactly the same proportions for each batch. A hoe and a deep wheelbarrow work well for hand-mixing, provided you mix thoroughly. Add the last amount of water cautiously; once the mix is nearly wet enough, even a little more water will turn it all into a liquid slurry that you cannot use. To test the consistency, use the hoe to pull the mortar up into a steep, nearly vertical face. If the mortar stands a few inches high on its own and maintain a smooth face, the mix is correct. If you are laying a lot of brick and develop reasonable speed, consider renting an electric mixer. Keep the tools clean—mortar is corrosive and bonds tightly to steel.

Several types of mortar are available. Depending on the climate, the type of brick, and the location, different mixes are preferred.

❏ *Type M.* This is a high-strength mortar suitable for general use and in walls that will bear a load. Use this type when the masonry comes into contact with the earth. It is suitable for freezing climates.

❏ *Type S.* This is not as strong a mortar as Type M. It is excellent for general use, such as for a mowing strip or with masonry in contact with the earth. Do not use in climates with temperatures below freezing.

❏ *Type N.* This is a medium-strength mortar for use on projects above ground level (such as freestanding brick walls in mild climates) where high compression or lateral strength are not needed.

❏ *Type O.* A low-strength mortar, Type O should be used only for interior brickwork or where brick will be exposed to little weathering and no frost.

Because mortar sets fairly quickly—particularly in hot weather—don't mix more than you can use in about an hour. If the mortar begins to set before you have used it all, you can add a little water and remix it for more plasticity. However, do this only once for a given batch; repeatedly retempering (adding water) weakens mortar.

Bricks vary in their capacity to absorb moisture. Some are more prone to wick water out of the mortar, weakening the joint. To defend against this, you may have to dampen the bricks before laying them. To test their absorption level, pick one brick at random and pencil a circle on its face about the size of a quarter. Pour half a teaspoon of water onto this circle and time the rate of absorption. If the water is absorbed in 90 seconds or less, the brick should be wetted before using. The easiest way to do this is to lay out a few rows of bricks on a clean surface and spray them on all sides with a garden hose. Let the bricks absorb the water before laying, as wet bricks won't bond with the mortar.

Bricklaying Techniques

Bricklaying is more complicated than it looks. At first, the coordination of handling the brick, the trowel, and the mortar simultaneously will feel awkward. But bricklaying is a very repetitive exercise, so the technique will soon become a comfortable sequence of events.

Placing mortar on a brick with the trowel is called "throwing." Begin by placing a shovelful of mortar on the mortarboard. Cut a section from the edge of the pile and, using the trowel, roughly shape it to the length and width of the trowel. Pick it up by slipping the trowel under in one quick motion. As you pick up the mortar, snap the trowel slightly to bond the mortar to the trowel. That amount of mortar should bed about three bricks.

Now comes the part that takes practice. The mortar should be thrown from the trowel in a sweeping motion so that it slips off the trowel and spreads along the bricks. Avoid dribbling the mortar along the bricks a little at a time. Start by trying to cover a couple of bricks simultaneously and increase to three or four as your skill develops.

Spread the mortar to an even thickness of about 1 inch, then use the trowel to cut off the excess mortar along the edges. Add that mortar to the brick or put it back on the mortarboard. Once the mortar is in place on the wall, lightly furrow the center of the bed with the tip of the trowel. This allows the mortar to adjust to an even thickness when the brick is placed on it. Avoid making too deep a furrow, which may leave an air space under the brick.

After the mortar is spread, the end of the next brick to be placed

BRICKLAYING TECHNIQUES

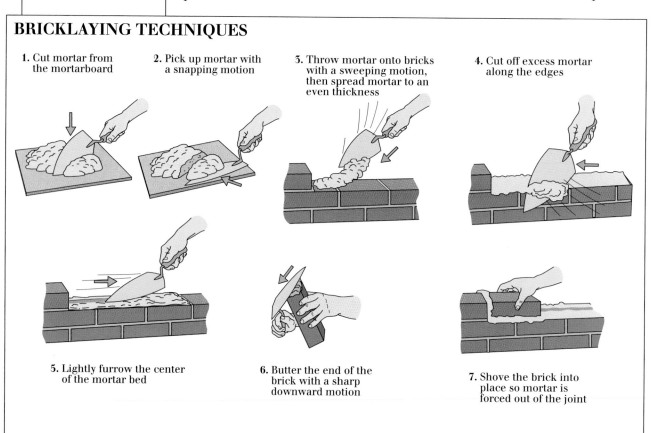

1. Cut mortar from the mortarboard

2. Pick up mortar with a snapping motion

3. Throw mortar onto bricks with a sweeping motion, then spread mortar to an even thickness

4. Cut off excess mortar along the edges

5. Lightly furrow the center of the mortar bed

6. Butter the end of the brick with a sharp downward motion

7. Shove the brick into place so mortar is forced out of the joint

must be "buttered." Hold the brick in one hand, with the end to be buttered tipped up at an angle of about 45 degrees. Place a small amount of mortar on the trowel and apply it to the end of the brick with a sharp, downward motion. Slapping the mortar onto the brick in this way causes it to bond.

Now place the brick on the mortar bed and shove it firmly against one already in place. When done correctly, mortar will be forced out the sides and top of the vertical joint. Use the trowel to skim the excess off and use it to butter the end of the next brick. Rap the brick with the end of the trowel handle to set and level it. If a brick is too low, do not simply pull it up a little bit; this will leave a gap where water can enter, freeze, and crack the mortar. If you place a brick incorrectly, pull it out, replace the mortar, and lay the brick again.

Building a Single-Wythe Wall

Now that you know how to work with mortar, you are ready to build a brick wall. One of the easiest types to build is the single-wythe brick planter box, which makes an attractive and functional feature. Normally, you wouldn't build a single-wythe wall more than a foot or so high, because it could be knocked over fairly easily. However, once you put corners on such a wall, it becomes much stronger. If you live in a cold climate, you'll likely need double-wythe walls. Because soil swells when it freezes just as water does, it can push out the sides of a single-wythe brick planter.

Laying Out the Wall This example is a three-sided rectangular box built against a house, with the concrete house foundation forming the back wall. Dig a trench about

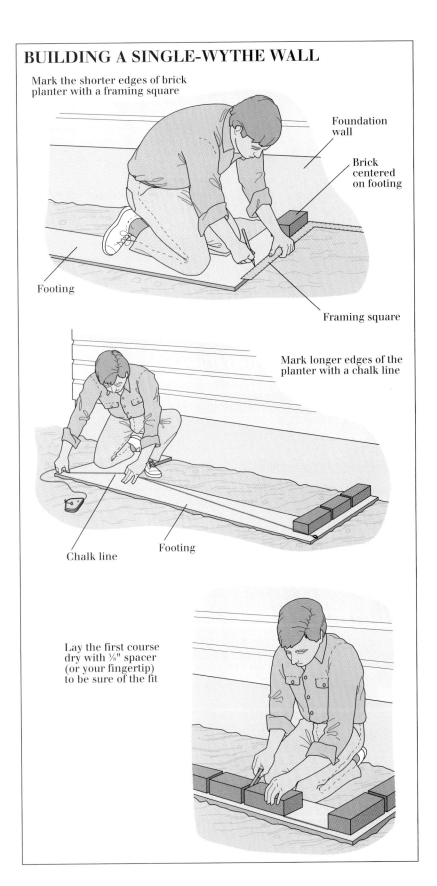

BUILDING A SINGLE-WYTHE WALL

Mark the shorter edges of brick planter with a framing square

Foundation wall

Brick centered on footing

Footing

Framing square

Mark longer edges of the planter with a chalk line

Chalk line

Footing

Lay the first course dry with ⅛" spacer (or your fingertip) to be sure of the fit

14 inches deep. Add a 6-inch bed of gravel. Pour a reinforced concrete footing twice the width of the wall and at least 8 inches thick. The top of the footing should be level. Cover the footing with plastic sheeting to prevent moisture loss and allow five to seven days for the concrete to cure.

BUILDING A SINGLE-WYTHE WALL (continued)

Shove the first brick into the furrowed mortar against the foundation wall

Try not to slop mortar over the guideline

Check each coarse often for level with a carpenter's level and a straight 2×4

The next step is to lay out the exact position of the wall on the footing. Brush the footing clean of any dirt, so that the mortar will make a tight bond. Center the brick on the footing next to the foundation and make a pencil mark where the outside of the first brick will be. Lay a steel framing square flat with one edge against the house foundation and the tongue next to the pencil mark. Using the square as a guide, snap a chalk line on the footing, then complete the layout, making sure that both sides are parallel with each other and square with the house.

Laying the Bricks With the wall dimensions outlined on the footing, lay the first course as a dry run to check the fit. Space the bricks with pieces of ⅜-inch plywood, or use the old mason's trick of spacing the bricks with the tip of your little finger. If the footing is laid out correctly, the bricks should fit without cutting. If they are off a little, adjust the lines on the footing to avoid having to cut a lot of bricks.

Using the troweling technique (see page 248), lay a bed of mortar for a distance of about three bricks. Try not to cover the chalk line with the mortar. Make a shallow furrow in the center of the mortar. Butter the end of the first brick and shove it against the foundation and into the mortar bed. Lay the rest of the bricks in the same manner, then use a carpenter's level to check that the course is true and level. If a brick is too high, tap it down with the trowel handle; if one is too low, remove it and lay it again using fresh mortar. Use the trowel to remove excess mortar on both sides of this first course, then use the tip of the trowel to smooth and firm up the mortar on the footing.

At the first corner, spread mortar on the footing for three bricks.

Butter the end of the first brick and push it into place against the side of the last brick, using care not to push that brick out of alignment. Continue to lay bricks down this second side of the planter. Since this leg of the planter is almost surely longer than your level, place the level on top of a straight 2×4 to check your work. For longer walls use mason's twine and line blocks for keeping each course true and level.

When starting the second course, be sure to begin with a half brick so that this course will offset the first one. The corners of each course will be offset also, as illustrated on the opposite page. Start at one end of the planter and keep working your way around, course by course, until you reach the desired height of 1 to 2 feet. Remember to tool the joints before the mortar sets.

Tooling and Finishing Joints

If you are new to bricklaying, you will probably be working more slowly than a professional might. Because of this, it is important to keep a careful watch on the mortar and to tool the joints before they get too hard. Joints should be tooled when the mortar will just accept a thumbprint with firm pressure. Tooling the joints compresses the mortar, which is necessary to completely fill the voids and prevent moisture from entering. Always tool the head joints first, then the bed joints. If there is not enough mortar in the joint, place a small amount on the trowel, pick up some of it with the jointer, and press it into the joint. A slightly concave joint is the best for weathering and for cold climates where freezing is common. In the more temperate regions, numerous decorative joints can be used. Check patterns and joint textures in your area and ask the brick supplier for a practical recommendation.

TOOLING AND FINISHING JOINTS

Tool the head joints first . . .

. . . then tool the bed joints

Capping the Wall

Walls are commonly capped for protection and a finished appearance. Walls can be capped with brick or with a contrasting material such as flagstone, pavers, or cast concrete. A common way to cap a double-wythe wall is with a header course or rowlock header of bricks. To do this, lay a course of mortar on the top course. Then, depending on the pattern you are using for the cap, butter either the edge or the face of each brick and put it firmly in place. This will be a particularly visible part of the wall, so watch carefully that the joint thickness remains consistent.

When you are within about 4 feet of the end of the wall, do a dry layout of the remaining cap bricks to see how they will fit. If the last brick extends over the end of the wall, it will have to be cut to fit. Don't place this cut brick at the end; rather, bury it 3 or 4 feet from the end, where it will not be noticed.

If you use pavers or flagstone to cap the wall, use the same principles as for brick. Although the mortar joints for the wall may be tooled in any pattern you wish, the joints along the cap should be struck flat and smooth so there is no depression that will collect water.

BUILDING LEADS

Fill in the area between, using line blocks and mason's twine to guide you

Line block

Mason's twine

Line block

"Tail the lead" with a level; the corners of the bricks should line up against a straightedge

Building Leads

The brick planter described in this section is an easy introduction to laying a brick wall. Its corners were built as part of the running course of each wall. However, for most brick walls, the corners—called leads—are built first and then the bricks between them are filled in. Leads are built first so that mason's twine can be stretched the length of the wall to keep each course straight and level.

There are two commonly used types of leads: the straight lead for the ends of walls, and the corner lead. For a basic single-wythe wall with a running bond pattern, corner leads would be built in the following manner.

Begin by remembering this rule: The number of bricks in the first course of the lead equals the number of bricks in the finished corner. If, for example, the wall will be 11 courses high, you will lay out 6 bricks down one leg of the corner and five bricks down the other leg. Once the lead is built, you will see that it forms stair steps of half a brick at a time. To make sure that the bricks are all properly placed, put a level or straightedge diagonally along the lead. Every brick course should just touch the straightedge. If a brick is out of line, tap it gently into place without moving the top or bottom brick.

Since bricks are laid from the leads toward the center, the last brick in each course must be fitted between two previously laid bricks. Butter the ends of the bricks already in place and then butter both ends of the last brick in the row; then, placing the brick directly over the opening, force it into place. A considerable amount of mortar will be squeezed out, but this is necessary to form a tight seal.

WORKING WITH STONE

Whether you are building a patio, a stone wall, or a rock garden, stone is an interesting and challenging material to work with. Although expensive, it has a permanence that few other materials can rival. Creating beautiful stonework requires patience and an artistic flair, but with care and consideration for the material anyone can produce an acceptable finished product.

Obtaining Stone

There are two types of stone: dimensioned (or quarried) stone and fieldstone.

Dimensioned Stone Dimensioned stone has usually been quarried as a block or large piece and then cut into a panel, slab, or other shape according to a specified measurement. It is normally cut at the site and sometimes is left with a natural face. Cutting is an expensive process that requires specialized equipment, which is why dimensioned stone is so much more expensive than fieldstone. The types of quarried stone commonly used in residential applications are granite, limestone, sandstone, marble, and slate.

Some concrete products are manufactured to look like quarried stone. This material is available in many patterns, textures, and colors. Some of it looks like real stone from a distance, and it is quite durable, much less costly, and reasonably colorfast.

Fieldstone As the name implies, fieldstone is uncut natural stone that is found in fields, along streams and rivers, and at the seashore. Sometimes it is rough faced; it may be water-washed and smooth. It has no specific dimensions. Fieldstone

Dimensioned stone has flat, straight edges, making the pieces easier to fit than flagstone.

Fieldstone, being irregular, is much more difficult to work with than quarried or dressed stone. However, its rough, informal appearance adds a natural charm to any landscape.

is divided into two categories: rubble and roughly squared. Rubble is just that—rough, random, natural rocks. Roughly squared stone is fieldstone that has been "dressed," or chiseled, to remove irregular or rounded sides. Dressed stone is more expensive but easier to work with. When selecting fieldstone, choose flat stones—they are much easier to work with than rounded ones. Fieldstone makes wonderful dry-stacked stone walls and can be used for random paving accents, stepping-stones, or edgings.

Finding Stone If you collect your own, the easiest place to find it is along rivers, streams, and highway or road cuts. Be sure that you obtain permission from the landowners or authorities before gathering stone. If purchasing stone, go to several different stoneyards in your area and compare prices and the

materials they have on hand. Be sure to inquire about the price of delivery. If buying rubble, check that the stones have at least one flat side and that the faces that will be exposed are attractive. For more information on obtaining and working with stone, see pages 85 and 89.

Cut stone such as ashlar and flagstone are the most expensive. Roughly squared stone is less costly, and fieldstone the most inexpensive of all, providing it comes from local sources. In areas where natural fieldstone is unavailable, transportation from long distances has increased its price to exceed that of cut stone from nearby quarries.

Estimating Quantity
The amount of stone you will need varies, depending on the project and the type of stone you are using. A flagstone patio bedded in mortar

will require stones that are between ½ and ¾ inch thick. Based on the total surface area, a stone supplier can tell you how many pieces (or tons) are required. See page 89 for more information on ordering stone.

To estimate the total volume for a stone wall, multiply the width times the length times the height. If working with fieldstone, allow more than 10 percent for waste, as many stones in a random load simply will not fit your pattern. If using cut stone, have it delivered on pallets and unloaded with proper equipment; cut stone chips if handled roughly.

Cutting Fieldstone

When cutting fieldstone, place the rock to be cut on a firm but resilient material—the ground, a bed of sand, or a piece of thick plywood. Do not set the stone on concrete; the reverberating shock waves can cause the stone to split in the wrong place.

All kinds of stone have sedimentary layers, veins, and faults. If possible, cut the stone at these places. Sometimes these faults will be adjacent to irregularities or protuberances. Once you have decided where to cut, mark it with a piece of chalk or crayon. Use a chisel to score the stone along this line, turning the stone so that the scoring is as continuous as possible. Then position the chisel on the scoring and give it a sharp blow with a sledgehammer. Dress the edges as necessary. Use a pointing chisel to remove any bumps or sharp irregularities by placing the tip at the bump and rapping sharply with the sledgehammer.

Some stones will not cut easily, if at all. Set the hardest stones aside or find a place to use them without cutting. For cutting flagstone, see page 210.

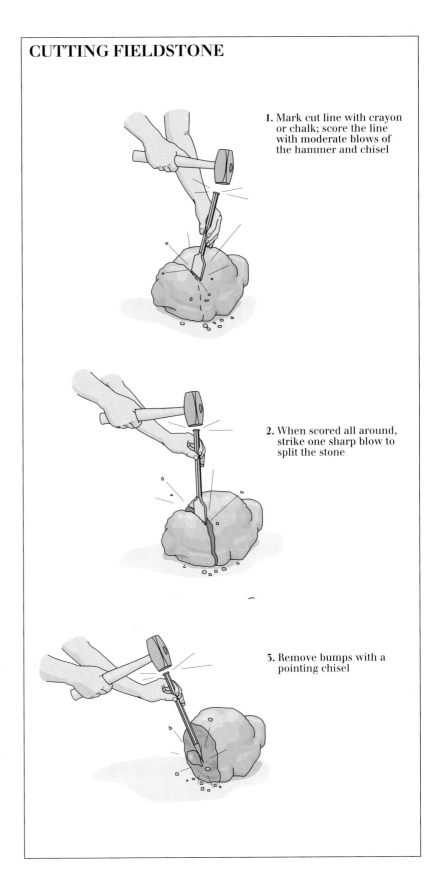

CUTTING FIELDSTONE

1. Mark cut line with crayon or chalk; score the line with moderate blows of the hammer and chisel

2. When scored all around, strike one sharp blow to split the stone

3. Remove bumps with a pointing chisel

Vertical retaining walls, if they are more than one or two courses of stone high, must be mortared to hold the weight of the soil behind them. Retaining walls higher than 3 feet might support tons of weight and should be installed by professionals or experienced masons.

BUILDING A MORTARED STONE WALL

If your yard has not been landscaped and numerous rocks are lying about, put them to good use. By using existing rock to build a stone wall, you will not only clear the land but also gain an attractive freestanding or retaining wall.

You can build a stone wall with or without mortar, depending on the desired appearance and strength. Mortared stone walls require considerably more work, because you will be dealing with sizable amounts of mortar. A mortared stone wall is not only more permanent than a dry-stacked wall but appears more finished.

The height of the wall may be regulated by local building codes. Generally, you are free to build a wall up to 3 feet high without a permit. Higher walls require a permit and possibly even an engineering study, so consult the building department first.

Construction Preparations

A mortared stone wall is inflexible and must be supported by a continuous concrete footing. The footing should be at least 2 inches wider on each side than the width of the base of the stone. It should also be reinforced with at least two ½-inch-diameter steel rebars running the length of the footing.

To prepare the footing, first lay out the wall site with stakes and mason's twine. The footing should be at least 8 inches wide. In regions with no frost, the footing trench should be 12 inches deep. The top of the footing should be level and the sides cut accurately into the earth—a clean-edged trench uses less concrete than a rough one. It is not necessary to form the sides of the footing unless the soil is very sandy or wet. Allow the footing to set for a couple of days before laying the stones.

Mixing the Mortar

The mortar mix for a stone wall should be a little stiffer (drier) than that used for brick so that it will support the heavy rocks. You should also add a little hydrated lime to make the mortar stick to the stone better and reduce staining. A standard mix is 1½ parts portland cement, ½ part hydrated lime, and 6 parts sand. Mix thoroughly, then carefully add water, mixing all the while, so that the mix is stiff but holds together. When you trowel on the mortar, it should stay in place, not ooze down the side of the rock. For general information on mortar, see page 245.

Applying the Mortar

Before applying the mortar to any stones, it is important to clean them of any dirt or sand. Either brush them off or wash them with a forceful stream of water.

Dry-fit each stone before you place the mortar. Mortar is not glue—it does not stick the stones to each other; it simply fills the natural voids in the wall. Stones should be supported by other stones. When you are sure a stone fits, remove it temporarily and place the mortar. Do so by actually throwing the mortar off the trowel. Work the mortar with the tip of the trowel so that all the voids are filled. Then firmly bed the stone so it touches the stones supporting it. Excess mortar should be scraped off and placed in the center of the wall so that there are no cavities left there.

Laying the First Course

Stones should be laid as they would fall if thrown on the ground. A stone will not naturally stand on end and should not be laid that way. Dry-set a base course of the heaviest stones until you are satisfied with the fit. Then remove them and place a 2-inch bed of mortar.

Remember that you are building a wall that is two wythes wide (in essence, two parallel walls), with the center portion filled with smaller rubble and mortar. Do not allow vertical mortar joints to be continuous. Offset the stones or the wall will be weakened. A good motto for a stonemason is: One rock over two, two rocks over one.

Building the Ends

After you have set the first course in mortar, start building up the ends. Stretch mason's twine between two stakes set at the ends of the wall and set the line 3 or 4 inches above the top of the next course. Keep the line taut and use a line level for proper horizontal alignment. Use the flattest stones with the smoothest faces for the end wall construction, interlocking the stones as much as possible.

MORTARED WALL

The first course should be the largest stones; set in a 2" layer of mortar on the footing

2" mortar bed

Footing

As you continue, dry-fit 2 or 3 stones at a time before setting them in mortar

String with line level

Stake

With the ends built up, start laying courses in the middle section.

Laying the Middle Courses

Dry-fit several stones at a time, then remove them, apply the mortar, and fit them back into place. When fitting stones against each other, spread mortar on the one already in place.

As you work your way up, remember to lay bond stones—rocks that span the width of the wall—to tie the two wythes together. Place bond stones about 4 feet apart horizontally about halfway up the wall (or more often if you have good bond stones). If the wall is high, add a bond stone every 2 vertical feet. Stones are heavy, and if the mortar is holding them up it is subject to crushing forces. Never lay more than two vertical courses a day so the mortar has time to develop some supportive strength.

Capping the Wall

A beautiful way to finish a wall is to cap it with a row of flat bond stones, but it is not often that you have enough of these. Instead, mortar the flattest stones you have along the top of the wall. Do not rake the top joints as described below, but leave them flush with the top edges of the stone for a more finished look.

Jointing a Stone Wall

The mortar in the face joints of a stone wall can either be left flush with the rocks or raked out. Many people prefer to rake the joints because the shadows cast by the stones above the indentations add definition to the wall. You can remove an inch or so of the surface mortar without weakening the wall. This is most easily done with a shaped stick or dowel.

Timing is important. The joints must be pointed (smoothed) or

MORTARED WALL (continued)

Don't be delicate in placing mortar—throw it from trowel to rock, then work it in with tip of trowel

Place bond stones every 4 feet or so about halfway up the wall

Bond stones

Cap stone

A row of flat bond stones makes the best cap stones for a wall

raked after the mortar is firm but before it is set hard. If you press your thumb firmly against the mortar, it should make a slight indentation. This is usually about half an hour after the stone has been set in place, but it will vary with the weather and the actual mortar mix. If you are building a long wall, check regularly and don't allow your previous work to set too hard before jointing. After raking the joints to the preferred depth, brush away the excess mortar. Smooth the surface of the mortar with a jointer for a hard finish.

BUILDING A DRY-STACKED STONE WALL

A dry-stacked stone wall is built much like a mortared stone wall—though of course the mortar is left out. This type of wall takes a lot of patience and care. Select the pieces for the best possible interlocking and mutual support. If a stone does not fit properly, it will eventually work out of the wall, and part of the wall will collapse. Properly constructed dry-stacked walls will stand for centuries. If you live in a cold climate, a concrete footing or series of large base stones should be placed below the frost line; otherwise the wall will heave and collapse.

Stone walls can be laid straight or curved, with vertical or battered faces. Battering (setting the top back a few degrees from the edge of the base) creates a more stable wall. Make a batter board from a 1×2 to use as a gauge. Slope the face of the wall a minimum of 1 inch for every 2 feet of height.

The base width of a dry-stacked wall will be in direct relationship to the height, usually 2 feet at the base for every 3 feet of height. However, low retaining walls only a couple of feet in height are often only one stone thick. Lean stone retaining walls into the berm at a batter of 3 inches for every 1 foot of height.

Laying the Base
Whether you pour a footing or not, the base of the wall must be on firm, undisturbed soil. If possible, dig through the topsoil to a firm underlayer below the frost line. Dig a trench with a smooth bottom for the footing or the base stones (see page 243). To start the wall, first lay out the largest and flattest stones for the base. Set them so that they are firm and stable. Sometimes it is necessary to wedge them with small shards of rock. Base stones should slope slightly inward so that gravity wedges the stacked stones tighter together rather than tending to topple them out of the wall.

This dry-stacked stone wall shows the skill of its maker. The stones are fairly flat on all sides, making a close fit possible.

Building the Ends

The most challenging part of good wall construction is building the ends or right-angle corners. As with brick mortared stone walls, it is common practice to build the ends and corners first and then fill in the rest (see pages 252 and 257). Use the longest and flattest rocks for the ends and corners. Place the stones so that each one interlocks with the others. Select the rocks with the smoothest faces to give the wall a finished appearance. Take your time, because careful construction at this point is important to the long-term stability of the wall. If you can't find rocks that will fit tightly enough, try cutting some. The wall is going to be around for many years, and you want it to look right and require minimum maintenance.

Laying the Other Courses

Lay each course of stone as described for the mortared stone wall (see page 257), using mason's twine to show you where to raise or lower wall sections. Check the face of the wall periodically with the batter board and level. Remember to tie the wythes together with bond stones, not more than 2 feet up, placed about 4 feet apart horizontally.

Capping the Wall

For a finished appearance and to hold the wall firmly together, lay a series of flat bond stones across the top of the wall. Mortar them together as a continuous bond to increase the strength of the wall. If you have a lot of irregularly shaped rocks left over, consider mortaring them in place along the top of the wall as a finishing touch.

DRY-STACKED STONE WALL CONSTRUCTION

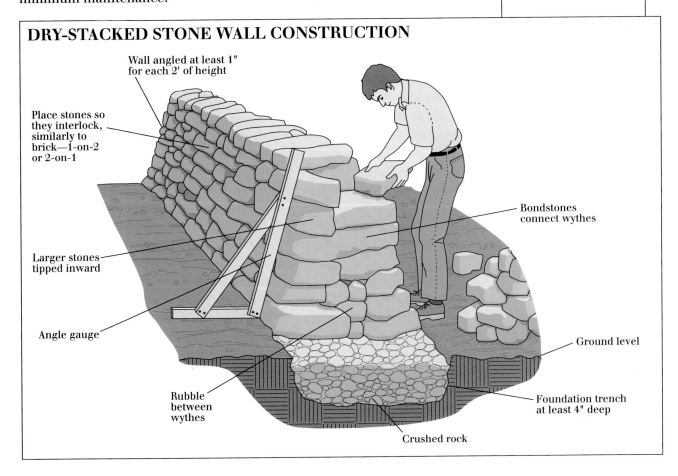

Wall angled at least 1" for each 2' of height

Place stones so they interlock, similarly to brick—1-on-2 or 2-on-1

Larger stones tipped inward

Angle gauge

Rubble between wythes

Bondstones connect wythes

Ground level

Foundation trench at least 4" deep

Crushed rock

OVERHEAD STRUCTURES

Lath makes one of the least expensive shade structures as well as one of the most simple to erect. Lath fencing is available in 4×8 panels and requires only the lightest of supports. As with any overhead structure, they should be anchored firmly and braced well.

Pergola, gazebo, arbor, trellis—the names for overhead structures often sound exotic. But whether composed primarily of sculpted redwood beams or of Elizabethan climbing roses, all perform the simple function of providing shade and sanctuary. Overhead structures are natural companions to decks and patios.

Almost any type of building material can be used for an overhead structure. A few simple beams on posts can support a roof of vines that will provide shade, color, and fragrance. Fabrics ranging from sailcloth to some of the new "miracle" plastics can shade a patio or cover a stadium. Roofing materials range from the age-old hand-split wood shake to state-of-the-art rubber membrane. Lightweight, reinforced concrete can be used for thin, elegant shells capable of covering modest patios or sprawling summer markets. Most, if not all, of these methods are within the range of do-it-yourself skills.

CHOOSING A DESIGN

There are two basic considerations when deciding on a design. The first is the practical one: Will the structure do what it is supposed to do? If it's a patio roof, will it provide shade where it's needed? If it's an arbor, will it be a suitable point of transition between lawn and garden? Such practical requirements shape the basic layout of the design.

The second consideration is aesthetic. A purely functional design can be an eyesore in the wrong setting. An ideal design fits naturally into its surroundings, provides a feeling of comfort and shelter, and reflects the style and taste of its owners. These considerations, along with basic elements of scale, proportion, and choice of materials, can lead to a delightful impression of inevitability. It often comes down to a certain something, difficult to define yet impossible to ignore, that makes one particular design seem right.

CHOOSING A SITE

The selection of a building site deserves special attention. Where you place a structure will affect not only the usefulness of the structure itself, but also the character of the surrounding area.

The possibilities for adapting an overhead to your site are limitless. Use long, narrow trellises to cover walks, protect windows from unwanted sunlight, or provide shelter for shade-loving plants. Raised portions of the canopy will focus attention on the area below. Cover an expansive area, such as a large patio or deck, by adding more posts, beams, and joists. If you'd like to leave some areas sunny, you can usually use the same post-and-beam arrangement as for the rest of the overhead, but omit the lattice covering.

The local building department can simplify the task of choosing a site by telling you what you *can't* do. Most municipalities have specific requirements for setbacks from property lines, maximum lot coverage, and maximum height of outbuildings.

Even if you have already settled on a location, there are certain things you can do to get the most from an outdoor room. Use your bubble diagrams to consider traffic patterns and how the structure will be used. If you'll be dining outdoors frequently, it's desirable to situate a barbecue area for easy access to the kitchen. If privacy is a consideration, take advantage of trees, fences, or an out-of-the-way location in the yard.

Pay attention to the patterns of sunlight and wind. Study how the sun affects the site at different times of day and different times of year (see page 25). This is particularly relevant for overhead structures, where you may want shade during the hottest part of the day and sunlight in the morning and evening. Consider the effects of prevailing winds on the proposed

An overhead structure not only protects from the sun, but also helps to enclose an area, increasing the sense of an outdoor room and adding structural interest to a landscape.

site. A cool afternoon breeze may be welcome on a hot summer day, but strong, gusty winds in an unprotected area can make an outdoor room uninhabitable.

Finally, use your choice of site to establish the architectural character of the new structure. Using materials, colors, and detailing that match or complement existing fences, outbuildings, or the house itself will help the new structure blend naturally with the existing ones.

PLANS AND PERMITS

Find out from the local building department if you will need a permit for your proposed project. Some detached outdoor structures do not require a permit, but most attached ones do. If a permit is required, you'll most likely have to prepare a site plan showing the location of the structure on the property, and detailed drawings that demonstrate that it will conform to building and safety codes. You will also have to pay a fee, which will be based on the estimated value of the improvements. For a discussion of such legalities, see page 49.

You can use this book as a guide to prepare your own drawings, or you can have them done by a professional. If you will be making any structural changes (increasing a beam span, for instance) or if you have to deal with snow loads, you should enlist the help of an architect, a landscape architect, or a structural engineer.

BUDGET AND SCHEDULE

Before jumping into construction, find out how much the project will cost and how long it will take to finish. Try to set aside enough time and money to complete construction within a reasonable time

frame. A project that sits half-finished for months can become weathered and deteriorated on exposed areas before it's even completed. In addition, if a project is idle for an extended period of time, the building official has the right to revoke the building permit.

Figuring the cost of materials is usually a straightforward proposition. When you have completed the plans, make a detailed materials list (see page 93).

The physical design of an overhead structure depends on climatic conditions as well as aesthetic ones. In temperate regions, building codes dictate that an overhead structure have a load-bearing capacity 30 pounds per square foot. This allows for 20 pounds live load per square foot for normal wind loading or a worker or two on the roof, and 10 pounds dead load per square foot for the actual building materials. This is probably more than necessary, but building codes are conservative and allow for safety factors in the design requirements.

Snow loading is an entirely different matter. Many regions in North America experience regular snow loads of more than 60 pounds per square foot—that is equivalent to parking heavy trucks all over the roof! The entire structure, including the footings, must be appropriately designed for climatic conditions.

Footings for Overhead Structures

Most soils will carry a load equivalent to 2,000 pounds per square foot. This includes firm sand, firm clay, and most loams or compact silts. Filled soils, some clays, and soils containing a large amount of vegetable matter will bear lighter loads; soils heavy in gravel will carry larger loads. Check local building codes for the allowable

FOOTING DIAGRAM

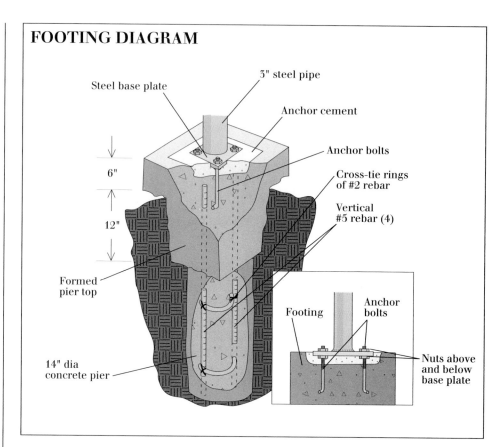

3" steel pipe

Steel base plate

Anchor cement

Anchor bolts

Cross-tie rings of #2 rebar

Vertical #5 rebar (4)

6"

12"

Formed pier top

Footing

Anchor bolts

14" dia concrete pier

Nuts above and below base plate

The substantial footings for this heavy structure are hidden by the concrete patio and the lawn.

bearing capacities for various types of soil.

As an example, let's calculate the size of a footing for an overhead structure in a mild climate. Suppose that the corner post is carrying an 8-foot-square area of roof. (This would be the case if the overhead were 16 feet square and resting on four posts.) Using the code-specified load-bearing capacity of 30 pounds per square foot, this would be $8 \times 8 \times 30 = 1,920$ *pounds.* A 1-foot-square footing under the post would be adequate, assuming soil types of an average bearing capacity of 2,000 pounds per square foot.

If this same structure were built in a location with a snow load of 60 pounds per square foot and a dead load of 10 pounds per square foot, the weight equation would be considerably different: $8 \times 8 \times 70 = 4,480$ *pounds.* In this case, the post will require a footing of 2.24 square feet, or 18 inches by 18 inches. If the same footing were also supporting a deck of the same area, the load would double and so the footing would have to double in surface area to 4.48 square feet, or 26 inches by 26 inches. Concrete footings should be at least 8 inches thick. Remember that footings must bear on firm, undisturbed earth. If possible, footings should be below the topsoil line.

If you are building a new concrete patio, all you will need to do is to thicken the concrete at post locations—unless there is a danger of frost penetration. If freezing and heaving is a problem, structural footings will have to be established below the frost line. In temperate zones it will be sufficient to thicken the concrete to 12 inches in an area 2 feet square (see calculations above) and set steel straps or post anchors if the support columns are to be wood. If the supports are to be steel, set an appropriate number of bolts in the concrete.

Load-bearing capacity is not the only factor that determines overhead design; there are other considerations to bear in mind. Wind, for example, can cause an overhead structure attached to a house to lift vertically as wind hitting the house is diverted upward. Numerous methods of "tying down" roofs are on the market; check the local building-supply outlet for pre-shaped steel ties for increasing horizontal and vertical strength.

SHADING

Often the primary function of an overhead structure is to provide shade during the hottest part of the day. There are many creative ways to accomplish this. A simple frame can support vines for beautiful and effective summer shade. If the vine

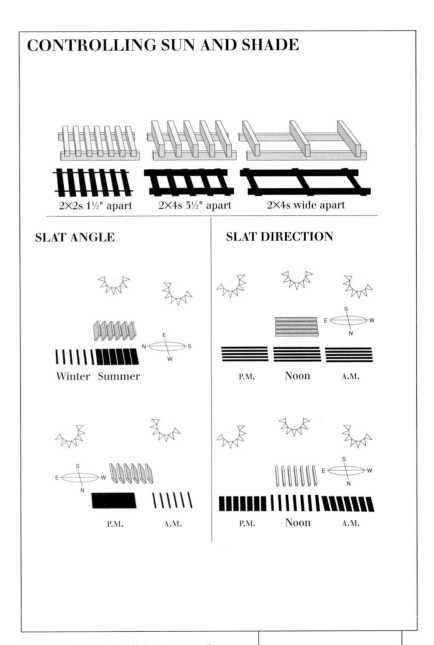

CONTROLLING SUN AND SHADE

2×2s 1½" apart   2×4s 3½" apart   2×4s wide apart

SLAT ANGLE

Winter   Summer

SLAT DIRECTION

P.M.   Noon   A.M.

P.M.   A.M.

P.M.   Noon   A.M.

is deciduous, it will let some of the winter sun through the fabric of its branches. For example, grape arbors provide dense shade in summer, dappled sun in autumn, and delicious fruit in between.

Canvas or nylon sailcloth panels can be mounted on sliding tracks or tied in place as awnings. Lattice panels are lightweight and, depending on the pattern, can provide dappled or nearly total shade. Their open structure guarantees air

LATTICE DETAIL

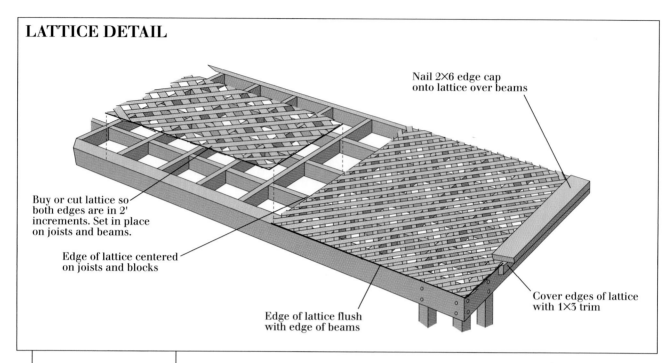

Nail 2×6 edge cap onto lattice over beams

Buy or cut lattice so both edges are in 2' increments. Set in place on joists and beams.

Edge of lattice centered on joists and blocks

Edge of lattice flush with edge of beams

Cover edges of lattice with 1×3 trim

movement and cooling breezes on hot days.

Woven bamboo blinds can be installed permanently or so they roll up or down in frames. The life span of these lightweight slats is short, however; you can expect a couple of seasons if you put them away for the winter. (To avoid mildew, make sure they are completely dry before storing.)

Louvered roofs can be used to control the amount of light and sun emitted, which is determined by the angle of the louvers and whether they are fixed or movable. Fixed louvers are simple to build. The most common types are 2×4s or 2×6s set on edge over wood beams. Depending on the spacing of vertical louvers, shade patterns can be controlled somewhat, with the most sun coming through at midday. Angled louvers can be constructed so that only the morning sun will penetrate the structure. Like latticework roofs, louvered roofs allow air to pass through relatively unimpeded and can be used to divert prevailing winds if desired.

FREESTANDING GARDEN STRUCTURES

Garden structures that are not attached to the house or some other fixed building, or structures that extend 6 feet or more from an existing building, are subject to forces that could cause them to sway. Excessive swaying will eventually result in collapse.

Like all buildings, lightweight garden structures need bracing to prevent side-to-side motion caused by wind, earthquake, or even the pressure of someone leaning against a post or wall. Effective bracing can be accomplished with a short section of rigid wall, such as masonry, or framing sheathed with plywood or a similar material. Sometimes adequate bracing can be achieved with a simple diagonal timber or by extending posts or columns into the ground.

Bracing does not necessarily have to be under the roof. Sections of fencing or decorative screens can extend outward from the structure, as can masonry walls, so long as

PERSPECTIVE VIEW

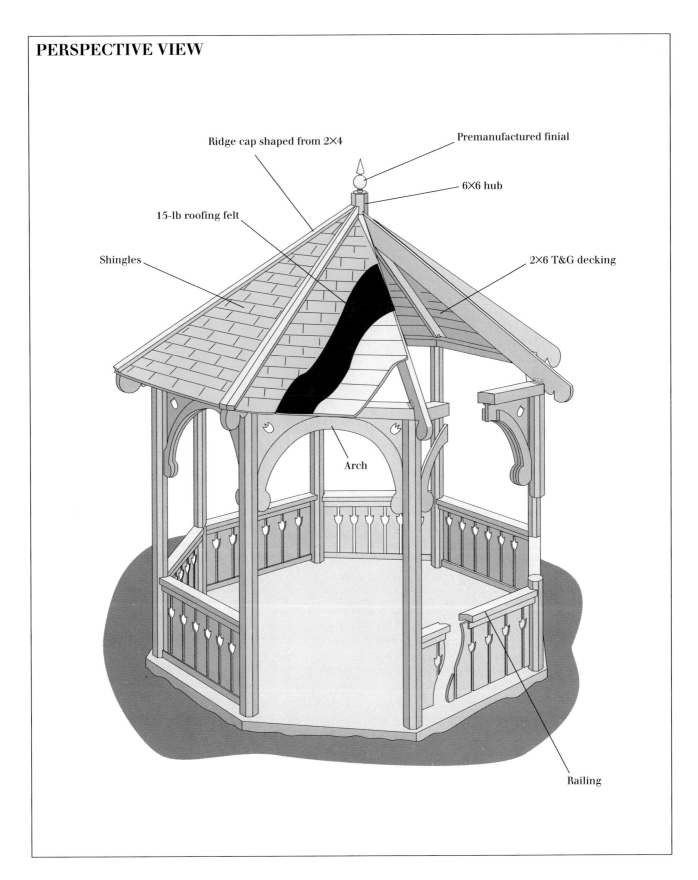

Ridge cap shaped from 2×4

Premanufactured finial

6×6 hub

15-lb roofing felt

2×6 T&G decking

Shingles

Arch

Railing

POST BASE AND POST-AND-BEAM DETAIL

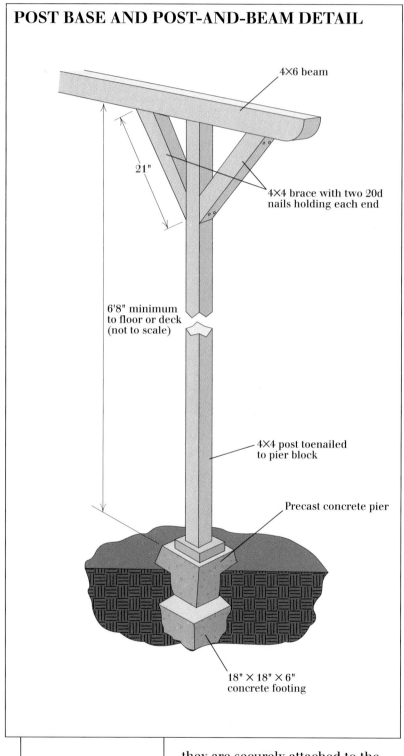

4×6 beam

21"

4×4 brace with two 20d
nails holding each end

6'8" minimum
to floor or deck
(not to scale)

4×4 post toenailed
to pier block

Precast concrete pier

18" × 18" × 6"
concrete footing

POST FOOTING DETAIL

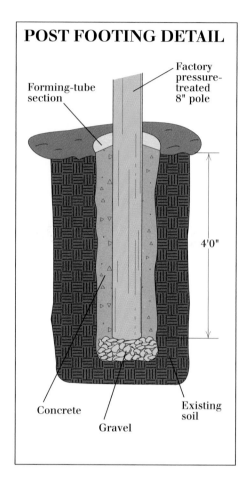

Forming-tube
section

Factory
pressure-
treated
8" pole

4'0"

Concrete

Gravel

Existing
soil

the design elements required to
eliminate sway.

COLUMNS

Columns are simply posts whose
purpose is to support a roof structure. They can be round, square,
octagonal (or any other multisided
shape), and they can be decorative
or plain.

Columns can be made of almost
any building material—concrete,
stone, brick, steel, wood, fiberglass,
or plastic. Composite columns can
be constructed with a combination
of these: wood trim can enclose
a steel center, masonry can face a
concrete column reinforced with
steel rebar.

Two factors—structural integrity
and aesthetic integrity—are of
prime importance and neither is

they are securely attached to the
vertical supports.

As with all design solutions,
structural or otherwise, appearance
is important. Consider carefully

Columns are substantial architectural elements and should be used only if they are supporting a weight that appears proportional to their size, as is the case here.

really more significant than the other. A column must be capable of holding the load imposed on it and it must look good too.

Proportion is relevant as well. A column should *appear* to be strong enough to hold up the structure it supports. A 2-inch-diameter pipe column might be more than adequate to support a 6-inch by 16-inch wood beam holding a massive shade structure, but it would appear out of proportion, incorrect to the eye. A reasonable design rule of thumb is to size column areas to match the area of the beams they support.

LIGHTING, SPAS, FENCES & PLANTERS

Besides its obvious advantages of safety and visibility, lighting sculpts a space at night. The night view, with its drama and strong shadow patterns, can appear very different from the day landscape.

Once you've successfully planned your deck or patio, it is time to think about those delightful features that make them truly livable. Outdoor lighting, portable and permanent spas, windbreaks and fences, planters—all can enhance the beauty and functionality of an outdoor living space. Lighting extends the use of a deck or patio and can dramatize features and increase security. Spas add the year-round potential of a watery spot in which to socialize and relax. Fences and planters screen, divide, soften, and brighten an outdoor room. Here is how to plan and install the finishing touches that will make your deck or patio enjoyable for years to come.

Lighting shouldn't make the outdoors look like the in-doors. Light the areas that need it, but leave pools of darkness, allowing shadows to add mystery to the areas where visibility is less important.

WHY INSTALL OUTDOOR LIGHTING

Light is an important, powerful element and tool. It can create moods of happiness or gloom, serenity or anxiety; it can also have a physical impact, a feeling of warmth or cold, excitement or re-laxation. It can make a place safe at night, extend a welcome, guide the way, or widen the use of an area that might otherwise have limited appeal. If well planned it will be in-visible—only the features and func-tions you choose to emphasize will shine forth.

Designing a Lighting System

As you design your lighting system, remember the main purposes for outdoor lighting—function, visual impact, and practicality. Lighting levels vary according to purpose. Generally, lower levels are for viewing; higher levels are for activ-ity areas. Light is sometimes diffi-cult to control in a small yard, and it is surprising how much even a dim light can spill over the property line; be careful about beaming light into a neighbor's yard. Use louvered shields so that light from bare bulbs or spotlights will not

shine into neighbors' homes or onto their outdoor living spaces.

Study the natural light on your lot. Notice how the sun and the moon cast shadows and reveal textures and tracery, or how the light looks on bright, cloudless days as opposed to cloudy ones. For night lighting to look right, it should simulate natural light as much as possible. The quality of light in a yard depends directly on the surfaces and materials in the spaces to be lighted.

Do not overlight your yard. When in doubt, err on the side of too little light. Lower levels create effects that look more natural. Carefully select techniques and fixtures that are in scale with the spaces, and avoid glare at all costs.

Bear in mind that insects are attracted to light. If insects are a problem in your area, try using pink or yellow bulbs sold as "bug" lights. If the quality or color of these is unappealing, at least place standard-colored fixtures away from windows or doors so you don't invite insects into the house. Avoid lights near outdoor dining areas as they may attract insect dinner guests.

The smaller the yard, the simpler the lighting system should be. Try to stick with one type of lamp for continuity within the landscape. In larger spaces, you can use a variety of techniques and lamp types. Carefully analyze what areas and elements require illumination, and determine light levels and fixture types accordingly. Use bright lights for safety along paths and in entryways, and arrange softer, more subtle accent lighting for special features. You can also use lighting to mask or black out areas that are unsightly by placing bright lights in front of the space. You may want to black out scruffy plants, an unfinished structure, a fence that needs paint, or a storage area.

Place switches and controls in protected, easily accessible locations. Hide light sources to the extent possible, concealing fixtures under plants or other objects; position them so light bounces off surfaces or is diffused through leaves, to avoid glare. Always direct the light beam away from the viewer.

Choose fixture locations carefully so they don't interfere with walkways or yard maintenance. Paint fixtures to blend in with plants or nearby structures. If you are installing the landscape in phases, consider using portable fixtures until permanent locations have been determined.

Make the lighting system as flexible as possible. A landscape is a growing, changing thing, and a lighting scheme that looks good when first installed may not look right once plants mature or your needs change. You can gain flexibility by using some portable fixtures, running several circuits (rather than one), and providing switches and dimmers. This is particularly easy with 12- or 24-volt systems.

Check local codes, rules, and requirements before embarking on a design. Have an electrical inspector, consultant, or contractor check both your plans and your work for conformance with these regulations. They are intended for safety. Do not jeopardize life and property by attempting shortcuts.

Drawing a Lighting Plan

Overlay your final site plan with a piece of tracing paper to sketch out ideas for using light in your yard. Pencil in ideas for using lights to highlight features, for illuminating the deck or patio, disguising what you want hidden, and enhancing safety and security. Start by sketching in the effects and areas of illumination you want before

To achieve the maximum impact, put as much careful thought into the lighting plan as you would into an irrigation or planting plan.

planning circuits and the location of lines.

Emphasize Features Consider lighting landscape accents, such as a particular plant, statue, or constructed element. Light a favorite view by figuring out where you would sit or stand on the deck or patio to see it best. Plan lighting for special needs, placing a soft, relaxing light outside the bedroom window, for example, or creating a well-lit area for guest parking.

Survey the yard for plants that have textures and colors that light can emphasize. Certain plants look especially good under night light. Keep in mind that many plants have different shapes in different seasons. You may want to light a flower bed for spectacular spring color, but you may not want to see it when it is covered in snow. Just remember to put that light on a different circuit than the deck or patio light, and you will have the effect you want throughout the year.

General Illumination Think of how you plan to use the deck or patio and consider the types of lighting needed. Determine the light levels for entertaining versus viewing, for example. The light level required for dining on the patio will be different than that needed for a night game of croquet on the lawn. As you plan a lighting system, note what light already exists in the yard. Light may spill onto your patio from a neighboring yard, the streetlights, or the interior of your house.

Take the sketch of your lighting plan into the yard and test your ideas. Set flashlights or portable lamps where you are considering placing outdoor lights. When all seems workable, draw up the plan on a clean overlay of the final site plan. Indicate all of the circuits, switches, fixtures, methods of attachment, and all other items related to outdoor lighting.

Next check elements that you will use light to hide. Look at your least favorite features. Think about hiding power lines, your neighbor's motor home, and other visual nuisances in the landscape. Use light to hide bothersome views of the street, nearby houses, and storage and garbage facilities. Try to light only those features that are attractive and that will help mask out the undesirable ones.

Planning for Safety and Security As you plan an overall lighting system, do not overlook the safety and security benefits of outdoor lighting. If an entrance to your home is difficult to find, add light along the walkway to direct guests. Light-sensitive switches turn lights on when it gets dark, automatically illuminating areas you wish to secure. Timers set for random or fixed times can be an effective deterrent to intruders when you are away from home. To discourage potential trespassers, install heat-sensitive fixtures whose switches turn on lights when body warmth is detected. These can be installed near rear entrances, driveways, and parking areas where illumination is necessary only when someone approaches.

Remember that not all of your lighting needs may be permanent, but these must be planned for as well. If you decorate the front of your house with specialty lights to celebrate winter holidays, or if you want to add festive lights around the deck or patio for summer parties, remember to include some kind of electrical access for these lights as you plan other lighting needs.

Downlighting gives the most natural look. Place the light source high above branches to cast shadows on the ground.

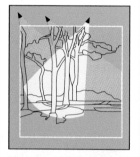

Lighting Techniques and Special Effects

Lighting techniques vary as to the position of the light source and whether it is pointed up, down, or across. Each technique brings a different focus to an area. Each of these basic lighting techniques can be employed for a variety of purposes. You will probably need to use a combination of techniques to light various elements appropriately and create the desired ambience. Safety, security, and nighttime activities will dictate the majority of lighting needs, but lighting can be used for a number of special effects as well. Choose from among the following lighting techniques to accent different elements of the landscape.

Downlighting Simulating natural illumination from the sun or the moon, this refers to the illumination of plantings, surfaces, and objects from above. The light source may be a floodlight for safety or security, several lights set high in a tree or on a pole or rooftop, or light diffused through an overhead lattice, canvas, or arbor.

Uplighting This is the illumination of a tree, wall, or object from below. Light is cast upward in either a broad spread or a more concentrated beam. This can have a dramatic effect and, since uplighting rarely occurs in nature, its appearance may be somewhat unnatural. Hence, areas of uplighting should be carefully planned and selected to illuminate special features.

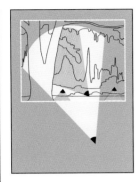

Uplighting empha-sizes parts of plants we don't normally pay attention to, changing their ap-pearance at night and creating a mag-ical, mysterious air.

Backlighting dramatizes the plant or accessory being lit. If the lighting is on the wall behind the plant, the plant is seen in stark silhouette. If the lighting is on the plant itself as well as on the wall, strong shadows are cast on the surface behind.

Backlighting Essentially, backlighting involves casting light (in any direction) behind plantings or objects. It reveals textures, creates long shadows, and gives a feeling of depth to the landscape.

How to Figure Light Levels

Ask five people what they perceive as "dim" light and you'll get five different answers. Although it is difficult to define standards for perceptions that are so thoroughly personal, you can use the following guidelines.

Brightness is measured in footcandles. Footcandles are a function of the brightness of the source and the distance from the source to the surface being lighted.

Dim Generally about 0.4 footcandles or less, this is the equivalent of full moonlight or the light on a street between streetlights. Silhouetting or moonlighting techniques produce about this level of light.

Medium Bright Anywhere from 0.5 to as much as 8 footcandles, this is less bright than interior house lighting. Low-voltage landscape lighting is usually from 3 to 5 footcandles. Most standard yard fixtures fall in this range. This level of brightness is used for uplighting, downlighting, and area lighting.

Bright About 8 footcandles or brighter, this is the illumination level of most interior rooms. Lighting in office spaces ranges from 60 to 150 footcandles. Bright lights are used for safety lighting, security lighting, and spotlighting. Except for security lighting and certain areas (a sports court or play area, for example), it is rarely desirable to light any part of the yard brighter than 20 footcandles, and 5 footcandles is a good average maximum. Be aware of glare caused by bright lighting. Use multiple low-wattage lamps (25 to 50 watts) rather than a few high-wattage fixtures.

Planning Specifics

Measure the length of the circuits on the plan. Make a list of the different types of fixtures and the quantity of each. Then estimate the cost of materials and installation. Check that the lighting plan fits into your budget. If not, rather than downscale, see whether you can put off some of the lighting installation until finances permit.

If you are not sure of your lighting plan, consult a licensed electrician or the local building department to be certain that all components are legal and safe. Schedule the installation in conjunction with construction for other utilities, keeping in mind that work should be done during good weather.

Outdoor Lighting Costs

Low-voltage (12-volt) lighting systems are the least expensive for the home landscape. The composite cost of a 12-volt system includes the electrical service, the distribution system, bases for the fixtures (usually concrete), the light fixtures and standards, the control switches, the transformers, and the lamps. Because of strict requirements for grounding and wiring standard 120-volt electrical service outdoors, a low-voltage system is much less expensive.

Low-voltage systems have the advantage of being quite safe, but because the electric current drops off

somewhat, no line can be longer than about 100 feet, and you cannot have more than three or four 100-watt fixtures per line.

A standard 120-volt system is less limiting. If your property is large and you intend to use the grounds at night for such activities as swimming, badminton, or tennis, or if you plan to light deck, patio, or lawn areas with multiple fixtures in order to minimize glare, you may

Low-voltage systems are simpler and less expensive than systems using household current. They are also easy for the homeowner to install.

wish to consider a 120-volt system. Because of the high voltage, this type of system is much more expensive to install, and because of the amount of electricity consumed, it is more expensive to run.

In either system you can set all the fixtures and dig all the trenches. Codes may require that an electrician do all the wiring and connections for a 120-volt system. Electrical cable should be snaked through a PVC (polyvinyl chloride) pipe for protection, but that cost is nominal. Fixture costs vary, and the choice is dependent on your budget and overall landscape style.

Spas and hot tubs can be purchased as ready-made units, as was this spa, or custom-constructed, like the large spa on the opposite page.

PLANNING FOR SPAS

Hot water to soak away the body's aches have been a luxury and a joy to humanity since before the dawn of civilization. Many cultures have incorporated the bath into their social fabric. Archaeologists have discovered 2,000-year-old baths built into hot springs in Japan. Spas are popular there still. Legend has it that Blalud, the father of King Lear, discovered the therapeutic properties of Bath's hot springs in the ninth century B.C. Roman invaders built baths on the same site about A.D. 50. Spas

It's easier to maintain healthy plants around a spa if you plant them in containers rather than in permanent beds. Then you can rotate them from time to time so they are not always exposed to the potentially damaging steam, wet, and chlorine.

continue to rejuvenate body and soul to this day.

Before deciding where to locate a spa, check with local officials for codes regarding spas or pools. Some jurisdictions are very specific about fencing requirements, sanitary facilities, and safety in relation to electrical grounding. You will also want to consider the need for privacy and wind protection by using appropriate screening. Vegetation will sometimes provide the screening you want, but often fences or windbreak structures are more practical in the short term—particularly while new plantings mature (see page 288).

Spas are heavy when filled and require structural support. Do not build a pool structure on or in filled earth unless it has been properly compacted by machine methods. It is structurally preferable to build a spa into a deck, providing a solid concrete base for it, rather than simply install it on top of the deck. If this cannot be done due to steepness of the site (or a deck on the roof of your house), consult an architect or structural engineer to design the deck. Water is heavy and when agitated can develop substantial horizontal momentum.

Study the sun and shade patterns of your yard as well as the microclimate (see page 25). A spa in the desert might benefit from some

midday shade, but in a cooler climate you might prefer that it be located in full sun. These are questions that only you and other users of the spa can answer, but consider them carefully—it may be very difficult to relocate a spa after it is constructed.

Outdoor spas can be used the year around in any climate, although heating costs will invariably rise during the winter. Although special problems arise in regions where winters are severe, they don't necessarily preclude year-round enjoyment. In snow country an overhead structure would be advisable along with underfloor heating cables around the spa to prevent ice buildup. Insulation is essential to prevent pumps and piping from freezing. Include an insulated cover to minimize heat loss and evaporation.

Plants and Spas

Nestling a spa into a lushly planted surrounding is an appealing idea, but not appropriate for every situation. Most plants don't like to be wet all the time—and they might be constantly soaked if planted immediately next to an active spa. In addition, plants are allergic to chlorine, the most common pool and spa disinfectant. Small spas, from which there will be minimal splashing, can be surrounded by plants, but if the spa is primarily for entertaining and will get a lot of use, consider decor other than live plants around the immediate perimeter. The fig family (*Ficus* species), including a wide range of decorative rubber plants (*Ficus elastica*), are quite tolerant and their bold tropical look will enhance most spa settings.

Plants that shed leaves or flowers heavily should not be used to decorate a spa. Some seeds are borne on fluffy parachutes that clog filters. If you can't live without such plants, locate them on the lee side of the spa, where the wind will move the detritus away from the water.

An in-ground spa should not be placed near a tree with large or invasive roots. The shell of plastic spas and even concrete structures can be damaged by the force of roots and their inexorable growth.

One of the best solutions for plantings near spas is container gardening. Planters, pots, hanging baskets, and trees on wheels can decorate the environs of the patio or deck spa without incurring any of the negative aspects of attempting a long-term relationship between plants and chlorinated water.

PRACTICAL MATTERS

Because the area surrounding the spa will be wet much of the time, the surface should ideally be wood decking or paving—not earth or mulch materials. A clean perimeter prevents debris from being tracked into the water. Even lawn immediately adjoining a spa or swimming pool will become mud in a short period of heavy usage.

Walking surfaces around a spa should be as skidproof as possible. Consider using indoor/outdoor carpet immediately adjacent to where people enter and exit the water, if there is a specific location. Otherwise use materials with some texture, such as Arizona sandstone, exposed aggregate paving, or concrete pavers. Avoid glazed ceramic tile and polished marble or granite on horizontal surfaces. Wood that is exposed to the sun will oxidize a little and develop a "tooth" that minimizes slipping, but beware of finishes that are made to shed water. Pressure-treated lumber decking will need less maintenance and is not subject to mold.

FENCES AND SCREENS

Fences and screens can mark boundaries, provide a sense of security, offer shelter from the elements, and give climbing plants vertical room to grow. They can also be decorative features.

To be truly comfortable, a deck or patio must be sheltered from the neighbors' view as well as from the elements. Ideally, this protection is provided by vegetation. Strategically placed hedges and trees will shelter the outdoor living space from wind and noise and provide shade and privacy while maintaining a natural link to the yard. When foliage is not an option, a vertical fence or screen is the next best choice.

Before giving free rein to your imagination, however, check local codes for restrictions on height and location. Some jurisdictions allow only 5-foot-high fences on boundaries but do not limit the height of structures inside the setback lines. In some cases, a fence isn't considered a structure unless it has an arborlike top. Almost all jurisdictions limit the height of fences at some level, and fence heights in front yards are usually the most restrictive.

Designing and Installing Screens and Fences

Use your imagination when deciding on a fence or screen. You can use wire mesh, expanded metal, boards, plywood, shingles, metal roofing, decorative tile, fabric,

A fence doesn't have to be just a backdrop. It can be a major garden feature if designed with imagination.

bamboo, beads, or plastic sheeting. Combine this with shrubs, trees, and vines as a foil, and you have a wonderful range of possibilities from which to choose.

A permanent screen is more effective than a wall because it protects the deck or patio while preserving an open, airy feel. Such a screen can be made from a number of materials. A roll-down shade of woven wood or fabric, for example, works where protection is necessary only occasionally—it can be lowered and raised as needed, so it is largely unobtrusive.

A freestanding wood screen, on the other hand, gives a stable, permanent feel and adds an attractive decorative element to a deck or patio. It protects without constrict-ing the space or blocking ventilation. It can also be used to conceal such unsightly necessities as air conditioners, utility meters, trash cans, and pool pumps. A wood screen makes a strong visual statement, however, so it must be designed to harmonize with the deck or patio and the house and yard. Structurally, a freestanding screen is fairly simple to build. It consists of a wood frame filled with lattice-work or diagonal slats of lath, batten, or lumber. The closer together the slats, the more solid the screen and the more protection it provides.

Surprisingly, solid fences and screens do not provide good wind protection. A swirling, spillover effect causes severe turbulence on the lee side of the barrier. A baffle-type

A lattice fence, such as this one, actually gives more shelter from the wind than a solid fence. The wind swirls over the top of a solid fence, making eddy currents behind it.

structure allows some of the wind to pass through. This forms a cushion of gently moving air that will deflect the stronger wind whistling over the top. Thus, a wire fence thickly cloaked with vines is an attractive and effective windbreak.

What makes a good fence? It must be well built, easy to maintain, and long lasting. But it also has to be attractive and look like it belongs. Perhaps your budget is limited and the fence must be simple. Focus your design attention on the gates, which you regularly see and touch. Whether you choose to incorporate a design sawed into the boards, a bit of sculpture, or a fanciful paint job, a gate can give a plain fence a point of interest and style.

Constructing a Wood Fence A wood fence is an easy do-it-yourself project. The most common construction for a vertical-board fence is to use 4×4 posts set 8 feet apart.

Begin by laying it out carefully with mason's twine and plumb bobs so that the posts line up and are truly vertical; set the corner posts first. Set the posts in concrete but, to ensure that moisture can drain out the bottom, do not encase the bottom of the post. Place 6 inches of gravel in the bottom of the hole, set the post on top of it, and then pour the concrete collar.

Painting the posts with creosote or some other wood preservative will do little good—the chemical layer is too thin. Instead, soak the posts in preservative for as long as possible where they will be in contact with the earth. An alternative is to simply buy pressure-treated posts; those that are not cut after treatment will last many generations.

A top rail is set on top of the posts, and a bottom rail installed between them. The fencing boards are then nailed to one side of the framing or the other.

BUILDING A FENCE

Chalk line marks top of boards

Guide strip for saw

Kickboard keeps fence from sagging and animals from squeezing under

1×2 guide strip to set boards on for nailing

Bottom stringers toenailed in place

Chalk line marks position of bottom stringer

Mark stringers for cutting by holding them in position

PLANT CONTAINERS

Planters add color, fragrance, style, and that delightful softening effect every deck or patio requires. Next to outdoor furnishings, they are the finishing touch that truly clothes the deck or patio, lending a definitive mood and style. The range of containers is almost as wide as that of the plants that will flourish in them. Which containers will suit your outdoor room is up to you. Size, cost, usefulness, beauty, and durability all need to be factored into the equation.

One way to get exactly what you want is to hire someone to build tubs and planters to your specifications. Another way is to use inexpensive baskets as cachepots and collect garden ornaments and planters as you happen to come across them. Yet another way is to determine what sort of containers you like best, say, blue-and-white Chinese ceramic pots, and each year add one or two more. Like decorating a home, furnishing the outdoor room is a long-term process.

Wood Planters

Planter boxes of redwood or cedar weather to a handsome silvery gray. They require no maintenance and last for many years. When the expense is amortized over the years of usefulness, the higher initial cost is easily justified. Plants grow well in wood planters because, like earthenware, they breathe and usually drain well. Painted wood planters have an attractively crisp look, although they do require some maintenance, usually a fresh coat of paint every few years to

Wooden planters, such as this one, can be made by most amateur carpenters. They can be as simple or as unusual as the builder's imagination suggests.

Wheelbarrow planters are a venerable garden tradition. Originally they were old wheelbarrows given new life; today most, like this one, are made to be planters from their inception.

keep them looking their best. Specimen trees and topiary are shown off to splendid advantage in smart, white Versailles tubs.

Fiberglass
Fiberglass containers last a long time, endure all kinds of weather, don't require repainting, and are not nearly as heavy as wood. They also tend to hold moisture well, since little is lost to evaporation. Be careful not to overwater, however.

Heavy Metal
Planters made of cast iron and lead are often very beautiful, but they are also very heavy. They last forever so long as they're not cracked by a sharp blow or by being dropped. Cast iron rusts and will need annual painting to keep it looking handsome. The rust can also stain patio paving and wood decks. Over the years, lead ac-

quires a magnificent patina and grows ever more beautiful.

Concrete
A wide variety of these durable planters are available as well. Beautifully designed to drain well and breathe, concrete planters do have the disadvantage of weight, making them a somewhat permanent installation. Plan ahead to allow for their weight if intending to use multiple concrete planters on a deck (see page 294). Use some caution when planting acid-loving plants such as rhododendron and azaleas in concrete planters, as they tend to be alkaline when new and may leach lime into the soil.

Found Containers
Almost anything can be used as a planter—from a weathered wheelbarrow to a clawfoot tub. Some "found" containers have proven

Unlike wheelbarrow planters, half-barrels usually have had an earlier career, holding wine or whiskey. Unsuitable for aging liquor after one or two uses, they can be recycled as garden containers.

themselves such excellent planters that they have become classics in the pot and planter lexicon. Old wine half-barrels and Chinese egg jars with their wonderful swirling dragons are classic examples.

Half-Barrels Not only are half-barrels superb planters (once the bottom has been drilled with four or five drain holes), but they have enough volume to accommodate trees, large shrubs, or a mini-garden of herbs or flowers. Garden centers often offer them seasonally for quite reasonable prices. They require no maintenance, last for years, and develop more character as time goes by.

Chinese Egg Jars Chinese egg jars are no longer inexpensive or easy to find (the antique dealers have discovered them) unless there is a Chinese community nearby, in which case you may be able to get them directly from grocers that sell preserved eggs. They are deep enough for growing small trees— a pair of neatly trimmed bays (*Laurus nobilis*) or privets (*Ligustrum japonicum*), perhaps, framing the access from patio to lawn. They look terrific with large shrubs such as camellias, and also work wonderfully with morning glory vines that twine over the French doors to the deck. Once they've been drilled

Almost anything that can be made to hold soil can serve as a container. Containers have been made from vegetable crates, as shown here, ceramic vessels of all sorts, old buckets and tinware, worn-out pots from the kitchen, and even old shoes.

long as half-barrels or Chinese egg jars, but are good for several years of service.

Preventing Leaks and Drips

Proper drainage is a necessity for planted containers; without it, plants can easily become waterlogged and die. Dripping water or fertilizer, however, don't have to be a fact of life for your new deck or patio. Fortunately, there are lots of ways to control drainage. The simplest is using waterproof saucers of sufficient depth and diameter to catch any overflow; both glazed ceramic saucers and plastic saucers are waterproof. Terra-cotta saucers, being porous, tend to absorb water, and though they may not necessarily drip, they will leave circular water stains on decks. Inexpensive, clear plastic liners can be put inside clay saucers to prevent them from absorbing water or inside baskets to keep the bottoms dry.

Considering the Loads

Decks must be designed to meet code requirements for floors, so usually live loads will present no structural problems for a deck built to code. Live loads are defined as the weight of snow, people, furniture, planters, and so on. Dead loads are the weight of the structure itself. Large and heavy iron or concrete planters may not be appropriate unless the structure is designed specifically to support them. Concrete weighs 150 pounds per cubic foot, and wet soil should be calculated at about 100 pounds per cubic foot. A 4-foot-square wood planter that's 3 feet deep will weigh more than 2 tons when wet—more than a large automobile. Use discretion when considering large planters on decks and check with the building inspector or a structural engineer before proceeding.

for drainage, they require no maintenance. When filled with soil, they are very heavy and should be put where they are going to stay.

Other fine containers are shipping or packing crates. If you live near a seaport or airport, find out where the freight comes in and ask what they'll let you haul off. These sturdy wood boxes are usually quite large and are often marked with intriguing foreign writing. Even if they say nothing more than "This end up" or "Handle with care," they still look wonderfully exotic. To make packing boxes and shipping crates last longer, line them with the heaviest plastic you can find. Don't forget to drill drain holes in the bottom and slit the plastic just over the holes for drainage. Shipping crates don't last as

Window Boxes

If you want to avoid or augment plantings on the deck or patio surface, planters under windows on adjacent house walls or on a deck railing make an attractive and convenient alternative or accent.

Window boxes are best supported by sturdy wood brackets under the box. They may be filled in either of two ways: with soil and herbs or flowers, or with pots already in bloom. Since annuals give the longest period of bloom, most window boxes are planted for a bright spring and summer display, especially in cold climates. Trailing plants are especially effective in window boxes, and bulbs can be planted under vines to come up with their welcome flowers every spring.

Using the window box as a sort of cachepot for pots of flowers at the peak of seasonal blooming solves the problem of the window box not always being in display condition. As one set of flowers begins to wither, the next set of seasonal performers takes its place. Using pots is a better bet when the window box overhangs a deck, as the drainage, and potential water staining, is much more easily controlled (see page 294).

If you use window boxes to provide color around a deck or patio, be aware that they can be heavy and require substantial support. To avoid damaging the walls, build them with an air space between the box and the wall, and design the box so that it drains away from the wall.

INDEX

Page numbers in boldface type indicate principal references; page numbers in italic type indicate references to illustrations and photographs.

U.S. MEASURE AND METRIC MEASURE CONVERSION CHART

	Formulas for Exact Measures				Rounded Measures for Quick Reference		
	Symbol	When you know:	Multiply by:	To find:			
Mass (weight)	oz	ounces	28.35	grams	1 oz		= 30 g
	lb	pounds	0.45	kilograms	4 oz		= 115 g
	g	grams	0.035	ounces	8 oz		= 225 g
	kg	kilograms	2.2	pounds	16 oz	= 1 lb	= 450 g
					32 oz	= 2 lb	= 900 g
					36 oz	= 2¼ lb	= 1000 g (1 kg)
Volume	pt	pints	0.47	liters	1 c	= 8 oz	= 250 ml
	qt	quarts	0.95	liters	2 c (1 pt)	= 16 oz	= 500 ml
	gal	gallons	3.785	liters	4 c (1 qt)	= 32 oz	= 1 liter
	ml	milliliters	0.034	fluid ounces	4 qt (1 gal)	= 128 oz	= 3¾ liter
Length	in.	inches	2.54	centimeters	⅛ in.		= 1.0 cm
	ft	feet	30.48	centimeters	1 in.		= 2.5 cm
	yd	yards	0.9144	meters	2 in.		= 5.0 cm
	mi	miles	1.609	kilometers	2½ in.		= 6.5 cm
	km	kilometers	0.621	miles	12 in. (1 ft)	= 30.0 cm
	m	meters	1.094	yards	1 yd		= 90.0 cm
	cm	centimeters	0.39	inches	100 ft		= 30.0 m
					1 mi		= 1.6 km
Temperature	°F	Fahrenheit	⅝ (after subtracting 32)	Celsius	32° F		= 0° C
	°C	Celsius	⅝ (then add 32)	Fahrenheit	212° F		= 100° C
Area	in.²	square inches	6.452	square centimeters	1 in.²		= 6.5 cm²
	ft²	square feet	929.0	square centimeters	1 ft²		= 930 cm²
	yd²	square yards	8361.0	square centimeters	1 yd²		= 8360 cm²
	a.	acres	0.4047	hectares	1 a.		= 4050 m²